PENGUIN F
A DOUBLE

Why did Princess Di compare her life to the Hollywood studio system?

How do you make a condom sexy?

Why did the emperor lose his clothes in the play Tughlaq?

Can a tramp be the perfect gentleman?

How did a house agency become a creative hotbed of advertising?

How can Corporates put back into society a little of what they take out from it ?

a double life answers these as well as many other questions while tracing the career of Alyque Padamsee — spanning a hundred years in his twin professions of theatre and advertising. It takes you behind the curtains with the Director of the Theatre Group of Bombay and former Chief Executive of Lintas: India. Unlike traditional autobiographies, **a double life** does not move chronologically from A to B to C. Rather, it's an insider's view of two diverse but inextricably linked occupations.

Go backstage with the man who has been dubbed India's Communications Guru as he unfolds thrilling scenes from his high voltage life. With acute human insights that illuminate the book like flashes of lightning, Padamsee reveals the hidden stories behind blockbuster productions like *Evita* and *Jesus Christ Superstar*, and megabrands like Liril and Kama Sutra.

a double life

My Exciting Years in Theatre and Advertising

Alyque Padamsee

with

Arun Prabhu

PENGUIN BOOKS

Penguin Books India (P) Ltd., 11 Community Centre, Panchsheel Park, New Delhi 110 017, India
Penguin Books Ltd., 27 Wrights Lane, London W8 5TZ, UK
Penguin Books USA Inc., 375 Hudson Street, New York, NY 10014, USA
Penguin Books Australia Ltd., Ringwood, Victoria, Australia
Penguin Books Canda Ltd., 10 Alcon Avenue, Suite 300, Toronto, Ontario M4V 3B2, Canada
Penguin Books (NZ) Ltd., 182-190 Wairau Road, Auckland 10, New Zealand

First published by Penguin Books India (P) Ltd. 1999

Copyright © Alyque Padamsee 1999

All right reserved

10 9 8 7 6 5 4 3 2 1

Cover design: Mukti Dave
Front cover photograph: Suresh Natarajan
Theatre photographs: Madhu Gadkari

Created, designed and printed at Repro India Limited, Prabhadevi, Mumbai 400 025.

This book is dedicated to

the Durga Mata

of my life, my mother

Kulsumbai Padamsee,

who was both a figure of

fear and admiration

at all times.

CONTENTS

Is there a nexus between theatre and advertising? Who are the practitioners of this double art?

How does one defy one's parents to marry the girl one loves? And how does one escape the advertising strait-jacket of Unilever International?

Which was my real family? The Padamsee clan or the Theatre Group coterie or the Lintas: India empire? And what are my relations with Lalitaji, Cherry Charlie, the Liril nymph, Tughlaq, and Evita?

Death, flops and marketing disasters open one's eyes and force one to face reality. The critical reception of *Vultures* and the consumer rejection of Dettol Antiseptic Cream taught me more than many of the successes I have enjoyed.

Improvising the Hindi version of *Marat/Sade* was not half the *Pagal Khana* that the preparations for the Opening Event of the Asian Track & Field Meet turned out to be.

INTRODUCTION

*B*ack in the eighties, there was a joke that was doing the rounds in advertising circles. Alyque Padamsee, CEO Lintas, also known as 'God', had a secretary called Jenny Pope. The joke said, that in order to meet God, you first had to meet the Pope.

Over the years, as I've got to know Alyque closely, I've often wondered why he was called God. I think I've understood. His perspicacity, his vision, his creative genius, his inimitable organisational abilities, his unending energy and his uncanny omnipresence – any one man who is endowed with all these qualities certainly qualified for the post of God. Today, as I write the introduction of the book on India's greatest English theatre and advertising man, I'm honoured. From being my boss in Lintas, to being my friend, guide and perpetual pace setter, Alyque has inspired, motivated, sometimes bullied but always encouraged me in my endeavours.

My earliest memories of Alyque are those of an incredibly casual but very focussed professional. He gave 100 per cent of himself to the issue at hand. He wandered around Lintas in rubber chappals (when he had a heel problem), equally at ease in the canteen and boardroom, giving freely of his advice to anyone who cared to listen. The smart ones not just listened but made mental (in my case written) notes. His organisational abilities amazed me. He always carried a little dictaphone into which he spoke all the time, making comments. He also had his little note pad (which he carries even now) that was more deadly and infallible than the most complex electronic diary.

Some of the famous one-liners, which he's fond of quoting even today, remain the Bible for any number of business aspirants, creative folk and people in general. Let me quote a few of my own favourites.

'Running an agency does not mean running the show. It means running the people who run the show.' The truth of this line has become even more blinding for me as I realise the extent of Alyque's genius in managing both the creative and business angles of Lintas over decades. I always believed that creative and business acumen don't go together. Alyque disproves that. I've yet to meet a more creatively driven individual – and I've yet to meet an individual to whom the bottom line matters more.

Alyque brought new meaning to the word motivation. He motivated in the most innovative ways. When Lintas became too large for everyone to meet every day, he instituted the concept of 'Prayer Meetings', where everyone got together and 'broke bread', as it were, under his aegis. His Monday Morning Meetings were legendary, and I carried them with me to every organisation I joined; today, they are an integral part of the organisation I run. His SRBs (Strategy Review Boards) were exacting, demanding every person involved to do his homework thoroughly. 'When execution comes before strategy, you are courting disaster.' His Creative Reviews sent hotshot Creative Directors scuttling for cover, while at the same time bringing a junior visualiser out of his or her shell, with a shy, tentative idea getting pride of place in the Lintas Hall of Fame.

The Lunchtime Stimulation Session was another custom (Alyque likes to call them customs, not systems, because he believed Lintas was a family, not a corporation) where all of us were exposed to the most unlikely stimulation – right from classical music reviews to discussions on Goscinny's and Uderzo's genius. Alyque always believed in cross-fertilising. *'Media buying must be disciplined. Financial systems must be creative. Servicing must be imaginative. And the creative must be brand driven.'* He believed in flexibility, not anarchy.

Theatre must have taught him that lesson. Whenever he worked on a new play, people stayed out of his way as Opening Night approached. His temper was famous. As famous indeed as his generous praise for everyone who performed. 'The term Director is a misnomer,' he would say. He is an evoker, a stimulator.

And evoke and stimulate he did. Not just by word, but by action. His indefatigable energy would see him going on and on and on till he reached perfection.

There are many of his tenets that I've successfully (some not so successfully) adopted in my own organisation today. 'My assets take the elevator every day at 5 o'clock,' was Alyque's favourite quote when he was asked to sum up Lintas' assets. Looking after his people is something he's passionate about. 'Start with the loo,' he's advised me over and over again, whenever I've tried to discuss my own corporate structuring with him. 'Focus, focus, focus,' is his constant refrain whenever I've indulged in flights of fantasy about entering new areas of business. He's as excited as a child whenever there's a new idea for him to chew on, always adding dramatic value to anything he discusses.

His philosophies are simplistic. Sometimes blindingly so. He derives a tremendous amount of inspiration from his background – 'middle-class Gujarati', he's fond of saying. That Lalitaji, the famous Surf mascot, was modelled after his mother is no secret. His awareness, and even more than that, his determination to be abreast of technology never ceases to surprise me. He's spoken to me with the same zeal of ten-projector audio-visuals as he has of using modems and links and internet and other hi-tech gizmos.

The one thing that irritates him more than anything else is the acceptance of mediocrity. 'India's largest industry is the follow-up industry,' he's often heard quoting. Woe betide the person who's 'forgotten' a meeting, or even an action point. Alyque comes down like a ton of bricks, but leaves with a few well-chosen words of advice that are bound of soothe, heal and inspire.

I could go on. His enthusiasm for a dance party could put a teenager to shame. His clarity of thought, his creative genius, his sense of humour, and above all his desire to make a difference makes him uniquely himself.

He's made a difference to hundreds of people – like me. Zealous account executives who are today running successful businesses. Young theatre hopefuls who are today stars in their own right. And tentative copywriters who have today written their own books. Look beyond these people, and you'll see Alyque standing in the wings. Encouraging, frowning, nodding, smiling.

Dushyant Mehta
Director
Repro India Limited, Bombay

FOREWORD

*A*lyque Padamsee is a most extraordinary man. In earlier days, his prolific range of gifts and activities might have been surprising, but in our own age of specialisation, the combination is rare indeed.

I first met Alyque in London in 1980, when we were both senior managers in the Lintas advertising network. He was running India's leading ad agency and I was managing our largest client, Unilever's food business worldwide, before going to Sydney to lead the Australia and New Zealand operations. Arriving in Sydney, it was clear to me that I needed completely new approaches to revive a slumbering company, and I started looking around for ideas. What about that man Padamsee? He was managing a very obviously successful business with a wonderful reputation in the key area of creativity. What was he doing to achieve it? So I started a dialogue (and a friendship) which progressively revealed over the months and years the amazing scale and scope of his world.

Alyque's brief, that anything you imagine can be achieved, has made him an acknowledged guru, not only in the world of business, but also in the world of theatre and film – a double life indeed! What's more, between those twin poles, and drawing on skills from both ends, lies another whole area of passion for him — the use of mass media to address most, if not all, of the major issues confronting Indian society in the latter part of the twentieth century: hunger, drug addiction, disease, social inequality, racial and religious conflict, and much more.

Amidst all of this activity, there was so much to stimulate and inspire me — in the arts, in business and in public service. For me, perhaps the more tangible outcome came during my time as world president of the International Advertising Association, when I conceived and launched a global campaign to tell people everywhere the positive role advertising can have not only in the economy, but in society at large. Many years later, that initiative is still running.

I have so many memories of Alyque, so selecting just one or two is not easy.

Alyque had known that I was involved in the reconstruction of Shakespeare's Globe Theatre in London, the 'wooden O' of Henry V. On a trip to London with his family, I arranged for them to have a VIP tour of the nearly-completed work (at the same time as hordes of tourist groups from around the world). It so happened that just the previous week, the stage itself had been completed — a great wide apron, reaching out to where the groundlings would stand. Alyque enquired as to whether this stage had yet been performed upon. His guide told him: 'No, not yet.' So without further ado Alyque stepped forward and declaimed to the astounded throng, 'All the world's a stage, and all the men and women merely players…' So there he was, the first.

Many years earlier, Lintas: Worldwide had run a conference in Bangkok for their top managers from all over the globe. I had organised a competition, to be judged by the assembled creative directors, to identify the best TV/film commercial produced in the Lintas world. Entries poured in from all over — for a dazzling array of products and services, in a dozen or more different languages. The assembled creative directors were shown the work. Then they discussed it. Then they saw it all again. Then they voted. It was very clear to me that our American colleagues expected to win — and by a wide margin — with their spectacular (and very expensive) launch advertising for the very successful new product, Diet Coke. And, in fact, when all the votes were counted Diet Coke did come in second place. But in the first place was an intriguing, stimulating and very unusual commercial on an anti-smoking theme, conceived and produced by AP's Lintas: India. What's more, the commercial cost less than one percent of the Coke campaign to produce. How could this happen? There was deep consternation as our American friends realised that they had to go back to New York and explain to their colleagues that they had come second to an inexpensive Indian campaign they had never heard of. Perhaps there should be a new voting system? Surely the big markets (!) should have more votes? But no. The result stood — and Alyque Padamsee's Lintas: India walked off with the prize.

I hope this book will provide the kind of inspiration for others that Alyque has given to me.

Roger Neill
Managing Partner
Synectics Corporation, London

PREFACE : THE ROLE OF ROLE-PLAYING IN ADVERTISING AND THEATRE

*M*any people are amazed that I have two full-time careers, one in theatre and one in advertising, when they can barely handle one. Incredible as it may seem, I've spent most of my adult life helping to run Lintas — among the largest advertising agencies in India — while at the same time, producing and directing fifty full-length plays for one of the most active theatre groups in this country. 'How did you manage it?' they ask. 'Is there any connection between the two professions?'

As I look around Bombay today, I am forcefully reminded that there is indeed a connection. Theatre people dominate the ad scene. If it's not Sylvester da Cunha Amul-buttering his way to glory after being a cardholder of the Theatre Group of Bombay for decades, it is Kersy Katrak leaping off the stage after Hamlet and forming India's legendary advertising agency, MCM. Then there are Roger Pereira and the late Homi Daruvala, the twin thespians who took Shilpi Advertising from an elegant boutique to a Top Ten agency. And Usha Katrak who stunned audiences with her Medea, years before she stunned the ad world with the agency Radeus. Lintas, of course, has provided the stage for theatre stalwarts like Gerson da Cunha, Kabir Bedi and Dalip Tahil, and film novitiates like Shyam Benegal, Robin Dharmaraj and Sumantra Ghosal.

What is this weird nexus? And how did it come about? Though theatre is as important as breathing to me, I have to admit, godammit, it doesn't pay a living wage! Where else can one write words, shoot pictures and turn imagination into reality but in advertising, and get paid for it handsomely? No wonder then that creative icons like Ebrahim Alkazi of the theatre, Nissim Ezekiel of the world of poetry and dozens of others from the arts have been tempted into advertising at one time or the other. It's a fascinating profession which also pays for the bread, butter and BMW.

When I started out in advertising, I had come from a theatre background. But at that time, there weren't many other people in advertising who also came from the theatre. There was of course, the late Hamid Sayani, and I think he was the one who pioneered this trend that soon became quite common. He had been in theatre for many years and then joined Stronach Advertising. A little later, another theatre man, Sylvester da Cunha, too joined Stronach's and then moved to Advertising and Sales Promotions (ASP). His brother, Gerson da Cunha who was also from the theatre, joined J. Walter Thompson.

And then when I was strapped for cash and realised that theatre couldn't pay my bills, I too, joined the advertising business. And after that came a whole succession of people. There were also people from the Hindi theatre like Satyadev Dubey who joined Lintas for a short time.

And before you could say 'To be or not to be', it was very much, to be in theatre was to be in advertising. Strange to say, a lot of the younger theatre critics, who know nothing of the history of advertising in this country, erroneously chant the mantra, 'The world of theatre has been invaded by the advertising philistines.' And even earlier critics felt that 'the advertising boys', as we were so ignominiously called, were overrunning the theatre. In their words, 'Commerce, crass commerce, is invading art.' Nothing could be further from the truth. It was, in fact, hungry art taking over plush advertising. All the ravenous theatre boys wanted the good life and they thought what better than to join advertising. The outstanding reverse phenomenon was the ad man Satyajit Ray crossing over to the poorly paid art cinema from a cushy job as Art Director of Clarion, Calcutta.

And this trend has continued over the years. After the first group of theatre people had crossed over to advertising came the next generation, with people like the brilliant actor Vijay Crishna, 'Bugs' Bhargava Krishna, Bharat Dabholkar, Ravi 'Rags' Khote and Adi Pocha. In more recent times, the trend has continued with Rahul da Cunha, Kunal Vijaykar and Cyrus Broacha.

More important than the names was the attitude. Which was, 'My God! Someone is actually paying us money to create words and pictures. This is incredible! The same things that we do in the theatre for free, pay us big bucks in advertising.'

My advice to agency heads: grab young playwrights, set designers and actors.

My advice to any agency head looking for creative or client service people is: grab young playwrights, set designers and actors. They could be your Kersy Katraks, Rahul da Cunhas and Bugs Bhargavas of tomorrow.

In retrospect, the question I ask myself is, 'What is it that makes theatre people effective advertising people?' What is the nexus between the two professions? What is the overlap? What is it that allowed me to lead a successful 'double life'?

The first similarity between the two professions is obviously role-playing. In the theatre you try to put yourself into the shoes of the character you're portraying. Whether it's *Hamlet* or *Jesus Christ Superstar* or *Begum Sumroo* or *The Merchant of Venice* or anyone else. In advertising, every time you dream up an ad for a lipstick, if you're a male, you put yourself in female high heels. Every time you think of selling beedis, you put yourself in the bare feet of a manual labourer.

This ability to put yourself, not so much in the shoes, but rather in the mind and heart of the consumer, is the hallmark of a great advertising strategist. And this comes so naturally to actors. It seems absurd to me that this phenomenon of theatre people in advertising doesn't occur anywhere else in the world.

It certainly doesn't occur in London's West End or in New York's Broadway. I was recently told that it does happen in Sri Lanka, but in all my years of travelling around the world, I have never seen this syndrome repeated. Except for Don Wilde who was a theatre person working in Lintas: New York. Perhaps one of the reasons is that advertising is looked down upon by people in the arts abroad. They've never thought of it as a respectable way to make a living. There was a famous book by a Frenchman who said, 'I told my mother I was a piano player in a brothel rather than reveal that I was working in an ad agency!'

It could also be due to the fact that theatre people in the West are paid much more than here. There, there is professional theatre. And actors are paid accordingly. There are shows daily and even twice a day sometimes. So it's a full-time job and they are rewarded handsomely. But in India, it's really just amateur theatre. At least in the English theatre, to which I belong.

The next similarity between the two professions can be found in the processes. In advertising, you start off with an idea. Or what we call the 'big idea'. In theatre, you start off with the script. Which is your big idea. Then there's the delineation of the idea. In advertising you have to decide in what context to put your idea. Whether it's a family scene or a sports-field or just a girl frolicking under a waterfall. You're actually asking your models to delineate character, like you would ask your actors on stage. Sometimes, you even get your products to delineate character.

Theatre develops your imagination, while advertising develops your analytical powers. Using advertising as the theatre of fantasy and theatre as the laboratory of human behaviour is fascinating. And even if you switch them around, you'll find that they're equally valid.

I've always believed that the art of advertising is really the art of show business. In advertising you show off your brand rather than your characters. This show business aspect first came through with the launch conference of Surf in 1958. We demonstrated the power of this detergent on stage with a giant transparent bucket and a jet of compressed air, which formed oceans of instant lather. That was forty years ago. Today almost every brand launch is an Event using showbiz techniques.

Then there's the whole discipline of paying attention to detail in both professions. The models or actors, the lighting, the music, the scenery, the entire *mise en scène*. And everything has to be fine-tuned for maximum effect.

In theatre everything is geared towards opening night. And in advertising too, everything is geared towards your first release. Then there are repetitive performances. The play has repeat performances. The ad has repeat releases. There's a chance to correct mistakes, if any, and constantly improve.

Another aspect of the advertising-theatre nexus is presentation flair. An actor is a born presenter. So is an ad man. Both are able to use their voice and body to make an impact on the audience. This comes in very useful when you're at a client presentation. If you can act out your film, a client usually gets convinced. 'Hey! This one will probably work.' If you just hand him a dead script, even with a good pictorial storyboard, he may not get the impact of what you're trying to convey.

A lot of the success we enjoyed at Lintas was thanks to the professional theatre attitude we carried over into advertising. Everything was preplanned. Whether it was a pre-production meeting for a film or rehearsing before a client presentation. All of us in advertising, who came from the theatre, brought with us a certain discipline. For example, opening night is a cruel time to make mistakes. Similarly, a client presentation is not an opportune moment to realise that the lettering on your slides is so small that the client can't read what's on them.

It seems strange that theatre should teach advertising the art of discipline, when the latter outspends the former a million times over. After all, you would expect a high level of accountability in advertising, where you're spending so much of other people's money.

A pennypinching product manager once asked me, 'Why is the cost of the Liril film so high, when you don't have any costumes, except a bikini, and you don't have any sets, except a waterfall?!!' Being from the theatre, I had a ready reply: 'A location shoot actually costs much more than a studio set, because of air tickets and hotel accommodation for models and technical crew, transportation of camera and lighting equipment and fees paid to owners of the location. Add to that, pre-trips (better known as "recce trips") to find the right location. Would you like to come along for the ride? It will only increase the cost by another Rs. 10,000.' The poor product manager mumbled something incomprehensible and slunk away, my tale between his legs.

One area in which advertising teaches theatre is feedback. In advertising, you pre-test before you finalise the campaign. And that's certainly something I have learnt to utilise in my productions. I always have a preview of my plays before a trial audience, and make changes before I go in front of the Opening Night audience. Most theatre producers don't follow this necessary discipline.

And that's something that is fascinating about both professions. You get the chance to revise and re-present. In advertising, if you are working in a reasonably professional agency, the ad is always put to the test where the consumer might say, 'Well, the beginning of the ad was wonderful but my interest tailed off towards the end.' So you go back to the drawing board and try to iron out the creases. In a play, you may suddenly realise that you've miscalculated. And the audience is not picking up what you thought they would. So you go back to rehearsals and you revise your production. In that way, they are both malleable media.

And they are both audience driven. There can be no theatre without an audience. It's wonderful to rehearse a play, but when you go into the auditorium and you realise you haven't sold a single ticket, there's no way you'll feel like performing. It's also wonderful to create a campaign, but if you realise that no one's watching the program that you've slotted your ad in, or if no one is responding to your ad, you're going to withdraw your commercial and put it some place where there's a larger audience.

I also discovered that both professions are actually in the business of 'manufactured reality'. When you produce a play or create an advertising campaign, you are in effect manufacturing reality. An interesting question arises: Is 'manufactured reality' truth or lies? Or is it, as Shakespeare puts it, 'Lies like Truth'?

When Kabir Bedi donned black make-up to play Othello, was it the same as Karen Lunel donning her green bikini to play the Liril girl? When people view actors, whether they are in a play or in a commercial, there is a willing suspension of disbelief. The audience knows they are watching something that is play-acted and not real, but if well done, it still sweeps them off their feet. These are the 'lies like truth' that power both theatre and advertising.

The other area where I find great similarities between the two professions is teamwork. You cannot produce an ad without a team and you cannot produce a play on stage without a team. On the stage you have the actors and the stage manager and the make-up man and the lighting guys and so on. All of them work together for anything between six weeks and six months towards the big opening night. And in advertising, you have the copywriter and the art director and the client-servicing guys and the media chaps and the studio and production guys, all working together as a team towards the big campaign release.

There's a great amount of team spirit. And with team spirit comes a certain bonhomie, a friendliness, a camaraderie. Which you rarely find in most other professions. There, it's more a vertical structure, whereas in advertising and theatre, it's more a horizontal structure, where you have one man as the director of the play or head of the agency and all the people below that are more or less equal. They may have different designations and various levels of salaries, but for the most part, they are all on equal footing when it comes to creating the ad or the play.

This gives one a tremendous sense of involvement. A sense that we're all in this together. Everyone is working hand in hand towards opening night or towards the break of a new campaign. There's a feeling of heightened excitement. I think I get an equal thrill from a campaign breaking as from a play opening. It's a heady rush of adrenalin and the butterflies in the stomach are very similar.

In fact, both professions are so absorbing and fulfilling that you barely have time for family and friends. I personally have been in rehearsal, sometimes, 200 days a year. This means skipping birthday parties, weddings and other ceremonial occasions. But I've never missed out on my social life because the theatre is not all work. There's lots of play as well. After-work parties are the order of the day, as they are in advertising. Each profession is a whole world, complete with intellectual stimulation, strong friendships and male-female bonding. No wonder, we often marry within our own profession. I've done it myself. To me, the theatre not only comes first, but is central to my existence. In a lesser sense, so is advertising. Between these two demanding mistresses...I am surprised, in retrospect, that I have had time for three wives!

To lead a double life like me, you need to be a master of time-planning. Particularly when you start at the bottom, as I did. As a trainee in advertising. You've got to juggle around your time in such a manner that if a client presentation and a dress rehearsal are both at the same hour, you somehow manage to attend both.

How the hell do you do that? The first thing is to see if you can reschedule the dress rehearsal. If the theatre says, 'No, sorry. That's the only time we've got,' then you find some way in which you make your part of the presentation to the client first, and then slip away quietly and unobtrusively. That is easier said than done. Especially if you make a splash and everyone at the meeting says, 'Yes, go on. Tell us more.' Then you're caught between the client devil and the deep blue mascara.

But if you do want to do both, you need to do your planning well in advance. And then at the last minute if a client changes his schedule, you say, 'I'm terribly sorry, but something personal has come up. I can't explain right now.' Never ever say it's the theatre. Because to them, theatre is fun and advertising and marketing is work!

I'll never forget the clash of interests I had when I was in school. I was playing cricket for my class, and at the same time, I had a bit role in Ebrahim Alkazi's *Richard III* at St Xavier's College. I had planned my schedule accordingly, so that I would be able to make it for both. Suddenly Alkazi decided to have a special Press viewing of the play at exactly the time I was supposed to be on the cricket field.

I was in a quandary. Since I was the pace bowler for my class, I couldn't miss the match. On the other hand, Alkazi, though small in stature, had a formidable personality that brooked no excuses. I prayed desperately that the match would end in a rout one way or another, so that I could rush back for the show.

As it turned out, it was a long-drawn-out match and I kept looking at my watch and wondering if the Press show had started. Unfortunately, I was on in the early scenes. As soon as the match was over, I dashed to the hall. Naturally, there was no question of taking a taxi on my schoolboy allowance. So I ran from where the Wankhede Stadium is now, all across Azad Maidan to St Xavier's College.

When I arrived, Alkazi was furious. The play was already halfway through, and I had missed my key scene. Someone had had to stand in for me, reading from the script. I tried to tell Alkazi that I would have been thrown out of school if I'd missed the match and he said to me, 'Well, in any case, you've been thrown out of something. You're out of the play.'

I was in disgrace for six months! And from that day, I learnt that time planning and having a good excuse up your sleeve are equally important. *A Double Life* traces my path from an advertising trainee to CEO while doing fifty full-length plays along the way.

HOW TO CUT
MAMA'S APRON STRINGS

*M*y most vivid recollection of childhood is the smell of cod liver oil. I was one of those spindly brats who had diphtheria and double pneumonia by the age of two. And because I was the first male in the Padamsee family after three girls in a row, I became a 'pleasure to treasure'. I wasn't the very first male. That honour went to my eldest brother, Bobby. But after three consecutive female offspring, I think my mother was quite pleased to have another son. And so I was given a protective massage by my dearest mother at the crack of dawn, without fail, every day.

My mother, Kulsumbai Padamsee, was a Madonna of relentless tenacity. Once she set her mind to doing something, she was inexorable as the proverbial irresistible force, steamrollering the hapless immovable objects that dared cross her path. A long time ago, my mother related to me how she managed to get our building in Upper Colaba, Chotu Terrace, back from the Navy, which had requisitioned it during the Second World War.

A Col. Temple was in charge of requisitioning buildings for the British Raj, and the British Navy had rented Chotu Terrace for a paltry sum of Rs. 5,000 per month for the entire building, which had more than hundred tenement flats. Kulsumbai felt that she was being denied her rightful dues and resented the fact that the Navy was holding on to the building even though the war was over.

She went to see Col. Temple, who listened very patiently to all her arguments and then said, 'Madam, I'm very sorry. The Navy still needs the building.'

'That's very unfair. It's my building. You requisitioned it during the war and I didn't object. But now the war is over and you must give it back to me.'

'I'm sorry. I can't do that as yet.'

'In that case, I'm prepared to wait.'

'Well, that's fine then.'

What Temple didn't realise was that she was prepared to wait in his reception room! She went and sat there. When Temple came out at lunch time, he saw her. 'Mrs Padamsee, what are you doing here?' And she replied, 'I'm waiting for you to give me back my building.' He laughed and thought it was quite amusing. He went off for lunch and when he returned, he saw her still sitting there. 'Have you had your lunch?'

'Oh yes. I brought my sandwiches, thank you very much.'

He smiled and went into his cabin to continue with his work. In the evening, when he came out to go home, he saw her still sitting there.

'Mrs Padamsee, I'm afraid you can't stay here any longer. We're going to lock up the office.'

'That's perfectly alright.'

She picked up her little sandwich box and trotted out. The next morning, when Temple came into the office at 9 o'clock, Kulsumbai was back.

'Are you still waiting for me?'

'Yes.'

He smiled again and went into his office. And the previous day's events were repeated at lunch time and in the evening. After a month or so, Temple began to get a bit fed up. While he was working in his office, he began to feel the pressure of this lady sitting just outside his door. Not saying anything. Not protesting. No morcha. No satyagraha. Nothing. Just sitting there and knitting. My mother was a great knitter and I think she must have knitted sweaters for all her eight children during this period.

Finally, at the end of a year, Col. Temple came back from lunch one day and when he saw her sitting there, he threw up his hands in despair.

'Mrs Padamsee, are you never going to leave me alone?'

'Not until you give me back my building.'

Realising he couldn't outlast her, he called her into his office and summoned the clerk to bring him the papers. He signed them and gave them to her. 'Now for God's sake, go home and leave me alone.' Determination evaporates without stamina, staying power.

Determination evaporates without stamina, staying power.

This real life story created such an impression on me that I learnt never to give up on my original goal. I must unabashedly confess that my fund of energy together with my twenty-five-hour-day stamina owes not a little to the daily pummelling I received from my maternal masseur as well as her own unrelenting example. Another weird and wonderful olfactory sensation of my infant era is the nuzzling nectar of mother's milk. This was undoubtedly because I was breast fed till I was two years old! Or is this the clichéd excuse every MCP trots out when accused of a breast fixation?

Growing up in a traditional Gujarati-Kutchi family could have been a strait-jacketing experience. But fortunately for her brood of eight progeny, Kulsumbai was a hurricane force that swept away the purdah of hypocrisy whenever it stood in her way. Whether her children and husband ran scared or scarred was the topic of local debate. She was an oxymoron beyond compare. A conservative with a rebellious streak several miles wide. Her children, though, adored her even when they were occasionally on the receiving end of her chappal or her sulphuric tongue.

Our branch of the Padamsee family had broken away from its roots in myopic Mazagaon (a suburb in Central Bombay), to blaze a trail of non-conformity across the genteel face of Colaba (in South Bombay), which in the thirties was a bastion of middle-class Parsi and Anglo-Indian values.

My great-grandfather had come to Bombay on a bullock cart in the nineteenth century. We hail from peasant Kathiawari stock. The name 'Padamsee' is derived from 'Padam', which means lotus, and 'See' or 'Sinh' which means tiger. A lethal combination. But my great-great-grandfather carried the simple surname Viru. (I am not sure when the family name switched to Padamsee.) Both my parents spoke Gujarati to each other, and only resorted to English when addressing their anglicised offspring. In a sense, they learnt English backwards, from their children.

The alienisation that most westernised Indians feel for their home country started for me at Miss Murphy's school. Remember, those were the days of the British Raj. And though we never felt the lash of the Empire on our backs, we understood very well that white skin meant *Burra Saab*. Besides good manners, we were taught good breeding: Look down on things native; speak only the King's English (even if he had abdicated); sing 'When Irish eyes are smiling' with feeling. Mercifully, we were spared the quaint, unhygienic customs of toilet paper and tub baths.

Those were also the days when clubs had signs that read: Dogs and Indians not allowed. I remember vividly umpiring a cricket match between our school and the Bombay Gymkhana junior team. I can still feel the flush of resentment when the all-British Bombay Gymkhana team muttered racist comments about the decision I made against them. You are rarely aware of being an underdog until an act of prejudice rears its nasty head.

I was seared again some years later in London, when I went to look for digs while I was studying at the Royal Academy of Dramatic Arts. It was the winter of 1950, and I had innocently put £5 with an estate agent to find me PG accommodation. They gave me several addresses to phone.

I dialled the first one. A pleasant male voice asked me if I was married and I replied in the negative. The voice said, 'Fine, come over at once.' Within half an hour I was ringing the doorbell of Mr Pleasant Voice. The door opened and a burly gent stared surlily at me. 'What do you want?' 'I've come about the room. I phoned you a half-hour ago.' There was a dull silence, then Mr Nasty Voice spoke in a strangled tone, 'Are you married?' 'No. I am a student.' 'Sorry. We only take in married men. Never students.'

My jaw dropped. From within me whirled a geyser of protest. But just as it was about to surface, it dawned on me the reason why Mr Pleasant/Nasty Voice had metamorphosed from Dr Jekyll into Mr Hyde. The voice he had heard on the phone sounded English. But the colour he saw when he opened the door was distinctly colonial. It was a body blow to my ego. I flushed a deep brown. Tears sprang to my eyes. I turned on my heel, mentally slamming the East India Company door.

This trivial but wounding incident convinced me that I would never want to live abroad. Years later when I acted in *Gandhi,* I re-felt the same surge of bile in my throat when

Gandhi is thrown off the train for being coloured. Sure, I believe in non-violence, but there are times when one is tempted.

My life, I am inclined to believe, can be measured not in years, but in emotional scars. With my theatre background, I like to imagine that I am a hostage of time making marks on the cell wall and listening to the tramp of boots outside. 'And what about all we thousands of sensitive people wounded during the day and limping the lonely, lighted streets of our prisons at night, and crying in our clenched pillows until dawn? What happened to all our dreams along the way?' This fragment of a play I once read is a recurring coda that stomps through my head every so often. Even when you are rich and pampered, you can feel miserable and neglected.

As a rather spindly, pimply teenager, I went through a gruelling period in school when I felt unloved and unwanted. Fear of rejection hung like an ominous cloud over my head. One day, at the Cathedral School, a prestigious educational establishment in South Bombay, I was sent out of class for talking too much. The Principal, a lean and hungry Scotsman named L M S Bruce, who used to sneak around the corridors in rubber-soled shoes, suddenly pounced on me and gave me a sharp and nasty clip across the back of my head. This tiny incident ballooned in my mind and I went into a state of morbid dejection for the rest of the term.

But there must be something resolutely Gujarati about my DNA molecules, for I was bouncing back the next term to found the school newspaper, *Our Journal*, *Reaction to distress can be a powerful motivating force.* along with two other classmates, Jangoo Dubhash and Coover Gazdar. Reaction to distress can be a powerful motivating force. Like a mother single-handedly lifting a two-tonne truck off her child's crushed leg.

It seems absurd that a boy from a well-to-do family, spoilt silly by his mother, should suffer from an insecurity syndrome. But when you're cocooned from the world, the slightest misfortune becomes a mushroom cloud. For a mollycoddled youth who rarely strayed far from Mama's apron strings (or is it sari pallu?), risk-taking was not desired or demanded. Being born with the proverbial silver spoon in your mouth prevents you from speaking up. Your mother is there to speak on your behalf.

The security blanket I developed for myself was not the traditional old silk sari clutched to the cheek in the Parsi tradition. Rather it was an assertion of self through some positive action that my peers would respect. I am the tortoise who withdraws its head into its shell in anxiety, and then after an interval of introspection, emerges like the MGM lion with a king of the jungle roar.

The sheltering umbrella of Kulsum Terrace, our palatial home on the southern tip of Bombay, and the benign influence of my father, Padamsee-seth, who owned an empire covering ten buildings, precluded any necessity for courage or confrontation on my part. I snuggled cosily in the Kulsum Terrace womb. From Miss Murphy's school to the Cathedral School to St Xavier's College to the cushy swivel chair at the Padamsee Estate office in Colaba, was all one effortless glide.

Then fate knocked rudely on my door. I fell in love. Diminutive Pearl Chowdhary (née Waiz), with her vivacious charm, was the woman for me. Talented, supportive and crazy about the theatre. Alas, my Juliet was divorced with two children. But that didn't faze me. In my innocence I popped the question to my dear Mama. A withering look followed by an ice cold 'No!' slapped across my face. My bed of roses, I realised, had hidden thorns.

I learnt that a son can be a *ghar-jamai* just as easily as a son-in-law. Romeo was trapped. He couldn't elope because he didn't have the money to pay for a carriage, an *ayah,* a flat, schooling or even a crust of bread. It takes fire not only to make steel but to make steam as well. The burning resentment I felt at being treated like a kid, turned into a high-pressure resolve to be a man. I had to get a job. I had to become financially independent But the cold claw of insecurity grabbed my intestines. What if I couldn't find a job? What if years of slobbing around had jellied my spine? Did I really have the guts and gumption to start life as a poor man at the age of twenty-three?

It takes fire not only to make steel but to make steam as well.

The phone jangled. It was my dear friend, Gerson da Cunha. 'There's an opening for a trainee copywriter at JWT for three hundred rupees per month. Want to give it a shot?' The very next morning, I was at Lakshmi Building, in the office of J Walter Thompson's Copy Chief, Mark Robinson. I was first in a queue of two. My fellow candidate turned out to be Ossie D'Souza, a gangly youth with curly hair and a big grin. He later turned into one of the most likeable people in this hard-nosed profession of advertising. Mark, on the other hand, was a cold austere Englishman with rimless glasses that glinted icily like Jinnah's monocle.

Ossie and I both trembled through Mark's copy test, administered with Nazi precision. Besides the usual maze of grammatical testing, to separate the men from the morons, there was a dialogue one had to invent between a husband and wife stuck in a traffic jam, which I waltzed through.

After what seemed to be centuries, Ossie and I were both accepted as tyro copywriters. We sat shoulder to shoulder in a stuffy cabin with a ceiling fan blowing our fledgling copy in all directions. But that fan was kinder than Mark, who had a habit of flicking your sweat-stained efforts into his strategically positioned waste basket. In a cold arrogant voice reminiscent of Conrad Veidt in *Casablanca*, Mark intoned, 'Never write more than ten words without a punctuation mark. Never use ten-rupee words when four-anna ones will do.' Our British guru even published a book entitled *How To Make Your Copy Talk*. It was my Bible for many years.

But the man who really turned me on to advertising (which I was slightly ashamed of until then) was David Bernstein.

Simile allows the imagination to soar. Statement brings it to earth with a thud.

His article in *Ad Weekly* on 'Poetry In Advertising' was like a blinding light on the road to Damascus, which until that time, seemed more like the pathway to Sodom. He wrote, 'Both poetry and advertising make use of similes and hyperbole to enhance the reader's appreciation of the object being written about.' For instance, Byron could have said, 'She is a very beautiful woman.' Instead, he wrote, 'She walks in beauty like the night.' Simile allows the imagination to soar. Statement brings it to earth with a thud.

Years later, when I visited David at his agency The Creative Business, although I was a grizzled veteran by that time, I still felt a thrill at meeting such an icon. Besides pleasantries, we exchanged our favourite slogans like Kawasaki's 'Let the good times roll' and 'We make things people need, including profits', Which is the best defence of capitalism I've ever heard. We may be living in the age of electronic media, but the printed word is still king.

In the mid-1950s, JWT stood head and biceps over the other agencies which included D J Keymer's, Stronach's, Grant's and of course, Lintas. Subsequently, JWT evolved into HTA. Keymer's, out of whose womb Clarion was wrenched forth, evolved into BOMAS, which then traumatised into Benson's. Benson's became Ogilvy Benson and Mather (OBM), which was then abbreviated into O&M or Ogilvy & Mather as it is now known in the 1990s.

Needless to say, much blood has passed beneath the Keymer bridge during these past five decades. Holocausts were monotonous in their frequency at this beleaguered agency. Whether it was Wally Ollins or Sherry Mukherjee or P N Sarma, the new CEO's broom would sweep clean. Often, twenty or thirty executives fired in one shot. Finally it was a young S R Mani Aiyar who steadied the rudder. And except for a mild purge triggered by Ashish Mitra in the early 1990s, Mani kept the ship on a steady course till the time he retired in 1994.

Stronach's gave up the ghost in the 1960s, and Grant's was swallowed up by Contract in the 1970s. Lintas exchanged its London gown for an Indian sari with an American border in 1969 and became Lintas: India Ltd. Incidentally, it was one of the first foreign agencies to have an Indian Chief Executive in the soft-spoken but hard-nosed Razmi Ahmed in 1957. This was the start of the great Indianisation tradition of Unilever, who appointed the hawk-like P L Tandon as Chairman of Hindustan Lever in the early 1960s.

In those glory days, there weren't many big Indian agencies around. The London Press Exchange (LPE) teamed up with the Indian Aiyars Advertising to form LPE-Aiyars. To the best of my recollection, the trailblazer who showed a host of others how simple it was to start your own Indian agency was the dashing Bal Mundkur. In one swift stroke, he cut the umbilical cord that led to London and New York. Boldly, he flaunted the Sanskrit name, Ulka, which means meteor.

Until then, most agencies were named after their founders. J Walter Thompson, Leo Burnett, and even in India, Dattaram's and Aiyar's. No doubt about it, Bal was a pioneer. He went on to become one of the founders of the Advertising Club of Bombay, which today is probably one of the most active advertising clubs in the world. For this, Bal, and later the energetic Amol Bose, deserve full credit.

Meanwhile, back at the JWT ranch, a mama's boy was now getting his baptism by fire. Besides Mark Robinson who wielded the creative whip, there were giants of the stature of Ayaz Peerbhoy, a tall, wide, handsome man with a lovely deep booming voice, and Nuru Swaminathan, a small flamboyant lady with a huge bindi in the middle of her forehead. They handled with ease multinational clients like Johnson & Johnson, Geoffrey Manners, Standard-Vacuum Oil and Indian companies like Air-India, Voltas and TOMCO.

It never fails to amaze me that the Tatas have always been a part of my growing up. Whether it was writing ads for these three Tata Group companies or attending a New Year's Eve Ball at their Taj Mahal hotel or producing plays at their National Centre for the Performing Arts. The late J R D Tata was more than just a great industrialist. He is an icon for generations to come. He bestrides our narrow world like an unassuming colossus.

At JWT, a far less unassuming colossus stood above the giants: E J (Peter) Fielden, Managing Director, Proprietor, and in his own words, Chief Account Executive. Peter Fielden was known in the corridors of the agency as 'Papa', a term that inspired both affection and fear. As one panned up from his alligator shoes to his matching alligator smile to his arctic blue eyes, one was aware of the Raj in all its imperial majesty.

He ran the agency like Captain Bligh, but he never allowed any mutiny on his Bounty. He had long ago mastered the British principle of divide and rule. He kept Ayaz and Nuru and Mark at loggerheads with each other like in a Punch and Judy show. All the strings led back to the puppeteer. He enjoyed having his barons warring with one another. He never appointed a deputy. So, brilliant Subhash Ghosal had to wait till Greg Bathon, John Gaynor and Morris Mathias had completed their tenures before assuming the mantle of Managing Director.

The creative system at JWT reflected, I think, Peter's Principle: Fielden made the Copy Chief sit on the second floor with his writers, and the Art Chief sit on the sixth floor with his artists... and never the twain would meet. For instance, Nuru would charge into our room, her pallu streaming like a jet trail behind her, and declare, 'Bobby Kooka wants his Air-India ad on "three flights a week to London" in tomorrow's *Times of India*. I'll be back in half an hour for the copy.' That was the client service brief in those days. Very brief.

True to her word, Nuru would banshee back thirty minutes later, tear the copy out of my typewriter, hurtle off towards the sixth floor to instruct short, quiet Umesh Rao, the Art Chief (who, incidentally, was the man who drew the original Air-India Maharaja, under Bobby Kooka's inspiring gaze). Twenty-four hours later, I would be the proud father of an ad which, like a test-tube baby, had been created without human contact with the other partner. I'll say one thing for Nuru. She was a great midwife.

Some years later, when I was Creative Director of Lintas, I introduced the Creative Team concept, and was promptly accused of destroying the traditional bond that existed in the Copy department and separately in the Art department. For I insisted that the copywriter and the visualiser sit together, rather than separately. (I believe a few old-fashioned agencies still carry on this decrepit practice till today.)

To me, great communication is when there is fusion between the word and the picture. Not the words as a caption to the picture. Not the picture as an illustration of the words. Even though I am a copywriter by training, I tend to think in terms of visuals. The shot of the girl in the waterfall, in the Liril film, is more important than the forgettable headline, 'Come alive with freshness'. The prologue of *Tughlaq*, where the bare forked animal is dressed in the robes of the emperor says more than a caption, 'Man into myth'. The visual metaphor is absolutely essential in a country of sixteen major languages. A picture may speak a thousand words. But a symbol speaks a myriad languages.

A picture may speak a thousand words. But a symbol speaks a myriad languages.

Nevertheless, when it comes to wit, it is difficult to beat the word. My earliest recollection of a great ad was for Carrier air-conditioners in *New Yorker* magazine (which I devour till today). The ad is split in two. On the left hand side is a skinny young man looking at the reader with a hangdog expression. Underneath is the caption, 'I used to be a ninety-nine lbs weakling.' On the right hand side of the ad, we see the same young man with a slight smile on his face, 'I'm still a ninety-nine lbs weakling...but boy, is my bedroom cool!'

Creative geniuses were rare in India in the 1950s. The only genuine one I can remember, besides Bobby Kooka, was Philip Rose of Burmah Shell. I can still recall his 'Fill-up and feel the difference' slogan. Wasn't he also the author of 'Burmah

Shell in India's life. And part of it'? The Art Director we most admired was P N Sarma, for his Burmah Shell and Tata Fison campaigns.

Art Directors had to rely more on drawings than photographs because newsprint reproduction was abysmal. Anything less than forty-five screen was a no-no. The nearest you could get to colour were blotchy faces in *The Illustrated Weekly.* Copywriters had to beware of howlers like, '"This is what Lux does for my complexion," says Mala Sinha.' Because poor Mala's face would look like a poached egg!

'Surf washes whitest' caused our Art Directors endless anguish, until our Chief Art Director, Raj Arjungi, invented the famous 'dazzle' motif. By using a black background and surrounding the garment with a white spiky halo, he was able to create an optical illusion of whiteness, even on dirty grey newsprint.

Copywriters, too, had their hands cuffed behind their backs. Not only were ten-rupee words out, but even one-rupee words were viewed with suspicion by clients like Hindustan Lever, whose ads went into twenty or more languages. 'Will it translate?' was the battle cry. So Product Managers emasculated your copy until it was reduced to a basic English corpse.

But I was pig-headed. Perhaps it was the lesson I had learnt as rebel *ghar-jamai*. If you believe in something, go out and do it. After I left JWT and joined Lintas (and married Pearl in spite of my mother threatening to disinherit me), I plunged into a heady battle with Unilever Detergents Co-ordination in London.

Before you joined a giant corporation like Unilever (and in those days, Lintas was owned by Unilever, not by Hindustan Lever as is the misconception), you had to go through a gruelling series of interviews. It was a third degree cross-examination, but done with British Raj finesse. Fortunately I came prepared, and machine-gunned my interrogators with facts about rural India and Indian language copy that left them silent but apprehensive. 'What kind of creative wild man are we allowing into the hallowed precincts of Unilever advertising?' was the silent signal that flashed from one to the other.

It's interesting to note that even today the 'Suits' don't quite trust the Creatives. As Chief Executive, I've interviewed hundreds of creative crazies. The deciding question I've always put to them is, 'What will you do if a client rejects a brilliant ad?' The best answer I've heard is, 'I'll sell it to him again and again.' Contrary to popular but myopic belief, brilliant creativity has to be sold with twice the vehemence. The classic client putdown is, 'It's brilliant, but I can't risk it.' But to break through the clutter, you need to walk on the edge, take risks. In recent times, our Kama Sutra condom advertising did just that, but more of that later.

So keeping their fingers and toes crossed, the wise men of Lintas hired me. Disaster struck at my first meeting with Hindustan Lever. I put forward a film idea for Rexona soap which featured (hold your breath!) a girl bathing under a waterfall. Gian Bahl, the General Advertising Manager, was aghast. 'You are outraging the modesty of Indian womanhood across five hundred thousand villages.' I fought back, 'But sir, you yourself have said that a bar of soap is a bar of hope. I am only opening a fantasy world for them which is an extension of Hindi cinema.'

Gian gave me his most withering scorn, 'You Oxford dons know nothing about rural India. Bring me a script with a girl bathing in a bathroom. And make sure the bathroom has no fancy tiles!' Many years later, of course, I was to trot out my favourite fantasy of the girl in the waterfall for Liril soap, just beating Raj Kapoor to the punch when he had Zeenat Aman doing her titillating wet number in *Satyam Shivam Sundaram*.

In the 1950s, a company like Hindustan Lever believed in leaning over backwards to avoid talking over the heads of their consumers. This caused many of us to become creative contortionists. You had to be creative, but within a logical strait-jacket. You were always told that your creative brilliance would fly above the bewildered heads of the poor ignorant Indian consumer. It was then that I realised that David Ogilvy was wrong. The consumer is not a moron, he is your client. I maintain that just because a man can't read and write doesn't mean he is stupid. Illiterate audiences are visually very sophisticated, thanks to television.

Even in the 1970s, the sword of logic was wielded with fearsome accuracy by Marketing Directors like David Webb. With cold blue eyes and gingery hair, he pulled no punches and in fact reminded me of a middleweight boxer. He was always prancing around on the balls of his feet. In his first speech to the Advertising Club of Bombay, he said, 'I'm the kind of client who writes the words and draws the pictures. Which is not to say I'm not partial to brilliant creativity!'

Fortunately, this same David Webb had the good grace to say in his farewell speech four years later, 'Rin detergent bar has been our greatest advertising success, thanks to Lintas getting the ads approved while I was on home leave. Can you imagine me okaying white lightning striking people like a thunderbolt from Jove?'

In retrospect it is interesting to observe that though the Chairman's post at Hindustan Lever was Indianised a decade after Independence, the Marketing Director's job continued to be the prerogative of the British Raj till the mid-1970s. But even prior to Mr Webb's opposition to our crazy 'Whitening strikes' mnemonic for Rin, we had to do battle with Unilever coordination in London on the proposition itself.

When Levers wanted to launch Rin, which was India's very first detergent bar, we had decided on a platform of whiteness. But Levers was very keen on selling it on the platform of economy. They said that South Africa was the only country where they had successfully managed to launch a detergent bar. In all other countries, it had flopped. Detergent bars don't work, detergent powders do. Because detergent bars are seen as more expensive.

My gut feel told me the Indian consumer equated whiteness with superior washing products, not economy. So we girded our loins for battle. Hindustan Lever was adamant. Rin had to project economy first. I told them this wouldn't be enough to make the consumer switch over to a totally new type of washing bar. In India, whiteness is the key benefit to offer the buyer. I remembered my mother's words, 'If you believe in something, don't give in.' The hostilities raged for several months. Finally we got a curt reply from London, 'Since Rin has not been a winner in the world, let Lintas: India give the whiteness platform a try.'

Now I was in a fix. We had to decide how to make Rin-whiteness different from Surf-whiteness and also different from Sunlight-whiteness. 'Surf washes whitest.' 'Sunlight washes white and bright.' How were we going to pull a third rabbit out of the whiteness hat? I put my head in a noose and let my copywriters loose. I said, 'I want a hundred different approaches in the form of headlines.' They came back to me and I went through all of them. Call it instinct. Call it luck. I selected 'Whitening strikes with Rin' from the lot. It was one of two dozen written by Cossy Rosario, a senior copywriter at the time who later went on to become Copy Chief.

And then because the product had a build-up whiteness effect, which meant that the more you washed with Rin, the whiter your clothes became, we changed it to 'Whitening strikes again and again with Rin.' We turned this into a mnemonic lightning flash and the rest is history. It did extremely well and sales went through the roof. Rin became the biggest profit earner for Hindustan Lever within a few years. Cossy, along with his beard and swept-back hair, deserves to be inducted into the Copywriters' Hall of Fame. (His first piece of copy that brought his writing to my attention was a programme note he wrote for a Theatre Group play.)

To me art is the magic of transforming imagination into reality. The horror of war in Picasso's imagination was transformed into the distorted lines of his *Guernica* on canvas. Imaginative reality has more power and punch than documentary statistics. That's why three tomatoes being squashed into a jar and bursting through their skin, gives more impact and memorability to the family planning line '*Ek ya do bas*' (One or two, that's enough) than a million Government of India pamphlets.

I don't wish to quarrel with neurologists, but I find this claptrap about the left brain being logical and the right brain being emotional, untenable. As a practitioner of turning ideas into action, I believe that the creative artist is endowed with a middle brain. Where a fusion between logic and emotion occurs. This enables the true artist to think in concepts, rather than just words or just pictures. This middle brain is the 'no-man's land' between the conscious and the subconscious. And that is why, as a creator operating in the field of advertising, I believe in symbolism rather than reality. Whether it is escapism into a waterfall or whitening entering our clothes through the heavens.

My greatest advertising battles have been fought on the playing fields of Lever/Lintas. One of the most exhilarating of these was the great Dalda debate. The Hamurabi of the market place of the 1950s, was the revered ICS prophet Dr Maurice Zinkin, who looked a bit like a priest. In his quiet mellifluous voice, he expressed his anguish that his baby, Dalda Vanaspati, was being rejected by the Indian housewife. He believed that Dalda was a scientifically healthy, nutritious product with the added advantage of being half the price of ghee.

The creative artist is endowed with a middle brain. Where a fusion between logic and emotion occurs.

So he mounted a campaign, 'Dalda is good for you', in twenty-one Indian languages, covering every conceivable target group. From government officers to schoolchildren, from doctors to illiterate peasant women. Lintas was asked to invent new media: back covers of exercise books; display boards near village wells; flannel boards for rural lectures; in addition to advertising on matchboxes, State Transport Buses, umbrellas and what have you. I think we even had an abortive shot at skywriting and airplane leafleting.

There was not a nook or cranny of India left uncovered by the indefatigable Dr Z. We must have reached almost 200 million of the estimated national population of 400 million in the 1950s. (How easy it would have been in the 1980s to reach 200 million with one commercial spot on *Mahabharata*!)

Alas! In spite of two years of this extremely logical campaign which plugged that Dalda contained umpteen international units of Vitamin A and Vitamin D, the consumer feedback was 'Dalda gives me a tickle in the throat'; 'Dalda gives me an upset tummy'; 'Dalda gives me diarrhoea' and

'Dalda gives me constipation', almost in the same breath; and even 'Dalda is bad for eyesight'.

This last comment was born out of an unsubstantiated experiment done by a doctor who fed rats on a pure diet of Dalda for several months, depriving them of all other nourishment. Naturally they went blind. And probably deaf and lame too.

Our researchers also revealed that housewives who used Dalda, flatly denied that they did. The researcher would ask what the cooking medium was and the reply was usually, 'Ghee'. On examination of the kitchen, the researcher would find a large tin of Dalda near the stove, and not a trace of ghee anywhere in sight!

This unsettling research caused the ever alert Dr Z to set up a task force comprising (if I remember correctly) Dr Rajni Chadha of Lever Market Research, Gerson da Cunha, Lintas Deputy Copy Chief at the time, Balwant Tandon, Hindi Copy Expert, and myself, who had joined recently. We conducted what was known as 'Motivation Research'. Which was the buzzword at the time, thanks to Dr Dichter's and Vance Packard's book, *The Hidden Persuaders*.

It was Rajni who came up with the astute insight that housewives were ashamed of Dalda because it symbolised their fall in status, that is, they were unable to afford ghee, and had to use a substitute product. Thus they were transferring their resentment on to the ubiquitous Dalda. I have observed this transferred resentment syndrome when a client service director screams at his secretary when he should be screaming at his client, or when a housewife admonishes her servant instead of her husband.

At a client-agency pow-wow, it was decided that we would scrap the factual campaign and put our money on emotion instead. In other words, since the prejudice against Dalda was emotional, we would fight fire with fire and use an emotional proposition. Gerson, with his gift for words, put it succinctly, 'Let us wrap Dalda in the cocoon of motherly love. If Maa blesses Dalda, it becomes acceptable in the home by all.' It was Balwant who came up with the emotive headline in Hindi, *'Mamta ki kasauti par khara* — Dalda' (Tested on the touchstone of mother's love). The English equivalent, 'Mothers who care, use Dalda', we always felt, lacked the emotional punch of the Hindi line.

This was my baptism by fire into the gut-feel world of Indian language advertising. It has often forced me to go back and rethink my clever-clever western concepts in Hindi. When in doubt, I go back to my roots. The way my mother and father think and feel in Gujarati. How would my first cousin who lives on a farm in Kathiawar react? This enabled me, decades later, to fine tune 'Lalitaji' as an ethnic symbol for Surf.

When in doubt, go back to your roots.

Was it the *'mamta'* proposition that switched off the prejudice against Dalda? Or is it just the passage of time that makes substitutes acceptable? Whatever it was, Dr Z was ecstatic. He now turned his attention to the models we featured in our Dalda films. To focus us better, he brought to a screening of a retrospective of Dalda cinema commercials, his formidable wife Taya and his son John.

I'll never forget the occasion. It was at the Strand cinema minuet theatre. The whole agency was on parade. Razmi Ahmed, our Managing Director, John Walton, our Copy Chief, Roy Delgarno, Art Director, down to the man in the hot seat, me, as Films Chief. After the showing, there was a weighty silence. Thus spake Dr Z, 'The models featured as middle-class housewives are far too glamorous and beautiful.' Turning to his twelve-year-old son, he said, 'Isn't that so, John?' Up piped John, 'Yes. They should be more plain looking. Like Mummy.'

The silence that ensued, moved from weighty to bone-crushing. Without batting an eyelid, Dr Z turned to the Account Director (who shall remain nameless) and said affably, 'Quite right. They should be plain Janes. Like my wife, or yours.' The entire senior management of Lintas studiously stared at their shoes. Gerson and I exchanged Groucho Marx-raised eyebrows, simultaneously bolted for the door, and just about managed to reach the toilets, before bursting into raucous laughter.

The world of film commercials in those days was pretty amateur. Levers pioneered the cinema commercial with six hundred-foot films (six-and-a-half-minute long-winded storyline films which resembled mini features). They encouraged Blaze Cinema Advertising to set up a system of distribution all over the country. Blaze's Mohan Bijlani (popularly known as Bijjles) and Freny Variava, his partner, soon had a national network in place.

I had joined Lintas with the key intention of becoming India's first advertising Films Chief. After all, Lintas made over fifty cinema commercials a year, that is, one per week. When I took over the films department, Mr Narayanswamy was the film production manager. A solid brick of a man with iron-grey hair. He stopped pesky account executives dead in their tracks by swatting them down with a firm 'No!' before they could sting him with their unreasonable requests.

He was a man who understood the English language in all its magnificent exactitude. I appeared to him as a hotshot from Mars, full of wild ideas and crazy exaggerations. 'I've told you a hundred and fifty times, Mr Narayanswamy, not to say "No" until we have examined the request.' 'Mr Padamsee, you have told me exactly three times. Not a hundred and fifty times.'

I think my time as Films Chief was one of the most exciting periods of my life. Because models were usually secretaries or working girls, we had to shoot only on holidays or weekends or late at night. This meant innumerable cups of tea, dozens of cigarettes and next to no food. Consequently I developed an ulcer long before it was fashionable. This badge of ulceration was handed over to each of my protégés in the films department, including Shyam Benegal, Kabir Bedi, Mubi Ismail (Pasricha), Robin Dharmaraj, Dalip Tahil, and later Sumantra Ghosal.

Getting home with the doodhwalla every day was a heady experience. Working with producers like Hamid Sayani, Clement Baptista, Paul Zils, Fali Billimoria and G B Ghanekar sharpened my learning curve. There was the time I wrote a script for Sunlight soap which started with a close-up of an eye, and Paul Zils said, in his most Germanic tone, 'Vee alvays ztart vith an eztablizhing long zhot.'

Since I had to turn out fifty or more scripts a year, I became adept at thinking visually. Coming from the theatre, I insisted every film have a dramatic arc. In those days, we moved from 600-foot films down to 100-foot films, which still gave one plenty of room to manoeuvre. Today, a 30-seconder has to be much more condensed, and a 10-seconder has to be shorthand *in extremis*.

My long-term ambition was to become a feature film director by the ripe old age of thirty. During my two-year stint at the Royal Academy of Dramatic Arts in London, in the early 1950s, I had taken a course in film craft at the British Film

Institute. I was a voracious reader of *Sight & Sound* magazine. Orson Welles was my reigning God and *Citizen Kane* was my film Bible.

But it wasn't until 1979 that I got a chance to do my first film script based on Girish Karnad's play, *Tughlaq*. I had hoped to get Amitabh Bachchan to play the lead, and thereby raise the finance for what was estimated to be a one crore-rupee project at that time. Unfortunately, shortly after we spoke, Amitabh met with his near-fatal accident on the sets of *Coolie*. And that was that. My second attempt at a feature film was based on an original idea I conceived on the Hindu-Muslim theme. It is still a script in search of a financier. Any takers?

I haven't yet become a movie director, but in the 1960s, I was directing movie stars for Lux and movie stars-to-be for other commercials. I shot Zeenat Aman on the steps of the Town Hall for Signal toothpaste. Zeenat was a sprightly young teenager who had just come to Bombay from her Panchgani school. After a particularly difficult shot where we had to shoot take after take, she turned to me and said, 'My God! You're a slave driver. My calf muscles are paining having to walk up and down these wretched Town Hall steps.'

Then there was this very demure Parsi girl, Persis Khambatta, who was posing for a product called Trionise, in a mini studio at Hunnar Films. She had to wait long hours for her shot and under the harsh studio lights, she began to perspire. I was about thirty at the time, while she must have been sixteen or so. Very boldly, I took out my snow-white handkerchief and dabbed her upper lip to make the perspiration disappear. At which point, she glared at me as if to say, 'Getting fresh, huh?' I'll never forget that look!

For Lux, Mr Venugopalan was our film star contact executive. He had just successfully launched Hema Malini, as

Raj Kapoor's *Dream Girl*. Next on his hit list was a young starlet called Padmini Priyadarshini.

My crazy script called for a dance amid Diwali fireworks. The fireworks were lit and G B Ghanekar, the director, called, 'Action!' As the *anars* fountained upwards, Padmini began her delightful dance which was suddenly cut short by her agonised scream, because her bare foot had landed on a glowing ember. 'Cut!' screamed her protective mother. (All South Indian stars have their *amma* by their side to defend their precious little darlings against any monkey business.)

'What are you trying to do? Kill my child?' Ever solicitous of my leading lady, I rushed forward with the first-aid kit. Her mother beamed at me, and then scowled, 'Who has written this bleddy script?' I quickly changed the topic by shouting for the giant air circulators to be switched on to clear the smoke. At this, the mother screamed, 'Be careful! Last week at AVM, one bleddy fillow's head got chupped off!'

Fun and frolic. But lots of ulcerous moments too. The preview of the double-header was always a four Gelusil affair. Those were usually held in preview theatres situated at cinemas like Liberty, Eros and Strand. Later, the Blaze Minuet Theatre became very popular. At Lintas, we were fortunate when we moved from Khaitan Bhavan at Churchgate to Duggal House and eventually to Hindustan Lever House, where we built our own cinema auditorium. This was achieved by Razmi Ahmed and myself convincing P L Tandon that a lot of time and money of senior marketing executives would be saved by having an auditorium on the premises.

I devised a method by which we could show triple-headers instead of double-headers. We had a preview attachment fixed to a thirty-five mm projector which allowed the soundtrack to run in synch with the picture. This saved the expense of making a married print and avoided having to cut the original negative. I worked out an arrangement to play the music background on a tape recorder along with the double-header. This immediately conveyed the mood of the film and gave it emotional impact. I think it enabled me to sell my double-headers more convincingly and thereby saved the time, expense and harassment of having to do revision after revision after revision.

I've always believed that a creative craftsman must understand technology. I don't think it's enough for a theatre director to direct actors. He must be able to direct the set designer, the lighting man, the make-up specialist, the music director, the costume designer, everybody associated with the production of the play. He must know his craft inside out. When I dramatise a scene from a play, I must not only dream the impossible, but I must also know how to make it work on stage.

In my production of *Marat/Sade*, I visualised the guillotine chopping an actor's head off in full view of the audience. At the back of my mind, I knew this effect could be achieved because I had studied magic and misdirection. The scene was so realistic that the late Pravin Joshi, the Gujarati stage's most outstanding director, told me he leaped out of his seat thinking a genuine accident had occurred when he saw the severed head lying on the floor.

I have to confess. I am a sucker for magic. Peter Brook, my guru in the theatre, whose career I have followed since I was a drama student, said, 'The theatre is a place of magic. Directors are the great shamans of the arts. The magic men who create illusions that leave the audience wonderstruck.' My brother-in-law, the late Hamid Sayani, who charmed radio listeners for generations and came to be known as Mr Radio Ceylon, was also one of India's finest magicians. It was he who showed me how to turn the water into blood as Pontius Pilate washed his hands in *Jesus Christ Superstar*. When Evita raises her arms up at the end of 'Don't cry for me Argentina' and her silhouette remains on the cyclorama for an illusory instant, we are magicalised. Thousands of people still remember Kabir Bedi transformed from a nude innocent into a powerful resplendent emperor in the prologue of *Tughlaq*.

This same magic infuses great advertising. When the Kawasaki motorbike morphs into a cheetah, we are thrilled and excited. And in a public service film I made years ago, as the commentator's voice says, 'The greatness of this man was his simplicity,' Imtiaz Dharker's hand paints a simple line drawing of Gandhi. This is drama. This is magic. This is communication. This is where I have spent my entire life.

To me, Bill Bernbach is every bit as brilliant as Peter Brook. Of course, ads are trying to sell products. But don't forget productions are trying to sell tickets. In the arena of painting and sculpture, we recognise great art by its commercial value. Why this does not apply to other arts like poetry and theatre is a question to ponder over.

We recognise great art by its commercial value. Why doesn't this apply to other arts like poetry and theatre?

The finest flowering of advertising art we find in England. The iron curtain between Hard Sell and Entertainment seems to meld. The brilliance of the latest Hamlet Cigar commercial is talked about in sophisticated London drawing rooms with the same passion as the latest performance by Kenneth Brannagh.

Unfortunately, the same cannot be said for the crass advertising on the other side of the Atlantic Ocean. Only rarely does a Nike or a Federal Express or an Apple break through the mediocrity of American advertising. And yet, hold it! Bernbach was an American. To me, the golden age of American advertising was the 1960s, when Bill Bernbach, David Ogilvy, Mary Welles, Jerry Della Femina, George Lois and a dozen more advertising comets lit up the US skyline.

As we approach the twenty-first century, I predict that Indian advertising will move more towards the English pattern rather than the American one. Film directors like Ridley Scott, and before him, Jack Clayton *(Room at the Top)* and Richard Lester *(Hard Day's Night)* and scores of others crossed over into feature films from advertising.

In India we have already witnessed the career of Satyajit Ray from advertising Art Director to maestro of the Indian cinema. We note Shyam Benegal, Govind Nihalani and several more operate with equal facility in these two worlds of commerce and art simultaneously. When will Prahlad Kakkar, Sumantra Ghosal, Nomita Roy Ghose et al make the leap from thirty seconds to two hours?

Desire is the key to all action.

THE FAMILY AS A CORE VALUE

*A*nyone who's met me will tell you that I am a family man. And I can justly say that I belong to several families. There's my own family — my 'blood family' so to speak. Then there's the Theatre Group family and the advertising family. The blood family I grew up in was a family of eight children. Add my parents, and that's a family of ten. We did everything together. Whether it was going to the movies or to parties, it was always in a gang. Of course, the family divided into sub-gangs, but overall it was a very tribal culture. Every human being needs to belong, to be a part of the whole.

My eldest brother, Sultan (Bobby), my eldest sister, Roshan and my second sister, Zarina — known to one and all as Jerry or Jay — were one gang. Then my next sister Shiraz, or Bee, was kind of in-between, so unfortunately she felt very isolated. She was three years younger than Jerry, so they treated her like a *kachcha roti*.

Every human being needs to belong, to be a part of the whole.

Then my brother Chotu or Cho, who's a year younger than me, and my brother Bubbles, who was four years younger than Cho, and myself were another gang. And then after a long gap came my youngest sister, Dilshad, nicknamed Candy.

So Candy and Bee always felt a bit estranged. Of course, we didn't realise this at the time. It was only some twenty or thirty years later when we were all grown up, and one day, it suddenly popped up in the conversation: 'Oh, I felt that you all were excluding me!' We, who were 'included', never even gave it a second thought at that time. (Cruelty, thy name is thoughtlessness.)

My father Jafferseth was a tubby man no more than five feet tall. He had a perpetually pleasant expression on his face, and his gait was slow and measured. Unlike my mother, he was always willing to see the other side of things. If you were late, he'd excuse you. If you failed your exams, he would understand. And generally, he had a wealth of goodwill for everyone, which my mother felt that people took advantage of.

My mother Kulsumbai too, was rather short, but she had a very purposeful walk. Ever since I can remember she wore rimless glasses, which added to the effect of her stern demeanour. She could be extremely severe, but at the same time she could also be extremely loving. She had a smooth complexion and a serene face that gave her a calm look, unlike energy maniacs like me who always look harried and harassed.

With short parents, most of my siblings were on the shorter side. I was the only freak who grew to be more than six feet tall. Bobby was a burly five feet nine inches and his large shoulders always seemed as though they were too heavy for his size. But he had an aggressive face and his eyebrows had no centre. A very attractive, macho man with thick full lips and a mop of curly hair. But it wasn't Bobby's looks so much as his voice that intimidated you. When he spoke, you had no doubt that you were in the presence of a man who had a tremendous charisma.

Chotu too is a handsome man, and since he has lived most of his adult life in London, he speaks with a cultured English accent. Very dapper, he has an engaging charm which comes from the Padamsee side of the family. Bubbles, on the other hand, was most unKulsumbai-like. Curly haired and five feet six inches tall, he was very tolerant, very laid back and in no hurry to push people. He was cool long before the term was invented, and was always ready with a quick quip or witticism. He was the nearest thing to my father Jafferbhai.

Roshan is a very quiet, spry lady who bounces along with a girlish traipsing walk, even now in her seventies. We've always called her the absent-minded professor of the family but she has a heart of gold and will never raise her voice in anger. Jerry was always the most beautiful of us all. With film-star good looks, she was an absolute knockout when she was young. She had a slow metabolism and gradually became stouter and stouter until she was barely able to get off her bed. The weight of her body could hardly be supported by her slim aristocratic ankles and feet. Bee is very contained and I always got the feeling that she didn't like to reveal all of herself. She doesn't have quite the same bounce in her step that Rosh has, but she's still a very energetic person. And finally there's Candy who has an open face with very warm eyes. She's one of the kindest human beings in the world and has become the mother figure for all her relatives in the USA.

When we were all growing up, moving together as a family gave me a tremendous sense of unity. It was a security blanket that was wrapped around us. Considering that my father was almost invisible, it was my mother's powerful but benign influence that once again cocooned us in this quilt of family-ness.

Quite naturally, you'd expect such a large family to live in a large house. And so we did. We lived in a building called Kulsum Terrace, which is situated on the Colaba Causeway in South Bombay.

Kulsum Terrace. The very name conjures up a kind of vast mansion. Which indeed it was. My father built it in the 1930s and named it after my mother, Kulsumbai. He had an Italian architect who designed it with a lot of fancy fittings, including

Italian marble mosaic tiles, and doors and windows that are made of genuine Burma teak. But the grand thing about Kulsum Terrace is the top floor. Which is where the Padamsee family lived.

If you're in Bombay and you walk down Colaba Causeway, just opposite Electric House is a lovely little lane called Walton Road. When you reach No. seven, you'll see a large, pink, Italian-marble pillar with the words 'Kulsum Terrace' running vertically from north to south. (Sad to say the pillar collapsed just as this book was coming to life!)

You enter a rather dingy corridor and you come to the lift. Press the button, and it sounds like a gunshot going off. 'Bam!' Down comes the lift, you enter and you close the metal cage doors and press for the fourth floor. 'Bang!' You hear this terrible explosion again, and the lift begins to slowly trundle its way upwards. As you go up, you can hear the lift literally groaning, even if there's only one passenger. If there are four passengers, which is the very maximum you dare tax this relic with, the groans turn into anguished rumbles!

When we were young, the lift used to invariably overshoot the fourth floor landing and go up a further six inches or so. This used to terrify the b'jesus out of us kids. We used to scream because we were afraid that it would go right up and mangle itself in those two giant wheels that lift the cage and lower the counterweight.

As you step out of the lift, straight ahead is a solid brown Burma teak door. And in those days, the name that was very prominently displayed was Kulsumbai Padamsee. My father kept everything in my mother's name. (Well, actually, she saw to that. My father was a very hen-pecked husband.)

Then you ring the bell, and a funny little eye-hole opens. The old-fashioned kind, a little 2" x 2" metal grill. The door opens and you step into this enormous drawing room, with a ceiling that goes up about eighteen feet or so, topped by etched-glass skylights. All the windows in KT (as Kulsum Terrace is popularly referred to) carry the KJP monogram designed by my father.

From the centre of the ceiling hangs a huge cut-glass chandelier, echoed by mini-chandeliers all around the walls. My father had business dealings in glass, so he used to import these beautiful chandeliers all the way from Czechoslovakia. This was in the days of the British Raj, when there were no import duties, and you could bring in anything you liked if you had the money.

As you look around the walls, vast 8' x 10' portrait paintings look down at you. On one side is a picture of my mother sitting on a chair with my brother Bobby perched on the arm. On the other side is a picture of my parents, in a kind of wedding pose. Then there are other portraits of my maternal grandparents and paternal grandparents. These are rather traditional pictures. In those days nobody smiled for a portrait. They all looked rather severe. The idea was to inspire awe, rather than portray a friendly paternalistic attitude.

But yet, there were two paintings side by side that were always smiling. One was the Aga Khan (whom I had seen being weighed in diamonds at the Cricket Club of India), and the other was Lord Krishna. It says something for communal harmony in those days.

Since the drawing room is in the centre of the house, it has an unusually large number of doors. Nine, as a matter of fact. Including three sets of french windows that open out on to a veranda that overlooks the busy traffic of Colaba Causeway. When we were growing up, the veranda used to be where my father lived in splendid isolation. He became rather reclusive since my mother dominated the scene. Moreover, since all the children became English speaking, ours turned from a Gujarati-Kutchi family into a totally English westernised household... and my father didn't quite fit into that. I got the feeling he always felt a bit of a stranger in his own home.

So he kind of 'retired' into the veranda. All day long, like many Gujaratis, he would sit on his jhoola and rock back and forth. And our great thrill was to come round the back of the jhoola and clamber over it and sit on its comforting arms. Then my father would tell us funny little stories, and illustrate them with his little red-and-blue pencil. But within fifteen hilarious minutes, my father was exhausted. Then he'd shoo us out of his room.

My mother, however, adapted marvellously. She totally accepted our westernisation, which we got first from Miss Murphy's School and then later from the Cathedral School. Miss Murphy's was a private boarding school. And though it was in Bombay itself, my mother sent us there because she couldn't manage so many children. She kept having babies at an incredibly regular rate. Hardly had she finished nursing one, when the next was already on its way. (My father, like his sons, had a high libido.) So by the time each child was two years old, he/she would be packed off to Miss Murphy's school. This veddy Bwitish institution was run by a *grande dame* with the classic Irish name Murphy.

By the time I got to know Miss Murphy, she was already in the twilight of her life. But I remember she always stood ramrod straight. A tall woman, she had silver-white hair and blue eyes that were beginning to blur with cataracts. She, together with our governess, Barbara, gave all of us Padamsees our 'Christian' sense of values. Corny as it may seem, I have lived my life according to the proverbs that these two principled ladies taught me: 'Actions speak louder than words', or 'Try and try again until you succeed'. Barbara Walcott was a tiny Anglo-Indian lady who, in spite of her parentage had an extremely dark complexion. She played foster mother to at least six out of the eight Padamsee kids. She was a strict disciplinarian. And if you didn't toe the line, you would get a slap that would make your head ring for days. There is something to be said for a disciplined upbringing. It instills in you a sense of right and wrong. It removes all cushions of self-pity and mollycoddling. To Barbara two things were paramount. Her Catholic religion and her unswerving determination to do things the right way. The second, of course, arose out of the first. Is it surprising then that I developed a strong fixation at the age of nine about becoming a Catholic priest? In our boarding school dining hall, we were not allowed to put our elbows on the table or even talk during meals. On one wall, a large poster stared at us, featuring an ugly black crow, with the quote 'Wise birds live in the country'. I still hallucinate about the meaning of that enigmatic message. I still dream about the echoing rooms of Miss Murphy's School. Do you ever really leave your past behind?

Do you ever really leave your past behind?

The next strong woman in my life was, of course, my mother whom I only got to know after Miss Murphy died and we went back to live in Kulsum Terrace. Kulsumbai's rules were simple. You never wasted money. Which meant you either travelled in one of the two family cars or you went by bus. Never by taxi. We travelled third class by train to a seaside resort for the holidays. (However, a lorry loaded with a refrigerator, fans and other necessities for luxurious living, accompanied us.) We could invite as many friends as we liked to breakfast, lunch or dinner. But dining at a restaurant was a sin.

Roughhouse games were in, but bullying was out. Disobedience was met with a chappal on the fleshy part of your calves. Physical affection and cuddling were conspicuous by their absence. Maybe it's the inhibitions of Gujaratis or of Indians in general, but embracing or hugging family members was taboo. Yet, aunts would insist on kissing children on the lips. Something I dreaded at large family occasions.

Actually, I was unaware of this absence of physical closeness till a friend pointed it out to me. It was then, at the age of twenty, that I began consciously putting my arm around my mother and giving her a hug. What started out as a forced action soon became natural. As Myerhold, the great Russian theatre director, said, 'Do the action and soon you will feel the emotion.' In other words, tears help bring the sorrow, and not necessarily vice versa, as his great rival Stanislavsky insisted.

'Do the action and soon you will feel the emotion.' In other words, tears help bring the sorrow, and not necessarily vice versa.

My father, too, replaced physical affection with gifts. He would shower us with presents on any occasion he could think of. A sweet-hearted man with a great sense of humour. But though he was the President of the Chakla Glassware Merchants' Association for many years, he was less than Vice-President at home. He retired at the age of forty-five, and sat on his jhoola all day in his veranda, cut off from the rest of the house. He would appear only at meal times, like a benign ghost. Always ready to listen to a sob story, Jafferbhai was affectionately known as a soft touch up and down Colaba.

At the Royal Academy of Dramatics Arts, London, an Irish colleen called Brenda Murphy (the Murphys seem to haunt my life) remarked that she thought my father was dead, because

I never spoke of him. I seemed to be obsessed with my mother. On my return to India, I made it a point to spend time with Daddy.

When I married Pearl against my mother's wishes, it was he who supported me in my hour of trial. It was he who every Sunday groaned manfully up the steep stairs of Bella Terrace, where Pearl and I had moved to, loaded with chocolate cake and presents for Ranjit and Raell. It was also he who eventually rebelled against my mother's overpowering ways, and made a quiet exit from KT at the unbelievable age of seventy to assert his overdue independence. My weekly lunches with him and his lady friend, at his tiny little flat in upper Colaba, are treasured memories.

Since my parents were not on speaking terms long before he left the family mansion, my mother spoke to my father only through the children. 'Go and tell your father, dinner is on the table.' Even when my father sometimes asked my mother a direct question, she would reply, 'Tell your father that I have sent his new silk shirts for embroidering his monogram, not to the *darzi*, but to the old lady in Dongri.' Incidentally, this mania of my father's extended even to his hankies and underwear (which carried the monogram JGP), and even to the windowpanes at KT. In India, status and *izzat* are often indistinguishable.

In India, status and izzat are often indistinguishable.

After Miss Murphy passed on, we eight brothers and sisters were split up into various schools. My brother Chotu and I were enrolled in the Cathedral School, which even today is one of Bombay's finest educational institutions. I was in the class of 1947. The cusp of Independence. And fifty years later, when India celebrated its golden jubilee, our class got together for our own golden jubilee.

Of the original thirty-three, some have passed on and many are scattered all around the world, but we did manage to get thirteen boys and twelve girls of our class to come to Bombay in November 1997 for the School's Founder's Day Celebrations. Some were from Bombay itself, but others came from places as far away as Bangalore and Calcutta, and even England and Canada. And though we were a bit doddery with grey hair and lined faces, we staggered off to the Founder's Day Service at St Thomas' Cathedral in South Bombay (where, during the British Raj, we had gone every Wednesday in Lent and sung hymns together).

Even at St Xavier's College, which I joined in 1948 (school was British Raj... college was free India), we had an incredibly together group which is still together fifty years on. There is Gerson da Cunha, his brother Sylvie, Pearl Padamsee, Zarine Wadia, Kiki Watsa, Cedric Santos, Mehli Gobhai, Hameed Sattar and so many more. We all belonged to the Dramatics Club of the college and perhaps that's why we had such a great time. Theatre is a marvellous leveller, a social mixer. Because after rehearsal, you always tend to have a drink and a party and exchange 'guff', as we used to call it in those days. Any nonsense that comes into your head. Exchange your views, ideas, opinions, even prejudices. But it was all good fun.

Growing up in a family of eight with dozens of cousins plus hordes of budding thespians can be an inhibiting or exhilarating experience. Though I was an introvert by nature, this hurly-burly made me a people-addict. I am a teetotaller and seem to get my high at parties with lots of laughter and noise. At KT, you had to yell to be heard above the cacophony.

Though we were a close family and even today we still are, each of us has an independent streak. Because from the age of two, we learnt to live without Mummy, except on weekends. And we would look forward to the weekends because it usually meant an evening at the movies. At that time, the Metro cinema was the place to go. The Padamsee family would book the entire 'A' row in the stalls. Not the balcony, mind you. Our very Gujarati parents would never ever allow us to sit in the balcony. That was considered wasteful.

There were ten of us and we'd always have another five friends with us. In the interval, my father would rush out to Bastani's, which is even today a popular Irani restaurant in Bombay, and pick up patties.

It's a tragedy that the westernised elite are ashamed of their roots.

He'd come back with this huge bag and shout from the back of the stalls in his thick Gujarati accent, 'Aalake, Aalake, I have brought it. Bastani pattice.' Much to the embarrassment of all of us who would cower down in our seats because our friends were there. Then he'd stroll down the aisle distributing these patties to each of us. It's a tragedy that the westernised elite are ashamed of their roots.

Like her children, my mother was very influenced by the movies. And since we owned a furniture shop, she ordered a huge horseshoe table, built like something out of a historical movie she'd seen. The horseshoe is a marvellous shape because the domestic help can enter through the opening of the horseshoe and serve everyone from the inside. It was also large enough to accommodate the ten of us in addition to the guests that we invariably had over for dinner. We prided ourselves on being the Knights of the Horseshoe Table!

The drawing room is also the historic site of the birth of the Theatre Group of Bombay. Bobby had his first rehearsals here. And after he passed on, I, his brother who was ten years younger, had my rehearsals at KT. Later on, my brother Bubbles and my sister Candy rehearsed in the very same place.

And in more recent times, the next generation has carried on the tradition. My daughter, Raell, has her rehearsals in this same drawing room. And one day, I hope my second daughter Shazahn and my son Quasar will meet with their actors here. And continue the tradition that Bobby started in 1941.

Walk through the door to the right of the horseshoe table, and you are in the kitchen. Every day my mother would have enough food cooked to be sufficient for as many as ten guests if necessary. It was usually rich moghlai dishes — chicken curry and mutton curry and always an abundance of vegetarian delicacies (especially for my father).

Almost every night, half a dozen Theatre Group-wallahs would be invited to supper with us. Being a very theatrical family, there were always people who would stay over after rehearsal which would end at about 8.30 p.m. or so. They'd hang around chatting, talking, laughing, joking. Then one of the family members would say, 'Why don't you stay for dinner?' Bobby was, of course, the maestro in charge. Hilarious anecdotes of what went on at rehearsals were exchanged. The latest gossip. Plans for the next production. And the coming Saturday's Hunt party.

To keep the camaraderie of the theatre going, Bobby had devised a party every Saturday night. It was called the Hunt, after the Hunt Ball that the British nobility attended at the end of their foxhunts on Saturdays. After Bobby passed away, I sort of took over the organisation of these Hunts. I'd ring up all our theatre friends and say, 'Hey, we're having a Hunt this Saturday at Kulsum Terrace. Don't forget to bring a little something along.'

Everyone would come with some goodies. Some brought the chips. Someone else would bring orange squash. And still someone else would bring patties. Then we'd wind up the old gramophone and play the latest pop music, which in those days was Glenn Miller's *In the Mood*. And everyone would dance like crazy. Then my mother would appear magically with all sorts of dhoklas and puris and samosas and other Gujarati nibblets.

There was no booze at those parties and yet people came to have a wonderful evening, and the dancing would go on till the wee hours of the morning. These Hunt balls continued for fifteen or twenty years. It started in the 1940s and continued right into the 1960s. And the group spirit that was built up at these rehearsals and Hunts was unbelievable fellowship.

But the best part about Kulsum Terrace is, you walk out of the drawing room and on to a terrace. The top floor of KT is half-enclosed and the other half is open to the sky. That was the most wonderful part about growing up there. In fact there are three separate terraces. One is level with the flat. When you climb a somewhat rickety staircase, you're on the second terrace, which is above our flat.

Finally you go on to the third one, which is the terrace above the drawing room. This is almost like a swimming pool, and we naughty youngsters would block the drains and let the water fill up. And we'd paddle about and have a helluva time, not caring a damn that this might cause the roof of the drawing room to come crashing down. Mercifully, that never happened.

As the family got more and more involved with theatre, the cast of each play became an extended family to us. It was social as well as work oriented. In the great cause of culture, we were creating something together. So there was much laughter and music and dancing and falling in love. In fact my first three sisters all married into the Theatre Group.

Bobby's first lieutenants, Ebrahim Alkazi, Hamid Sayani and Deryck Jeffereis, married my sisters Roshan, Jerry and Bee, respectively. So the Theatre Group and the Padamsee family became one and the same thing. And the Theatre Group headquarters was the Padamsee family residence, Kulsum Terrace. I grew up in this atmosphere of being surrounded by people I knew and people I loved. Good vibes are good for creative growth.

Good vibes are good for creative growth.

So our family, which was already a large one to begin with, became even bigger once everyone started getting married and having children and in-laws. And every Wednesday and Sunday, my mother insisted that all the families and in-laws came over to KT for dinner. On Sunday, it was lunch plus dinner. And this was every single Wednesday and every single Sunday, unbroken for almost ten years. My mother was a great one for keeping the family together. She believed the family that breaks bread together stays together.

Unfortunately, it all broke up, principally because of my marriage to Pearl. Which my mother never accepted. Then the family began to fall apart. I feel quite guilty about that, but I'm glad I stuck to my principles. (Thank God for Miss Murphy and her Irish backbone.)

I'm also happy to say that my own separate families are now a kind of big 'joint family'. I know I've not been a good father in the sense that I've been divorced, separated from my ladies twice. But yet, Raell, who's my daughter from my first wife, Pearl; Ranjit, Pearl's son from her first husband; Quasar, my son from Dolly; and Shazahn, Sharon's and my daughter… after some years of misunderstandings, today can eat together at the same table, go to the theatre together and laugh and joke together. I guess you can say I'm a very lucky man.

Completely unlike me, all my children are very gentle. Raell has inherited the Padamsee good looks which come from my father's side of the family. Her most striking feature is her shy smile which indicates a very gentle approach to life and certainly to the children in her drama school and the actors at her rehearsals. Quasar has not only inherited his father's height, he's also inherited his father's academic capabilities. Like me, he too is not a very good student, but he loves to read and is absorbed with ideas. He has directed the St Xavier's annual play on two occasions and is captain of the college cricket team. Shazahn has a combination of her mother Sharon's and her Aunt Jerry's good looks, but mercifully she's growing up with no intention of becoming a fashion model; instead she is busy writing and directing plays with the neighbourhood kids. Ranjit, my foster son, has always been a delightful sprite of a human being. An impish person, both in size and personality, he's quick-witted and charming and has carved out an impressive international film career for himself as Ranjit Chowdhry.

I've tried to be a good ex-husband. And I've tried to be a good current father. Though he's my foster son, Ranjit is as important to me as Raell and Quasar and Shazahn. I love them all and I try to show it.

That's another very important thing I learnt. You have to demonstrate love. Initially I thought doing things for others was enough. Putting them in a play, giving them direction. But I never said, 'Hey! You're a terrific guy. You're a super actor. I love you.' I never put my arm around anyone's shoulders in the early days.

It's surprising how just putting your arm around someone and saying, 'You're a wonderful person', can mean so much. It's not that I didn't want to do it. Mentally I was doing it, but I was not doing it physically. And this is something I learnt.

You have to *show* affection. Not just feel it. You cannot keep the feeling inside you. You have to let it come out of you and your arm has to go around someone.

You have to **show** *affection. Not just feel it.* After I started doing that in the theatre, I found that my actors were much warmer with me. I've certainly done that in my own family. With my brothers and sisters and my children. I tried to do it to a certain extent in Lintas, but I can't say I entirely succeeded.

When I first joined Lintas, I once again found myself enveloped by a family culture. Lintas was not the kind of agency where it was dog eat dog. There was no stepping on each other's shoulders to get ahead. It was a very warm and friendly atmosphere. Unilever was very particular about looking after not only the individual executive, but his family as well.

One of the reasons I joined Lintas was I had recently got married, and my wife Pearl had a sick daughter, Rohini, from her first marriage. At that time, Lintas was the only agency that provided medical benefits to an executive's wife and children. And the short but commanding Razmi Ahmed, who was the first Indian Managing Director of Lintas, had a very warm and generous heart. He extended to my stepdaughter all the family benefits of Lintas. And to think I had only recently joined the company.

Gerson da Cunha, who succeeded Razmi Ahmed, was also a very paternal figure at the agency. He treated everyone in a very warm and affectionate manner. Sometimes I felt he overdid it. Because then he couldn't pull them up when they went off the rails. Since they had been to his house for dinner the night before, he couldn't be stern with them the next day as boss. And I fear some people took advantage of that.

On the other hand, as Creative Head of Lintas, I was the person who demanded a lot, and demanded that the work be disciplined. I was far too work-oriented and not people-oriented. But when I took over as Managing Director, I realised that people expected the MD to be a father figure and a much kinder, gentler person. I'm eternally grateful to Gerson because I absorbed a lot of this fatherliness from him.

I realised that the boss must have a human face and so I tried to make the place a little more cosy. Advertising is a 'people's business' and the first people I realised I needed to care for were my own employees. So we renovated the toilets, we renovated the canteen, we renovated the lobby. We wanted people to be proud to be members of the Lintas family. The first profits were spent in these areas.

Then my HRD man, the small but highly energetic, bespectacled Sumit Roy, and I brainstormed a lot of ideas. We came up with 'YEGs'. What is YEGs? Year-End Gifts. We felt that instead of giving executives bonuses, why not give them something that they could share with the entire family? Give a guy money, and he'll probably spend it on his girlfriend, then go to his wife and say, 'Oh well, I'm broke.' Or he'll go out and get drunk. We said, let's give gifts that would be useful to his wife and children at home.

We started off with giving suit lengths and saris. Then the next year we gave radios. Then we gave TV sets and washing machines and refrigerators and microwave ovens. And every year, the YEGs got better and better, and people talked about it. In fact, I'm told that the buzz in advertising circles in those days was, 'If you're getting married, join Lintas. Then you can fill up your new home.'

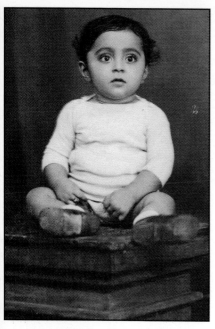

Alyque Padamsee as a youngster

As a young man

AP's father and mother after their wedding

The Padamsee clan

L to R: sister Bee at extreme left, sister Candy with garland, mother Kulsumbai, sister Jerry, sister Roshan and father, with brother-in-law Deryck Jeffereis behind him

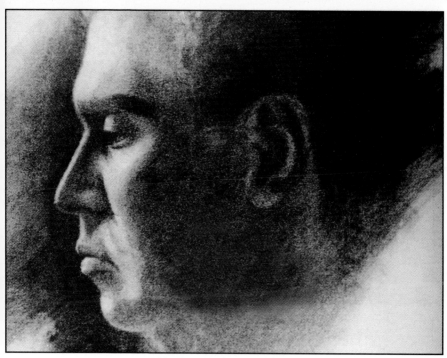

Elder brother Sultan (Bobby)

With Gerson da Cunha and Hassan Taj at Lintas in 1962

With Ranjit, Raell and Pearl

With Quasar and Dolly

With Sharon and Shazahn

With Sharon at rehearsal

Cathedral School Class of 1947
(AP in last row with specs)

With Rajiv Gandhi at Lintas Golden Jubilee, 1989

With Shunu Sen at 1974 *Reward* soap sales conference

Lintas Silver Jubilee group photo, 1964
In front row, L to R: Roy Delgarno with beard, Razmi Ahmed, Tim Green, Prakash Tandon

This was all part of the togetherness attitude. There was always a feeling that 'Wow! Lintas is our family.' And we'd have get-togethers where we'd invite wives and children as well. There was even an official Family Day, which was 15 August. Independence Day. You were invited with your family to a big jamboree. Balloons and streamers and kiddie games, a clown walking around, movie shows and lots of fun. This was the brainchild of Vivienne D'Souza, my Personnel Manager.

Later, when I went to London, I noticed that Unilever treated even their retired people extremely well. Every Christmas, they invited all the retirees (many of whom lived in Port Sunlight, a Unilever town where retirees could buy houses at knock down prices) to Unilever House in London, to celebrate the festival with the current employees. It brought tears to my eyes.

So I took that one step further. I said, 'Why should it be only people who retired from the company?' Anyone who'd been in Lintas for even two months should be invited. Now this was heresy in the Lever world. In those days (not any more), people who left Levers were treated like *persona non grata*. Who should never be spoken to. Leave alone invited to a year-end party. I thought, 'Frankly, this is nonsensical and self-defeating.' So I changed the tradition.

And so every year, we had the Great Lintas Get-together. To which were invited all current Lintas employees and all ex-Lintas employees, whether they had left fifty years ago or five weeks ago. We used to hold it at the Rangoli restaurant of the Tata Theatre. And then it grew so big, we had to have it at the Oberoi's Regal Room. All three rooms. I believed that Lintas was like your school, your alma mater. So the Year-End Party was your annual alumni meet.

This caused a kind of ripple in the industry. The buzz was, 'Lintas is a great place. Even when you leave them, they still love you. You're still part of the family.' And this had its own valuable spin-off. Twenty-five per cent of the top management in my time were people who had left Lintas and then rejoined. They were people who had looked at the outside world and said, 'The pastures are not greener on the other side of the fence. It's greener in Lintas.' Someone actually termed this as the 'Rubber Band Principle'. If you leave Lintas, there's a rubber band that pulls you back after a year or two.

Another interesting thing I learnt was how to smile. I was usually a non-smiler. And so when I was concentrating, people thought I was angry with them. Someone came up to me once and said, 'Why are you always angry?' It took me quite by surprise. 'I'm never angry,' I said. 'Yes! But you look so angry.' 'Oh, shit!' I said. I looked in the mirror and I found that when I was concentrating, I would tend to frown and hence look fierce.

So I began to actually cultivate the smiling habit. Even when I didn't particularly feel like smiling, I smiled. And today I find that I'm always breaking into smiles. It's become a habit with me.

To further inculcate the family atmosphere at Lintas, I insisted that everyone be on a first name basis with each other. Even the trainees who walked out of the IIMs with their MBAs. I would say to them, 'Okay, there's no "Sir" around here. There's not even a Mr Padamsee. You either call me Alyque, or if you find that too familiar, please call me AP.' Since I was so much senior to most of them, they'd feel a little embarrassed to address me as Alyque, so AP was what we settled on.

Of course, in the midst of all this family atmosphere, discipline was of vital importance. I absolutely discouraged laziness. I didn't want people to think that just because it's a family atmosphere, you can get away with whatever. I made it clear with my people as to what their objectives were and what their deadlines were. And once they agreed to them, there was no reason why they shouldn't be able to adhere to them in a happy atmosphere. I put up a slogan, 'A hardworking family is a happy family.' At our annual get-together I made it a point to say, 'Lintas is a Club of Professionals. We are friends not only with each other but with our deadlines.' This I got from the theatre with its warm friendly atmosphere combined with its implacable Opening Night deadline.

If executives in the Lintas Club couldn't meet a deadline, they had to have a very good reason for not doing so. Not an excuse, mind you. But a reason. If I found they were only making excuses, I'd admonish them with, 'Look here. You've got to pull up your socks. This is a performance-led agency. And if you're not comfortable with that, well, you know where the door is.'

I find in India many parents tend to mollycoddle their children. There's too much of *laad*, love and affection, and consequently we tend to grow up as *laad saabs*. My mother was not like that at all. She could be pretty tough when required and if you hadn't done what you were supposed to do, then out would come her chappal. Never across the face, because she had read somewhere that hitting someone across the face could damage the brain. She was very sensible in her own way.

But there was no fooling around with her. There was a lot of caring, but no careless caring. No spoiling or 'Give him what he wants. It's too much of a bother to argue it with him.' And no 'I'm too busy.' Never. Yet when you wanted something and you went to her and gave a good reason, you'd usually get it.

So when I was in Lintas, if people wanted to see the 'boss', the door to my cabin was always open. They were always free to walk into my office and say, 'Could I have half an hour or so of your time? I want some advice on my career.' So much so that my secretary used to complain, 'But AP, you haven't got a minute to see your clients. Where are you going to fit this guy into your schedule?' I'd reply, 'No, no. It's alright. I'll postpone that meeting. If one of my people wants to see me, send them in.'

However, I often have a guilt complex when it comes to my personal family. The kind of attention I gave the people that I helped groom to stardom, whether it was Sharon or Shiamak Davar or before that Shyam Benegal or so many others, took up more of my time than my family. Not only them, but even the other characters in my life, who are supposedly fictitious but actually have a strong personality and presence of their own.

Even though God has not blessed me with any grandchildren as yet, I am lucky I have a host of Brand Children. Brands like Liril, MRF, Dalda, Bajaj, Park Avenue, Captain Cook, Surf, Cherry Blossom, Spartek Tiles, Kitply Plywood, Reynolds Pens, Jet Airways, Timex Watches, Monte Carlo, Closeup Toothpaste and of course, Kama Sutra. These

The greatest advertising award of all is to have your brands live on after you.

Brand Children are still alive and kicking...in a marketing scene strewn with corpses that were nine-day wonders at one time. The greatest advertising award of all is to have your brands live on after you.

On the theatre side, there were characters like Hamlet and Evita, Don Quixote and Begum Sumroo. Gosh, the amount of time I spent with my actors, grooming them into their roles. All these brands and characters took a lot of my thought, a lot of my care, a lot of my guardianship.

Perhaps if I had spent less time with these characters and more time with my own children, then I probably would have been more of a good father than a godfather. Why does a man do that? I've often asked myself this question. And I think that somehow or the other, because of daily living with your children, they become more of a habit and less of a challenge and adventure.

I've noticed that creative people, particularly, often neglect their children and put much more time into their work, which in fact becomes their child. If you want to be a good father, you've got to rethink your priorities and look at your child as a work in progress. This can be the most rewarding investment of your life.

Strong mothers usually produce strong sons.
But strong fathers often create weaklings.

FAILURE AS A LEARNING EXPERIENCE

*T*he first big 'No' in my life was when my mother refused to let me go abroad to study because post-war England was too devastated. I wanted to follow in the family tradition set by my brother Sultan, who blazed like a meteor across the horizon of our lives. He awakened the dormant artistic spark of the Padamsees, that had been buried under several generations of making money.

It was Bobby, as Sultan was affectionately 'christened' by Miss Murphy, who laid the seeds of the Theatre Group of Bombay in 1941 at the St Xavier's College Dramatics Club. It was he who banded together a group of disciples like Ebrahim Alkazi, Hamid Sayani, Jean Bhownagiri and Deryck Jeffereis, and started a tradition of artistic excellence that already spans half a century.

I very badly wanted to follow in Sultan's footsteps and go to Oxford. My mother's 'No' was like a giant full stop that brought my academic ambitions to a complete halt. I was all of fifteen years old and had just stood second in my class. The disappointment was crippling. I sulked and dropped to fifteenth place. What was the point of studying like a lunatic when you knew you'd never become an Oxonian? Subsequently, I looked at examinations as a bore which interfered with my theatre work. This ensured a third class for me in my Senior Cambridge and in my BA. The groves of academe were never again to be my Garden of Eden.

But failure is a learning experience. When fate kicks you below the belt, you've got to fashion yourself a groin guard. You've got to get over the ego bruise and make a comeback.

But this is only possible if you analyse why you failed in the first place.

When fate kicks you below the belt, you've got to fashion yourself a groin guard. You've got to get over the ego bruise and

Even as a teenager, I realised that the kind of swotting-by-heart that was insisted on in Indian education was not for me. Somewhere I had read that education was expanding the mind. And the best expansion course one could take was reading. Consequently, I read anything I could lay my hands on. From my brother Bobby's collection of Shakespeare and Kraft-Ebbing to Richmal Crompton's *William* series to American and English comic books like *Superman* and *The Wizard.*

The great treat on Saturday afternoon at Kulsum Terrace was to take our pocket money and rush to Happy Book Stall, buy as many comics as we could and hurtle home to spend a lazy weekend devouring every frame. Not surprisingly, I started wearing spectacles at a very early age.

But the greatest influence on my taste in literature was my darling elder sister, Jerry. She served up a mixed bag, ranging from Peter Cheyney to Ernest Hemingway with exotica like the Australian *Saturdee* and Guy de Maupassant and Saki. It was undoubtedly Jerry who gave the Padamsee family its macabre sense of humour. She invented a vicious little character called Violet-Petal.

Violet-Petal went to bed.
Violet-Petal, her prayers never said.
When she awoke, she found she was dead.
The devil greeted her with a nod of his head.

These limericks, and sometimes playlets, were enacted on

the terrace of our family building Kulsum Terrace with a great deal of flourish, which is not unexpected, coming as we did from a theatrical background. My earliest triumph in this impromptu family theatre was a scene from a gangster movie called *Johnny Eager*. 'No, no! Johnny, don't shoot. I didn't mean to squeal. They made me do it, Johnny. For God's sake, Johnny, don't shoot.' At this point, I would give a heart-rending groan and spend the next sixty seconds thrashing about in my death throes, blinded by the dazzle of an imaginary Academy Award.

There's a lot to be said for a happy childhood. And a lot more to be said for discreet parents. I never realised till I was eighteen that my mother had not spoken to my father for twenty years. Some things are best kept hidden from children. A secure childhood certainly builds confidence. But being born with a silver spoon in the mouth can be traumatic when the spoon is rudely removed.

The next great 'No' in my life, as I have said elsewhere, was again delivered by my mother, when I told her I wanted to marry Pearl. And she gave me the ultimatum, 'It's either No or Go.' So I went. This traumatic exit from the Kulsum Terrace womb was certainly a learning experience. As you know, it breaks the 'Mama's boy' syndrome and makes a man of you. It puts steel in your spine. It certainly made me realise that most people have to earn a living, and don't get it handed to them on a silver *thali*. It sharpened my understanding of the consumer. It personalised for me the titles of classics such as *Lower Depths* and *Les Miserables*.

For those people who believe that Alyque Padamsee was born as the Godfather of Lintas and the Patriarch of the Theatre Group, I must throw some ice water on this cosy myth. When I moved out of the palatial family mansion to share a humble roof with Pearl and her two adorable children, Rohini and

Ranjit, I was earning the princely sum of Rs. 750. Of which, Rs. 300 went towards rent, and the balance had to cover food, clothes, transport, schooling and what have you. Tough times breed togetherness. The secret is to avoid whining. To have no regrets; as Edith Piaf

Tough times breed togetherness. The secret is to avoid whining.

sings, *'Je ne regrette rien.'* Because regrets murder the future.

Remembering life with Pearl and the two children in Scheherazade building, a hop, step and a jump away from Kulsum Terrace, fills me with nostalgia. It was the 1960s. Kennedy was in the White House. Nehru was in his decline. The flower children were beginning to blossom. The world was young and so were we. If this sounds like the flashback from *Casablanca,* please remember that it's one of my favourite movies. But unlike Bogart, I won't mutter, 'Play it again, Sam.'

Pearl and I went to England and America in 1961, mainly for my six-month stint at Lintas: London, to learn TV production. Pearl took the opportunity to join the London Academy of Dramatic Arts, and both of us saw as much theatre and cinema as we could cram in. I was like a sponge, soaking in anything and everything, from Shakespeare to striptease. This was the time Peter Hall was setting up the great tradition of the Royal Shakespeare Company at Stratford and the Aldwych Theatre in London. The New Wave of French cinema was beginning to crest and the Kennedy-Nixon TV debate was the great live theatre of that time.

A month after we arrived back in Bombay, Rohini, who had a dreadful kidney disease, nephritis, took a turn for the worse. We rushed her to hospital, and kept day and night vigil over her bedside for three months. I'll never forget the kindness of my boss, Razmi Ahmed, who gave me time off to be with our daughter. I don't know how many blood transfusions we gave Rohini, but it never seemed enough. Both her kidneys were failing fast. But I knew one thing. Rohini would not die.

I began sleeping nights at the hospital to relieve poor Pearl, who had become a shadow of her usual ebullient self. In the morning, I would go straight from the hospital to Scheherazade for a quick shower and shave, and then try to lose myself in my work at Lintas. But come evening, I was back to the life and death struggle of a ten-year-old child. It couldn't happen. It mustn't happen. These were the trip-hammers in my head. After all, I had succeeded against all odds in marrying Pearl. I would succeed in this crusade too.

But on 26 September 1961, the hammer blow fell. We were all devastated, and even as I write this, nearly forty years later, the tears fall afresh. Death is a humbling experience. It reaches in and twists your innards. I experienced a tremendous sense of loss, of failure. I was never quite the same again. You realise you are vulnerable. But it was only years later that this revelation brought a new understanding to my relationship with everyone around me.

Death is a humbling experience. You are never quite the same again.

On the other hand, my brother Bobby's death was something that happened to another person in another time. I was too young. I was too remote. With Rohini, it was hard and it was searing. It was not only the loss of a loved one, I think it was the feeling of impotence, of standing by and being unable to stop the inevitable. It took me months and months to recover my equilibrium.

Like an angel of mercy, Zarine Malik (née Wadia), Pearl's dearest friend, whisked us away to her home in Ahmedabad for a month. I remember Ranjit, who was only six at the time, being petrified when I went away to find a coolie at the station. He thought that I, like his sister, would disappear. In my stupidity, I had urged Pearl at the funeral not to allow Ranjit to see Rohini's dead body, thinking it would be a traumatic experience. Unfortunately, this had a reverse effect. His schoolmates told him that his sister had been whisked away and burnt. (She was cremated at the electric crematorium in Chandanwadi in Bombay.)

But I have always had this personal phobia of being unable to look at the dead body of anyone close to me. When my brother Bubbles and his two children were killed in a car accident on the Bombay-Poona road in 1974, I was shattered. Besides being my youngest brother, he had been my closest friend. Yet I was unable to look at his face, even at the *mooh dikhana* ceremony at the graveyard in Dongri. Still, by some quirk of fate, as he was being lowered into the grave, and they removed the winding sheet he was wrapped in, I inadvertently looked down and saw his face. And in his usual cheeky way, he winked at me. Or so I imagined.

The searing agony of death makes other failures less lacerating. For instance, failure in one's work in the theatre. Many audiences today imagine that all my plays have been successes. Well, pardon me, while I rip away that conceit. The very first play I did on the Bombay professional stage was an innovative production of Shakespeare's comedy *The Taming of the Shrew* in 1954. It was greeted by the late Mr M V Matthew of *The Times of India* with a cutting review, 'One or two laughs in the Shrew'.

After hiding my head in a wet towel for several days, I crawled out and took another look at the review. 'Yes,' I thought to myself, 'there's something in what he says.' I got my actors back into rehearsals and made several revisions before the next show. I then sat in the audience (something I had avoided doing, because of nerves, at the first show) and made notes of the audience reaction. In advertising, we call it feedback. But I was still in college, and more than a year away from starting in the ad business.

My next below the ribs came when I produced a play called *Bed Room,* written by my sister Jerry and her friend, Freny Bhownagiri, whose husband Jean was one of the founder members of the Theatre Group of Bombay. This was a fascinating experiment that started in an actor-cum-playwright workshop I conducted in 1967. It concerned a woman who was gradually withdrawing from reality and confining herself first to her house, and then to her bedroom and finally to her bed. She was retreating from the world in stages. *Bed Room* was heavily influenced by the European Theatre of the Absurd, which was all the rage in the 1960s.

This time, the critics without exception, brought out their long knives. But worse than that, the audience stayed away in droves. To the best of my knowledge, it is the only *A brilliant concept dies* play I have ever done that *without a brilliant execution.* lost money. However, I am glad I did it. It taught me more than most of my successes. A great idea doesn't in itself make a great play. A brilliant concept dies without a brilliant execution. This is one of the few plays I would like to redo as a film.

Mercifully, my next disaster took a decade in arriving. This was Vijay Tendulkar's *Gidhade,* translated into English as *Vultures* by Priya Adarkar. I had been mesmerised by the great Marathi actor Shriram Lagoo and his performance in the original version. A terrific vehicle, I thought, for Kabir Bedi in English. It should knock our audiences flat. I was grotesquely mistaken.

In spite of months of rehearsals, trying to capture the flavour of English spoken as Marathi (including not only Marathi inflections and intonations in the voice, but also the body language of Marathi speech), drama turned into camp! *Vultures* did all right at the box-office thanks to Kabir Bedi's fame as a movie actor, but artistically it was a lead balloon. As the Americans say, 'It was dead in the water.'

But again, this theatrical disaster was a textbook of learning for me. The brilliance of a Lagoo or a Shombhu Mitra or a Balraj Sahni can fool you into thinking that because the play works in an Indian language, it will dazzle the audience in English. What a crazy conceit! Language plays should never be transliterated into the English language, but rather re-worked utilising an English idiom. On the positive side, I learned how close Indian speech is to Indian dance. The language of Indian facial expression from the curl of the nostril to the wriggle of the brow to the downward slant of the mouth, is the equivalent of the *Abhinaya* in Bharat Natyam. Furthermore, we Indians speak with our whole body, not just with our mouths. A vehement 'Yes' can begin from the toes, arch its way through the spine up to the musical wag of the head. Which to most westerners could mean either yes or no or maybe.

When it comes to advertising, failure can turn out to be an expensive learning experience unless we move fast to repair the damage. I am a great believer in consumer insights. And so, flush with my success of extending the Dettol franchise from cuts and wounds, to shaving, baby care and sick care, I launched into a perfectly logical supposition about Dettol Antiseptic Cream. That the next extension of the Dettol brand should be in the area of burns.

On analysing the antiseptic cream market, I found that only one cream was acceptable to the Indian consumer: Burnol. I asked the marketing men at Reckitt's if Dettol Cream was good for burns. They were surprised at the craziness of the question. But I persisted. Their technical boys came back with a very positive response: Dettol Cream was every bit as good for burns as Burnol. I then outlined the new strategy: We would push Dettol Cream not only for cuts, but also for burns. It would be presented as the soothing white healer. How could we fail? We had the Dettol brand equity and a USP over Burnol in being white and non-staining.

In test market after test market, it bombed. Why? I had overlooked the fact that Dettol as an antiseptic was associated with a stinging quality. Quite *The consumer listens* illogically, but perfectly *logically, but* emotionally, the consumer refused *acts emotionally.* to accept any form of Dettol as 'soothing'. The thought of applying Dettol Cream to a burn was like covering it with hot coals. Lesson? The consumer listens logically, but acts emotionally.

Perhaps the biggest boo-boo in Indian advertising, equalling the disaster of New Coke in USA, was the launch of the New Foods division of Levers, under the brand name Hima Foods. This was a series of dehydrated products like peas, soups, gulab jamun mixes, etc. But dehydrated foods was an idea whose time had not yet come, and I think never will. It is the same kiss of death that hangs over any soya product in India.

With a blush of embarrassment, I admit I was deeply involved in the Hima project. I am now a lifetime believer that all food products must come out of the packet looking luscious, not shrivelled up and dehydrated. Above all, you cannot fool around with the Indian palate. It has an emotional life all of its own. Taste, and taste alone, is the significant choice factor when it comes to food products. Convenience is way behind. Clever copy is not the way to a person's stomach. Mouthwatering photographs are.

But even mouthwatering experiences of another kind can turn into embarrassments that teach you a lot about human behaviour. I will never forget my pungent interlude at the Cannes Ad Film Festival in 1976.

Clever copy is not the way to a person's stomach. Mouthwatering photographs are.

The Executive Creative Director of Lintas: Worldwide, Bob McLaren, would always hold the Lintas Creative Directors' conference at Cannes. So it was a double treat for us to review each other's work as well as see some of the best advertising in the world.

On the opening night of the festival, there was a big ball at one of the casinos. Dolly, who was accompanying me on this trip, and I were sitting at the Lintas table. Bob was regaling us with various amusing anecdotes. Also at our table was the creative director from Austria, who had a beautiful blonde, woman in tow. She was absolutely ravishing. And although most of us had brought along our wives, we couldn't resist giving her the glad eye and asking her for a dance.

Her name was Alexandra. And as the evening rolled on, she became quite friendly with Dolly and me. She was quite intrigued by Dolly's clothes. In a typically French accent, she said, 'Ooh, I lurve ze zaree. We French admire ze Indian culture. I've always wanted to wear a zaree and I lurve Indians becauze zey 'ave such a beautifool accent.' I thought, 'Mam'selle, not only do you have a beautiful accent, but you also have a beautiful body.' But naturally, I kept this to myself.

Then she asked Dolly, 'Are you familiar wiz Cannes?' and when Dolly replied that she wasn't, she said, 'Ooh, I weel take you shopping. Don't worry Dollee. I weel come zomorrow to your 'otel.' Sure enough, she was at our hotel the next morning and she took Dolly on a shopping expedition.

Now Cannes was very very expensive and all you could do was window shop, really. Especially for us Indians who were on a meagre foreign exchange allowance. We could barely pay our hotel bills, leave alone pay for meals! We were reduced to eating at the equivalent of the local MacDonald's. Then Alexandra said, 'Zomorrow evening I weel take you out for deenair. I know a beautifool French restaurant on the steps of ze old Cannes.'

So dutifully, Dolly and I met Alexandra for dinner the next night and we had an exotic meal with cheese and wine and the works. I hated it, of course, because for me, any food without chilli is non-food. But I made a pretence of enjoying it all. Suddenly in the middle of dinner, Alexandra stood up, 'Oh, here is my friend ze waiter. Ee as just bought a new bike. I must go for a speen.' So in the middle of dinner, she and the waiter just sped off!

I turned to Dolly, 'I say, do you think she's going to land us with the bill?' This was a frightfully expensive restaurant. Fortunately she returned and we continued with liqueur and coffee. Dinner seemed to drag on for hours and hours. Finally the waiter put the bill in the middle of the table. I yawned and pretended as if I hadn't seen the wretched thing. After all, she had said she was taking us out, and I had made it very clear to Dolly. 'Look, we don't have enough money to pay for a bill like that. If we do have to shell out, then the rest of our trip around Europe (which we had planned to do after Cannes) is off.'

But as it turned out, Alexandra reached for the bill and said, 'Allow me.' As she opened her bag, she suddenly cried out, 'Ooh la la. What a peety. I changed my bag at my 'ouse and I forgot to put my moneey is zis bag. If you don't mind...' I looked heavenwards and very reluctantly reached for my wallet and took out thousands and thousands of francs to settle the monstrous bill. Then she had the nerve to say, 'Ooh, wait a meenit. I weel pay ze tip'! When we staggered out of there, I had a huge scowl on my face as you can imagine.

After dinner, as were strolling down the waterfront, Dolly stopped in front of a shop which was displaying some wonderful bikinis. Dolly said she wanted to buy one. I said in Hindi, 'For God's sake, after that bill, we don't have enough to buy a monokini leave alone a bikini! Just then Alexandra piped in, 'Oh, zis beekeeni is nussing. I weel show you zumthing better.' And suddenly in the middle of the road, with all sorts of passersby, including many from Lintas and other advertising agencies, she lifted up her dress to show us her panties, 'Is zis ze style you want?'

I just hemmed and hawed while Dolly was delighted. 'Yes! That's exactly what I'm looking for.' 'Zomorrow, I weel take you to a beautifool shop where you will be able to buy all zees sings and zey weel geev me a spesil discount beecauze I am a resident of Cannes.'

We finally reached our hotel and just as we were saying good night to her, she said, 'You know, zomorrow is ze final ball at ze Caseeno. Can I come wis you? And Dollee you are so sweet. Can I wear one of your zarees? Zey are so beautifool.' I was looking daggers at Dolly by this time, but in all her innocence, Dolly replied, 'Yes, of course.'

As soon as Alexandra left, I turned to Dolly, 'Are you crazy? She just landed us with a bill for thousands of francs and now you're going to let her wear your sari?' 'Now, don't be silly. Stop being so suspicious.'

The next day I said to Dolly, 'Listen, the ball is beginning at seven o'clock. Let's get ready and leave the hotel by 6.30, before Alexandra descends upon us.' But just as we were about to leave, Alexandra bounced up the road, 'Ooh la la. 'Ow nice. I'm so glad I came a leetle early. Now Dollee, can I wear your zaree?'

So reluctantly we returned to our room and Alexandra proceeded to change. And instead of going into the toilet, she undressed in the middle of the room, with me standing there! Now, of course, being the gentleman I am, I turned my back... but I kept an eagle eye on her through the mirror. Dolly helped her get dressed and as she was taking off her blouse, she turned away to put on Dolly's choli...much to my chagrin. When she was finally ready, I must say she looked damn good. A blonde in a peacock blue sari with a bindi is a stunning sight.

Then Dolly made the ghastly mistake of telling her, 'Oh Alexandra, when we wear a sari like this for a special occasion, we always wear a bit of jewellery. Do you have any?'

'No, I didn't theenk of it.'

'It doesn't matter. I have a spare necklace here.'

By this time I was ready to strangle Dolly. Fortunately it wasn't a pure gold necklace and only gold plated.

As we walked the short distance to the ball, a thought suddenly struck me. 'Wait a minute. This woman has already taken us for a ride. What if she doesn't have a ticket to the ball?' The tickets were frightfully expensive, and you had to buy them on the first day of the festival itself. I had already picked up two for Dolly and me. So I asked Alexandra, 'Do you have a ticket?'

'Of course,' she replied.

We reached the gates where these big burly bouncer types were checking tickets. Alexandra opened her bag and exclaimed, 'Ooh la la, I must 'ave left eet on ze dresser in your 'otel.' I muttered, 'This is too much. Instead of the ticket, I wish she had left herself behind!' Aloud I said, 'Bye Alexandra. You're on your own.' I grabbed Dolly's hand, rushed forward, showed the doorman our tickets and we went in.

Behind us I could hear Alexandra trying to convince the doorman, 'But zat ees alright. Zat Indian gentleman...' Hearing that, we increased our gait to a trot and quickly disappeared into the crowd, found the Lintas table and sat down breathlessly. All of them were laughing away as they asked me, 'So how's your friend, the con woman, Alexandra?' 'I don't want to talk about it.' Bob turned to me, 'You Indians are real suckers. Anyone could see she was conning all of us.'

We were sitting there glumly when all of a sudden, Alexandra was at our table. 'How did you manage to get in?' I asked her. 'Eet's perfectly all right. I told ze man zat ze Indian gentleman 'as my teekit. At firs, 'e did not believe me, but zen 'e say okay.' I was aghast. 'Alexandra, how could you do that? I haven't bought your ticket.' 'Eet's alright. By ze time we leave, 'e weel 'ave gone.'

So, cool as cucumber, she sat down at our table. And as usual, she managed to delight everyone around her. I stared unbelievingly as everyone asked her for a dance, including Tony Perone, who was the creative director of Lintas: Hong Kong. Tall, handsome, elegant, with curly Italian hair and twinkling eyes, Tony was recently divorced but had come with a new girlfriend. Unfortunately, they were not getting along too well, so he was flirting outrageously with the charming Alexandra, and they danced away the whole evening.

After dinner we were all enjoying the fireworks display, when someone said, 'By the way, where's Alexandra?' 'I think she said she was going to the loo.' Then Bob turned to Dolly and asked her, 'She was wearing your sari, wasn't she?' 'Yes' 'If you expect to see your sari again, you're sadly mistaken. It's gone for good. Along with your jewellery.' Dolly went white as a sheet and rushed to the 'Ladies'. No Alexandra there. Then we looked all over but couldn't find her anywhere.

Tony Perone had hired a car and he said to us, 'Relax guys. Get in the car and we'll drive to your hotel. She's left her clothes there, so she's probably gone there to pick them up.'

We rushed to the hotel and went up to the concierge. With my heart in my mouth, I asked him, 'Have you seen a blonde lady in a sari?'

'Yes.'

'Did she ask you for the key to my room?'

(Bob had primed me for the fact that she had probably already plundered our room of all our cash, clothes and jewellery.)

'Yes, she did.'

'Well? Did you give it to her?'

'No sir, of course not. We never give the room keys to anyone except the resident.'

I heaved a sigh of relief and slipped him a small tip from what little money I had left.

'What happened then?'

'She went away, very angry, but I would not open your room.'

I said to Dolly, 'My God! He's really saved us.'

Next morning, we awoke early to leave for the airport, but before we did that, I thought let's try one last time. I wrote a letter: 'Dear Alexandra, I'm sure it must have been a mistake. My room was locked and you couldn't get your dress. I have left it in a plastic bag for you. We'd be most grateful if you could give Dolly's sari and necklace to the concierge. He will forward it to my London address which I have left with him.'

'Fat chance,' I thought, 'but worth a try at least. What the heck.'

I went to the manageress on duty and said to her, 'I have a package and letter for Mam'selle Alexandra.'

'Mam'selle Alexandra?'

'Yes, Mam'selle Alexandra.'

'Oh, but Monsieur, you've made a mistake.'

'You know Alexandra?'

'Yes, very well.'

'Why have I made a mistake?'

'Because she is not a mam'selle. She is a monsieur. You do not know? He is a famous transvestite.'

'What?'

'Yes, I thought you knew. I had seen you with him and everyone in Cannes knows that Alexandra is a man dressed up in woman's clothing.'

'Oh my God!'

'What happened?'

'Well, she took my wife's sari and jewellery.'

'Oh monsieur, you will never see them again. He is well known to be a con man.'

'Madame, if by any chance she, or rather he, does turn up, please give Alexandra this. I will call you from London to check.'

'Monsieur, I will try, but I tell you, it looks hopeless.'

I was feeling quite morose as we drove to the Nice airport, from where we were catching our flight to London. I kept wondering how we could all have been fooled. We all danced with her. My God! I was in the same room with her/him while she was changing. True, I never saw her chest, but she had lifted her skirt in front of me on the street and I had seen her panties and her beautiful legs. And all the while, none of us had a clue as to her true identity.

As we drove on, I began to relax and see the funny side of it all. I also had a naughty idea. When we got to the airport, and found out the flight was delayed by half an hour, I said, 'Marvellous. May I have some change for the telephone?' I went to a phone booth and dialled the number of the hotel where my friend Tony Perone was staying. The operator put me through to his room, and it was a blurry early morning voice that greeted me, 'Yes, what is it?'

'Tony, this is Alyque.'

'Alyque, for God's sake. It's six o'clock in the morning.'

'Yes, Tony.'

'By the way, what happened to Alexandra last night?'

'You danced with her, Tony. You should know.'

'Yeah, sure. She's a great dancer.'

'Tony, I've got news for you. You danced with "him". Do you know that Alexandra is a man?'

'WHAT?'

'Yes, she's a transvestite.'

'Oh my God! I don't believe it. But I danced close with her!'

'Yes, Tony. It just shows that your hormones ain't working the way they should!'

And I put the phone down. At least I got some laughs out of the episode!

Of course, when we reached London I called the manageress of the hotel in Cannes and of course she said, 'Sorry, sir. No, Alexandra has not turned up.' And that is how I got conned or is it Canned?

When you are looking for a cheap thrill, it often turns out to be expensive. The Alexandra episode taught me that the product does not always live up to the packaging.

> *When you make a fool of yourself,*
> *only your sense of humour*
> *can save you from drowning in self-pity.*

Chapter 4

THE RUN-UP IS MORE IMPORTANT
THAN THE DELIVERY

*M*any moons ago, I read in a translation of the *Upanishads,* 'He who does not enjoy the journey will never reach his destination.' That explained, to me at any rate, what is the meaning of life. Up to that time, thanks to my western education, I was entirely goal-oriented. I had not learnt that the cosmos is interlinked. To me there was only cause and effect within a narrow spectrum. You put the coin in the slot and out comes the packet of chocolate. What happens along the way was of little or no concern for me. Thank God it finally dawned on me that enjoying the work you do is as important as the result.

I think I first experienced this feeling on the cricket field when I was a pace bowler for the First XI in the Cathedral School. The exhilaration I felt as I started my long run-up to the wicket, with the breeze blowing in my face, tensing my body for the delivery, the swing of my arm as the ball flashed through the air. The run-up, I realised, was the joy. Getting the wicket was the satisfaction, mainly to my ego. This is the same exhilaration I get at rehearsals, when with my actors, we explore the text. Sometimes, we are involved in reinventing the whole play over a period of a year, enjoying the creativity so much that we almost forget about opening night. This is what happened to me and my actors when we got into production for the Hindi version of *Marat/Sade* entitled *Pagal Khana.*

The big-hearted movie director, the late Basu Bhattacharya, very kindly lent us his office space, off Tulsi Pipe Road (in Lower Parel, Bombay), where *Pagal Khana* metamorphosed from Ismat Chugtai's adaptation to an improvised socio-political theatre piece about revolution in India. That sincere actor, the late Nitin Sethi, transformed the original character of the Marquis de Sade into the essence of the Hindu ascetic, looking inwards, as opposed to Karan Razdan's Marat, the firebrand social reformer, a strange amalgam of Ram Mohan Roy and Subhas Chandra Bose.

After reading the text once, we launched into a series of improvisations over a period of half a year. As the dates we had originally booked at Prithvi Theatre came and went, Razdan, Kavita Chowdhury and a deputation of actors approached me anxiously. 'We are certainly enjoying the improvisations. But when do we open the actual play?'

When I told them that the improvisations would form the actual play, they went into a state of mild shock. But being good troupers, they soldiered on. When *Pagal Khana* finally hit the stage, it caused something of a sensation. Besides being vehemently anti-government, it was laced with savage violence. The play is set in a lunatic asylum. The governor of the asylum decides to impress on the audience the sanity of his inmates by allowing them to stage a play. He explains that the guards armed with lathis at the auditorium doors are there to prevent the lunatics from escaping. At a particular point in the play, one of the lunatics runs into the audience and begs them to protect him. Two brutal guards drag him away and beat him senseless.

After the interval, the audience returns to find that a steel-mesh fence has been erected around the stage area. The governor explains that this is for the audience's safety. During Act II, a food riot breaks out among the lunatics, who fling dal and chappatis through the mesh at the audience. At the climax of the play, when Kavita is supposed to stab Razdan (as Charlotte Corday stabbed Marat), she stabs the governor instead. Pandemonium breaks loose. One of the inmates switches off the main fuse. In the dim light of flashing torches, wielded by the guards, the inmates begin to scramble up the steel mesh, and leap into the audience to escape. They are last seen fleeing through the compound of Prithvi Theatre, and on to the road, screaming, '*Azadi!*' There is no curtain call. The audience stumbles out of the darkened theatre, moved and shaken.

Pagal Khana travelled to Pune, Calcutta, Delhi and where-have-you. My greatest regret is that I didn't videotape it. Nevertheless, the photos taken by Madhu Gadkari are amazingly evocative. (So is the audio cassette of the innovative songs composed by Asit Desai.) With his egg-shaped head and heavy horn-rimmed glasses, Madhu has photographed all my plays since *Hamlet,* in 1964. He is a brilliant artiste who understands the difference between reproducing reality and capturing the magic moment. (Most of the theatre photographs in this book have been shot by Madhu over a span of twenty-five years or more.) Furthermore, as an Art Director at Lintas, he has helped me produce over forty public service films (many of which won national and international awards).

You need to understand the difference between reproducing reality and capturing the magic moment.

Shakespeare, as always, puts it best, when he says, 'The readiness is all'. Preparing for an event is ninety per cent of the enjoyment. And this was the case with one of the largest live theatre events I have ever staged. The opening ceremony for the Asian Track & Field Games held in Delhi in November 1989. Sharon and I were requested by the late Indian Prime Minister, Rajiv Gandhi, and the organising committee to stage a spectacular event. One that would match the opening of the Olympic Games held in Los Angeles in 1984. A tall order.

I assembled a team consisting of the brilliant young dance director, Shiamak Davar, who had recently blown everyone's mind with his choreography for our production of *Kabaret;* Roger Drego, who started work with me in *Man of La Mancha* in 1976, and had since then gone on to become India's top sound specialist; Viraf Pocha, my trusted lieutenant on lighting and special effects; the ever reliable Rehmatali of Shobiz, who entered the theatre by constructing sets for our *Jesus Christ Superstar* in 1974; Leon D'Souza, whose musical association with the Theatre Group also started with *Man of La Mancha;* Arun Dhavan, Delhi's veteran theatre technician; Ajay Balram, who learnt the ropes of stage management with me in the 1960s; and of course Sharon, who exploded on the theatre and music scene as Evita in the 1980s.

A great team. Now all I needed was a great idea. How do big ideas come to one? My best creative time is either in the shower or in the half-awake period when I'm about to fall asleep. Sometimes it comes in a blinding flash. Most often it comes by constantly focusing your internal spotlight on the problem. This spot swings

The Big Idea is the one that inflames your emotions. But don't jump at it. If it still excites you after seven days, you've got yourself a winner.

around your idea box lighting up cliché after cliché. You have to be ruthless in rejecting *déjà vu* ideas. You also have to stamp out the corny ones. The Big Idea is the one that inflames your emotions and seems dead right for the project at hand. But don't jump at it. Sleep over it for a week. If it still excites you after seven days, you've got yourself a winner.

The big idea I dreamed up was this. A thousand silver butterflies, their wings shimmering in the sun, flutter on to the field to the strains of a jazz/pop concerto entitled *Tracks of Friendship*. They dance in ecstasy around a giant replica of the Indian National Flag. These 1,000 butterflies are joined by a hundred space-suited dancers who do an *Athletics as Art* ballet. As the music reaches a crescendo, the giant flag opens up, and Sharon, in a long white dress, emerges like a butterfly out of a cocoon and bursts into song: 'The spirit is moving. I feel it inside. We're coming together. With hearts open wide.'

As she continues singing, Sharon, like Alice in Wonderland, seems to grow taller and taller. She rises up above the 70,000 people gathered to watch the Opening. Eventually she is fifty feet high with her white gown cascading below her. She is now on level with the athletic flame at the top of the stadium. At the climax of the song, she points skywards. And a dozen skydivers drop out of a helicopter poised above the stadium and plummet towards the earth, trailing saffron, white and green smoke. At the last minute, their tri-coloured parachutes open and they float gracefully down to earth. And the crowd bursts into thunderous applause... if everything goes according to plan! (I think my greatest strength and my greatest weakness is dreaming the impossible dream and then, like a damn fool, trying to achieve it.)

Turning fantasy into reality. That's what theatre and advertising are all about.

Obviously I derive a lot of satisfaction in making ideas walk and talk. Turning fantasy into reality. That's what theatre is all about. And that's what advertising is all about. But this time, had I bitten off more than I could chew? I'm always doing this. Setting myself enormous challenges, which I then burst a blood vessel trying to achieve!

Whether it's trying to cram 120 singers and dancers on to the inadequate stage at the Birla Theatre for *Superstar,* or trying to take Lintas: India from Rs. 100 million to Rs. 2,000 million in ten years.

On analysis, I am a lazy person who is terrified of being called lazy! Therefore I set myself impossible tasks with impossible deadlines so that I have to leap my lazy bones out of the bed every morning and attack the impossible project with ferocious energy. Fear of failure is a great motivator, it acts like an electric cattle prod.

Fear of failure is a great motivator, it acts like an electric cattle prod. It galvanises you into action.

It galvanises you into action. Obviously, somewhere, lurking beneath the surface, I have a nagging insecurity, and therefore I have to prove to myself again and again that I'm not a failure.

But this does not explain why I try new and unexplored avenues. (Why don't I just stick to successful formulas?) Why did I insist on performing an anti-religious play like *Marat/ Sade* in St Xavier's College auditorium, against heavy opposition from the Catholic priests? Why did I stage Gurcharan Das's *Mira* as a play reading with live Mira bhajans and projections of Tantric paintings by Prabhakar Barwe? Why an interpretation of *Othello* as a return to Islamic-Moorish roots, which caused a furore among Shakespearean purists? Why a condom campaign that caused questions to be raised on the floor of Parliament?

The simple answer: Coming from a traditional Gujarati background, I get a kick out of provoking people. Sure, I enjoy success. But success is a bland meal, if it lacks a pinch of controversy.

So we embarked on this gargantuan Asia meet with a terrific team and a trembling heart. An absolute charmer, Shiamak scoured Bombay for a hundred volunteers whom he could train into accomplished dancers within sixty days. Sharon managed to get the Brabourne Stadium for rehearsals of this mammoth cast. Ajay Balram and his enchantress wife, Usha, made a giant Montech camera crane materialise out of thin air, to lift Sharon and her 200-pound dress, fifty feet into the stratosphere. The ever resourceful Sunoo Davar, our costume designer, set to work producing 1,000 pairs of silver foil butterfly wings.

Success is a bland meal, if it lacks a pinch of controversy.

The experienced Leon D'Souza was joined by the musical genius Ranjit Barot, and they spent dozens of recording hours putting together the *Tracks of Friendship* symphony with the sound of 1,000 violins, fifty sitars, dozens of tablas and dholaks, French horns, piccolos and even a harpsichord. (God bless the invention of the electronic Sampler.) Shiamak and I flew to Delhi to audition 1,000 school girls from a dozen different institutions to play the roles of the dancing *titalis*. Roger Drego used muscle and money to assemble over 50,000 watts of speaker-power to cover the enormous Nehru Stadium.

I then sat down to write the lyrics of the theme song. The first draft took me precisely two hours and seventeen minutes. I then proceeded to polish it up for the next fifty-nine days. Every day I'd get up and the devil on my shoulder would whisper, 'It's got to be better!'

After two months of blinding hard work, our huge entourage took off for Delhi with anxious mothers imploring me to take special care of their little Sita or their delicate Ram. We arrived in the Capital amid chaos. The accommodation provided for our hundred dancers and fifty technicians lacked running water and electricity. I exhorted my team to treat this nightmare as an exciting adventure into this unexplored Jurassic Park. They smiled weakly and Shiamak and his redoubtable assistants, Glen and Sita, organised a community singsong that lifted drooping spirits on that first harrowing night.

Meanwhile, back at the stadium, we had run into a rehearsal snafu. Amal and Nissar Allana, Kumadini Lakhani, Kamlakar Sontake and a score of other rehearsees were squabbling about dates and timings. Our troupe was in danger of being banished to some location on the outskirts of Delhi. But in my usual fashion, I bulldozed my way back into the Nehru Stadium.

Then the first major disaster struck. The stadium authorities refused to allow the Montech crane to be wheeled across the expensive astro-turf track on to the centrefield. The ever down-to-earth Ajay Balram solved this by putting rubber mats across the track. But hold it! Where the hell was the Montech crane? It had started its long journey to the stadium ten hours before. Ajay sped into action with his resourceful brother, Vinay. Late that evening, the Montech hove into view like Godzilla, in the gathering gloom. Apparently, the driver of the tractor that was hauling the Montech had taken a diversion to his farm to have a little *nashta*.

In a trice, I had Sharon on to the crane and began to raise it. Ten feet up in the air, Sharon screamed, 'Stop! Stop! I've got vertigo.' My son Quasar, who has an uncanny knack of timing his boarding school holidays to witness his father's crazy antics, gasped, 'She's going to fall!' With a feigned nonchalance, I commanded, 'Freeze!' The Montech operator muttered to Ajay, '*Kafi thandi hai. Phir bhi saab keh rehen hai*, "freeze"?'

Inexorably, the Montech continued its climb and my poor darling wife's screams became fainter and fainter as she approached the moon. Unable to stop Godzilla, I yelled, 'Look up, darling. Don't look down.' Fortunately, that dose of heaven-climbing cured Sharon of her vertigo, but then we ran into the problem of safety. The guardrail around the crane was waist-high, ideal for suspending the fifty-foot skirt of Sharon's dress so that it looked like it was around her waist. But this meant that Sharon had nothing to hold on to as she wobbled skywards.

Without batting an eyelid, ingenious Vinay constructed a canvas safety belt around Sharon's waist and latched it to the guardrail beneath the giant skirt. Furthermore, the inventive lad suggested he sit on the platform beneath her skirt, holding on to Sharon's thighs to steady her. (I insisted calves, not thighs!)

Hardly had we overcome this tricky problem when we faced another googly. The aluminium hoops that helped keep the skirt in shape got snarled in each other as the crane began to lift. Eventually Ajay arranged for two brave assistant stage managers to stand inside the suffocating skirt with fifteen-foot bamboo poles to whack the offending aluminium rings apart when they got entangled.

But our Montech nightmare was far from over. On the day of the show, the tractor we were expecting didn't show up, because it was required by the owner's family to plough his *kheti*. At the nth hour, Ajay commandeered the Nehru Stadium tractor to haul the Montech and its cupola across the rubber mats to the centre of the field, just as our item was being announced over the loudspeakers. God is truly on the side of the brave…or is it the barmy?

Problems were flying in faster than flies in the monsoon weather. Have you ever tried putting fragile silver foil wings on to 1,000 giggling schoolgirls? What's worse, have you ever tried taking off the wings after a two-hour rehearsal, when the kids are dying to get their hands on free Frooti? This superhuman feat was achieved rehearsal after rehearsal by the unflappable Honey Mani, our wardrobe mistress, whose nature is as sweet as her name. As we went along, this project was beginning to resemble the Titanic in her last hours.

The next major challenge was to coincide the skydivers' arrival with the climax of Sharon's song. Fortunately, I had an extra powerful walkie-talkie to instruct the helicopter pilot (who hovered thousands of feet above the stadium), when to make the parachute drop.

By this time, my team and I were totally exhausted. But the adrenalin of the deadline is like an energy pill, and when D-Day arrived we were recharged. We were told that Rajiv Gandhi had been especially looking forward to the show. *Tracks of Friendship* was to be the climax of the opening ceremony.

The adrenalin of the deadline is like an energy pill.

The final challenge was flung at us by the security guards an hour before the Prime Minister's arrival. Two of the four gates from where 500 silver butterflies were to emerge were blocked off because they were considered a security risk! My hats off to the teachers of my 'butterfly' students. They immediately re-organised their troops to make a circuitous entry, to avoid ruining Shiamak's carefully designed choreography.

Enter Rajiv Gandhi on the dot. Our event is one hour and thirty minutes after the start. The tension mounts. My friend Akash, the inventive TV director, has his finger poised on the video camera trigger and is sweating profusely in the cool November sun. The flags of all the participating Asian nations snap in the wind like the drums of doom. The item before us is the Cavalry Parade. On my walkie-talkie, I whisper hoarsely, 'Ajay, start the tractor.' Hidden by the dust kicked up by the horses, the fifty-foot circular platform trundles across the green sward.

It comes to rest on its chalk marks, and the tractor disappears under the cupola, where feverish activity is going on. Sharon is being harnessed into the Montech. Vinay is gripping her legs for dear life. Ajay is checking the recharged batteries of the Montech (which had stalled the crane in mid-air at the six a.m. rehearsal that very morning). A dozen assistant stage managers are flouncing out the giant skirt to keep it free from entanglements. Roger and I in the stands, are linked to Ajay and his merry men by an umbilical river of sweat, as our body salts desert us like rats fleeing a sinking ship.

Roger hits the play button. And 50,000 watts of sound engulf the 70,000-strong audience. I steal a glance at the Prime Minister. He is wearing his usual half-smile. At the first roll of the tympani drums, we hear a rustle of 1,000 pairs of wings. A shiver runs down my spine. I pray fervently that this thrill, in a less fearful form, is shared by the audience. On to the field stream four rivers of silver, glinting in the noonday sun like quicksilver gone mad.

A ten-year old stumbles and almost falls. But miraculously she recovers herself and races on. (Flash-cut to my dream the previous night: One child tripping up could cause a domino effect, and a whole line of 250 butterflies could be sprawled across the grass!) The bodies of the butterflies are in three colours. Saffron, white and green. While their wings are silver. A ripple of applause runs through the stands. Rajiv's hands are motionless, though the half-smile is still there.

Another roll of the tympani, and Shiamak's hundred dancers appear. They go into their *Higher, Stronger, Faster* ballet.

Another ripple of applause traverses the stadium. Rajiv's hands remain frozen. I still have another ace up my sleeve. On the third crash of the tympanis, Sharon emerges like Venus out of the waves of silver-coated butterflies in full-throated song. She floats upward on what seems to be a cloud of gossamer. For a heart-stopping moment her ascent comes to a halt and I scream over the walkie-talkie, 'Ajay, give the stubborn Montech a hefty kick!'

Miracle of miracles, the Montech continues its majestic rise and Sharon is wafted high above the athletic flame, singing her heart out to the now ecstatic crowd... who have never seen anything like this before. Rajiv unfreezes and is now on his feet, applauding with the rest of the audience. His half-smile has broadened into a boyish grin. In the excitement, I almost forget to give the signal to the helicopter. Fortunately, Roger yells, 'Helicopter cue.' From out of a cloudless sky, drop the paratroopers. The sky is filled with tri-colour parachutes.

Ajay and his crew have still to complete one more tricky manoeuvre. They must get the Montech down and off the grass fast, to avoid the parachutists accidentally crashing into it. They manage it in the nick of time. The music rises to a crescendo. And as the final skydiver hits the grass, there is a roll of applause that grows unto a thunderclap. Mission Impossible made possible. With a lot of luck, pluck and a little help from my friends, the gods above.

Cole Porter said it with wit, 'I get no kick from champagne, but I get a kick out of you.' Being a lifelong teetotaller like Morarji Desai (but without his craving for body fluids), I've managed to avoid champagne but get a kick out of life 365 days a year. As I look back, I realise that right from my school days, I deliberately set myself difficult tasks in order to enjoy the challenge of mastering them. Nothing ventured, nothing

a double life

gained. You've got to have stars in your eyes before you reach for them in the sky.

You've got to have stars in your eyes before you reach for them in the sky.

The year is 1968. The challenge I set myself is this: Produce a sales conference for Lux soap that will blaze a new trail. The task as Hindustan Lever saw it was simple. Enthuse the sales force about Lux in four colour variants. Too simple for AP.

I decided to do a multi-screen audio-visual, which had never been attempted in India till that time. Easier said than done. I got hold of Madhu Gadkari, who had helped me create the grand-daddy of single screen AVs on India entitled *The Changing Face of Tradition* (which later had a thousand reincarnations as *India: Adventure and Riddle, Continent in Chrysalis,* etc.). We then purloined Joseph St Anne from the copy department. This triumvirate was to break new ground every year for the next decade, in the field of AVs. The torch was then handed over to Homi Daruvala, Imtiaz Dharker, Etienne Coutinho and other young tyros who passed through the portals of the Lintas AV department.

I was bubbling with ideas, having just staged a Café Theatre experiment called *Trial Balloon* using the three walls of Chetana Art Gallery as screens with three primitive slide projectors, hand-operated to change their slides in time to the Beatles' *Lucy in the Sky with Diamonds.*

For this Levers conference, we decided to go in for three giant screens. One in the centre, and one each to the right and left. This meant that the audience was almost surrounded by the huge slide images. The opening AV was *The Changing Face of Tradition,* but now on three screens, with a stereo soundtrack. Most of the time, we used only the centre screen.

Then suddenly, for dramatic impact, we would start with the left screen, add on another image on the centre screen, and yet another image on the right screen. Sometimes, we repeated the same image on the three screens simultaneously. This seems pretty old hat now, but for the audience of those days, it was revolutionary.

To make matters more complicated, I insisted on using the gauze scrim device I had tried out in my Hindi production, *Shishon ke Khilone,* some years earlier. At the climax of the conference, Helen, the movie-star dancer, was to appear on a slide, which then dissolved into the real live Helen, who lifted her magic wand to cut through the gauze and walk through the screen and into the audience.

But as I've said before, an idea is only as brilliant as its execution. Because Helen was not available for rehearsals at the Taj, I took the gamble of demonstrating to her at her residence, how she would raise the wand and simply cut through the screen. For the dress rehearsal on the night before the morning conference, I was the stand-in for Helen and cut through the screen neatly. Unfortunately, at the actual show, Helen raised her wand to slice through the gauze, but the gauze refused to part (unlike the Red Sea for Moses).

She slashed away at the mosquito netting, which stubbornly withstood her onslaught. As a murmur ran around the hall, I zipped out from behind the projector I was manning, whipped out my penknife and rushed forward like Anthony Perkins in *Psycho,* with blade raised. Helen blanched. The blade slashed through the gauze. I proffered my arm to Helen, and with all the dignity she could muster, she stepped down into the auditorium to a standing ovation from our sporting sales force.

Two decades later, I repeated this 'Sir Walter Raleigh gallantry' for the late Princess Diana at a dinner hosted by the then Prime Minister, P V Narasimha Rao. It was a chilly winter evening and I was seated to the left of the Princess of Wales. I noticed that her chatting had turned into chattering as she shivered under the shamiana in the Prime Minister's freezing garden. Gallantly, I offered her my suit jacket. But even more gallantly, the sarod maestro, Amjad Ali Khan, whipped off his exquisite shawl and beat me to the punch, 'Try this, Madam. It is more suitable.' (I looked daggers at him.)

Later that evening, Princess Diana tried to return the heirloom shawl, but Amjad, being the true gentleman that he is, would have nothing of it. He said simply, 'Please keep it, Madam. It is a gift.' The Princess was overwhelmed, but insisted on returning it. At this point, I stepped in and said, 'In that case, Madam, you keep my jacket, and I'll keep the shawl!' Prince Charles shot me a Queen Victoria look, as if to say, 'We are not amused.' (Sadly, I kept my jacket and the Princess kept the shawl.)

Earlier I had asked Diana what it was like to be a princess. She replied, 'It is like being a movie star under the bad old Hollywood studio system. Your protocol manager decides how you dress, where you go and who you meet. I see my life as a long corridor with everything circumscribed within. Of course, my husband and my sons don't mind becuase they have been brought up to be princes. The trouble is, I haven't. I miss doing my own thing.'

In the theatre, there is no Take Two. The fear of making a complete ass of myself causes me to have umpteen technical rehearsals. I believe that it's better to be safe than suicidal. That is why I always keep Plan B ready, because Plan A invariably goes haywire. Nevertheless, Murphy's Law (whatever can go wrong will go wrong!) operates in spite of the most painstaking preparations.

For example, my production of *Hamlet* caused a sensation in ways I had not planned. The very trim and well-groomed veteran actor Farrokh Mehta had just completed his cameo as the gravedigger to heartwarming applause. As he bent down to pick up Yorrick's skull from the grave (which was cut into the platform), my super-efficient stage manager slammed down the lid of the grave in the blackout... entombing the hapless Farrokh underneath the platform for the rest of the play. In Bombay theatrelore, this incident is referred to as 'Yorrick's Revenge'!

Always keep Plan B ready, because Plan A invariably goes haywire.

The theatre has given me such an incredible variety of experiences that I often feel I've crammed a dozen lifetimes into one. Take the time when I was directing Irwin Shaw's *Bury the Dead* for the St. Xavier's College Dramatics Club.

This was in 1968, and I was very into Stanislavsky. So I insisted that my young cast undergo the rigours of army training. The play is about soldiers who refuse to die, and rise from the dead like zombies. So I arranged with an army friend of mine to show my boys how to march with a full pack, load a rifle and even dig a trench.

Bright and early one Sunday morning, as dawn was breaking over the military cantonment in Upper Colaba, my sleepy-eyed regiment of actors was six feet below ground level, shovelling away and sweating from every pore. At the end of this gruelling test, I was left with only six soldiers. The rest deserted me. But those who stayed had the thrill of a lifetime at the dress rehearsal.

At the climax of the play, the general orders his troops to open fire on the advancing dead men, who won't lie down.

Taking realism to its ultimate, I loaded the rifles with blanks. At the command of the general, the firing squad marched down the aisle, from the backdoor of the auditorium in perfect formation. They then lined up at the footlights, and on command, raised their rifles and opened fire.

The noise was deafening. Acrid smoke from the gunpowder blanks filled the hall. Three out of the four 'walking dead' continued to advance towards the firing squad (as planned). But one of the 'corpses' began to retreat in fear shouting, 'You crazy bastards! You're supposed to aim above our heads. You hit me with a wad of cardboard that is part of the goddamn blanks!' I almost had another deserter on my hands that night.

Accidents happen in real life, in spite of the best precautions. For stage effects, I make it a point to test every stage device myself before allowing my actors to risk their necks. In *Marat/Sade,* the famous guillotine effect required the heavy blade to fall with a thud, seeming to sever the neck of the victim. To achieve this effect, I had a guillotine built that had two safety catches to stop the blade three inches before it hit the neck of the actor.

With theatrical flourish, and a mock farewell speech to my cast, I placed my head on the block and asked my stage manager to release the rope that was holding up the blade. The blade came down like the sword of Damocles. It was neatly stopped by the two safety catches, and as I grinned with relief, a ripple of appreciation ran round the cast. 'Okay, positions please, everybody. Let's start the scene.'

The actor who was playing the aristocrat to be beheaded placed his neck gingerly in the slot. He looked up apprehensively at the gleaming blade, eight feet above his head. The drums rolled, and at the cymbal clash, the executioner released the rope. The blade flashed downwards. The aristocrat screamed as one of the safety catches gave way, and the blade hovered half an inch away from his exposed neck. I rushed forward shouting, 'I'm going to decapitate the carpenter who built this lousy guillotine!' The poor actor had nightmares for months afterwards and even developed chronic insomnia, according to his distraught wife. (I wonder if I unwittingly improved their nightlife!)

Kabir Bedi, who played *Othello* in my 1990 production, almost developed a nightmare syndrome too. My Othello doesn't suffocate Desdemona with a pillow. Instead, I planned he strangles her with the incriminating handkerchief. Since the hanky is vital to several characters, I insisted on having five identical hankies. One each, for Othello, Desdemona, Iago, Cassio and Emilia, so that the all-important hanky would never be missing.

As luck would have it, Kabir's dresser forgot to place the handkerchief in the pocket of his gown at one fateful show. At the climatic moment, where Othello growls, 'Down, strumpet!' Kabir reached into his pocket and groped desperately. Nothing there.

There was a deathless pause (pun intended) as Kabir's hand emerged from his pocket horribly empty. Sitting in the audience, I groaned audibly. My solicitous neighbour mistook my agony and whispered, 'It's only a play.'

The blonde and bubbling school-girlish Nikki Vijaykar was already halfway through Desdemona's last words, 'But while I say one prayer.' Kabir, with magnificent stage presence, raised his large hands, sans handkerchief, towards Desdemona's throat. Nikki desperately tried to extricate her own copy of the handkerchief from her nightgown, but Kabir thundered, true to the Bard, 'It is too late!' and proceeded to strangle Desdemona with his bare hands. After the curtain fell,

Kabir was tempted to perform a second strangulation on his dresser!

The best-laid plans of mice and men, as we know, often go haywire. The first time we shot the girl in the waterfall for Liril, was in Khandala, where the waters were balmy. But I thought the results were anaemic. So the producer, Kailash Surendranath, travelled all over India, and finally chose the Kodaikanal waterfall for a re-shoot. After weeks of preparation, the unit left for the location with Mubi Ismail, our Films Chief.

The next morning, bright and early, Karen Lunel – the diminutive water sprite with lovely dancing eyes and a dazzling smile that lights up her whole face – donned her lime-green bikini and stepped radiantly into the waterfall. Within a few seconds, the poor girl turned blue. It was freezing. The water was 4°C. So instead of the Liril girl's flashing smile, all we could see were her chattering teeth. In our innocence (or was it stupidity?), we had selected November as the month for the shooting. But no one had checked the temperature!

Still, Karen was a real sport. Fortifed with a few slugs from a bottle of rum, she gave the performance of her life, dancing and cavorting in the icy water like a Nordic sea nymph. For over a decade, Karen continued to thrill viewers with her seemingly effortless performance. Radiating sunshine and joy. (Did the naughtiness in her eyes reflect Liril or Old Monk?)

Karen gets my vote for the all-time top model. Besides her vivacity I love her professionalism. She takes pride of place in my Hall of Fame. I think the makers of Liril soap should award her a solid gold medal. Sometimes a model makes a product. Catherine Deneuve for Chanel. Isabella Rossellini for Lancôme. And, of course, Karen Lunel for Liril.

The run-up is more important than the delivery

While shooting for *Gandhi*, I learnt from Attenborough what it is to be cool under fire. When a hundred horses required for a scene failed to show up one morning, he didn't turn a hair. (In spite of a £1,000 per minute cost ticking away.) All he said was, 'We'll do Scene seventy-six instead. It's all indoors.' A crisis can either panic you or focus you. The choice is yours.

A crisis can either panic you or focus you. The choice is yours.

This little 'cool under fire' lesson came in useful when I fell off the stage during the dress rehearsal of Mahesh Dattani's *Tara* and broke my arm. Luckily I was not knocked unconscious, so I was able to yell for ice. My daughter Raell, who was the producer, rushed me to the Breach Candy Hospital next door to Sophia College auditorium. My arm was X-rayed and found to be fractured. A plaster cast was applied. And feeling very Attenboroughish, I went back, cool as cucumber, to complete the dress rehearsal...much to the annoyance of my cast who were expecting the night off! This incident has since come to be known as 'The plaster saint in a plaster cast!'

The most astonishing thing about growing old is that the voyage of discovery continues.

FOREIGN IMPORTS OR
INDIAN ADAPTATIONS?

*A*s India enters the global arena and readies herself for battle with multinationals, both at home and abroad, we are riding into the future with a big load on our backs. This is actually a colonial complex, which translates itself into 'Can we match their might, their money, their know-how?' We need to rid ourselves of this baggage before we can even step on to the international stage.

We may not as yet win sackfuls of Clios and Cannes awards (though Lintas: India did pretty well in the 1980s with over a dozen including the Clio Hall of Fame). Our creativity is as powerful as the best in the West, but it is different. Our advertising is designed to work in our own cultural context. The Clio and Cannes festivals celebrate American and European advertising culture and style.

However, when the multinationals from the other side of the Suez Canal enter the Indian market...they find their much vaunted creativity fails to work its magic on the *desi* consumer. Coke stumbles against Thums Up and the Indianised Pepsi. Kellogg's Big Breakfast is not sufficient for the Indian family, which demands a brunch-size meal. Mercedes finds their models are too old-fashioned for the NRI yuppies who are clued into BBC's *Top Gear* TV programme. Levi's gets shot down by Killer Jeans and their Indian clones. In order for MNCs to be successful in the Indian market, they need to rethink their 3 Ps: Proposition, Personality and Pricing.

Hindustan Lever, the unique local-multinational, has seven out of its ten most successful brands invented in India. Like

Fair & Lovely face cream, Dalda cooking fat, Liril bath soap, Surf detergent powder (especially the Lalitaji phase), Lifebuoy soap (*Lifebuoy hai jahan, tandurusti hai wahan* which means 'Where there's Lifebuoy, there's health'), Rin detergent tablet, Wheel detergent powder. That's because Hindustan Lever has been run by Indian chairmen since the early 1960s. And I am happy to say almost all the brands listed above have been created by the Indian Lintas with Indian, not expatriate, creative directors.

MNCs need to rethink their three Ps: Proposition, Personality and Pricing.

Similarly when it comes to foreign plays like *Evita* and *Jesus Christ Superstar,* instead of international touring productions, we need staging that is adapted to the Indian context. There is a mistaken impression even among our own theatre reviewers that productions of western plays in India are carbon copies of the Broadway and West End originals. I don't agree. Take *Evita,* for instance. What attracted me to *Evita* was, of course, the music. But, even more important, the theme. The fact that a woman could rise in a man's world and become the empress of her country. In my mind, this was so akin to Indira Gandhi.

So my production began with the premise that though I would use the music from the original *Evita,* as well as most of the words, my interpretation would be India-oriented, and most certainly Indira-oriented. So much so that Indians who went abroad and saw the production on Broadway or in London, came back and said, 'My God! The Theatre Group production in Bombay is so different. And we prefer it because the storyline is so meaningful.' Whereas in London and New York, they assumed that everyone knew about Evita and

Argentina, that is Eva Peron and Argentinian politics, here I didn't assume that at all.

Nobody here gave a damn as to who Evita was. Hardly anybody knew where Argentina was and no one cared a fig for South American politics. So we took the Indian Prime Minister, Mrs Indira Gandhi, and used her as a parallel for Evita. Now Evita, mind you, started as a poverty-stricken girl whereas Mrs Gandhi was a rich man's daughter. But we concentrated on showing how both ladies wielded their power. As soon as Mrs Gandhi got to the top, she began to behave very much like Evita did when she got there.

Both started off with good intentions. Evita came from the downtrodden and as she went up in life, she forgot the purpose for which she wanted the power. Mrs Gandhi wanted to do a lot for *garibi hatao*, but in the end she only managed to *hatao* Chief Ministers, so that she could remain in power.

My version of *Evita* reflected the reign of Mrs Gandhi. The script included slogans from the 1975 Emergency declared by Indira. These were still fresh in people's minds, and so we projected these slogans on screen as if they were Peronist catch phrases. Thus the line between Indira and Evita merged. The production had a tremendous impact because the play not only had excellent music but now the story had a parallel and an immediacy for the Indian audience.

I also introduced the role of Che Guevara as a *sutradhar*, a sort of narrator, which is not present in the western production. I wrote brief but bitter links for Che Guevara between the songs to give the audience a breather from the constant barrage of music, and to explain the storyline as the play unfolded (and, most important, to give my stage management time to change the sets!).

Che would come on and make some caustic comments about Evita, some of them obliquely referring to Mrs Gandhi's behaviour. However, there was no attempt to give the characters or the production an Indian look. The relevance was in the theme of the play. A woman in power, and how easy it is to be led astray from your noble objectives to baser ones.

Evita went on to run for about 150 shows and probably would have run for another 150 if we hadn't stopped. But by that time, I think the actors and myself were quite worn out. We opened in 1983 and took it to Delhi in 1984 after Mrs Gandhi had been assassinated. In fact, we invited her son Rajiv Gandhi, who had taken over as Prime Minister, but he could not make it as he was busy. The Delhi audiences who were very familiar with Indian political history, more than any audience anywhere else in India, burst into applause when the Emergency slogans were projected. There is no doubt in my mind that however brilliant the product, whether *Evita* or Surf, it needs a reinterpretation if it is to impact the Indian audience. In the case of *Evita* it was Indira and for Surf, it was Lalitaji.

The greatest kick I got out of *Evita* was not from the plaudits, but from the letter I received, out of the blue, from Harold 'Hal' Prince, one of the world's great theatre directors: 'I read in the *New York Times* about your production of *Evita,* and I'm fascinated that you based it on Indira Gandhi. As you may know, I did the original production of *Evita,* so perhaps the two directors of *Evita* could have a chat about our different productions of the play. If you happen to visit New York, please give me a ring and we'll have a drink together.'

I showed the letter to Sharon who was delighted. The next time we went to New York, I called Hal, and sure enough, he invited us over. We spent more than an hour talking about *Evita* and *Kabaret* and *Tughlaq* and *Faust,* which was the opera he was doing at the time. Just when we were leaving, he said,

'Aren't you the man who played Mr Jinnah in *Gandhi*?' When I nodded, he said, 'That is one of my favourite films and I truly admired your performance.'

Praise from a professional is the headiest wine of all.

Praise from a professional is the headiest wine of all.

Ever since I can remember, I've had an obsession about Mrs Gandhi. The first time I introduced her in my theatre work was when I drew a parallel between her and Julius Caesar in a mini production I did in 1977. I took the liberty of calling the play *Caesar* instead of *Julius Caesar*. I kept all Shakespeare's blank verse except I changed the word 'his' into 'hers' wherever it occurred. Because the fear of the Emergency had not yet died down, the impact of having a female dictator was terrifyingly real. I sometimes wonder whether this was my most prophetic production...Indira Gandhi like Julius Caesar was assassinated a few years later.

It has always been my contention that certain things which work in the West but are unfamiliar to Indian audiences, need to touch base with what Indians understand. Either as history or culture. That is critical. Like in *Jesus Christ Superstar* when I drew parallels with Mahatma Gandhi, but more of that later.

I have always felt that English theatre in India, most of the time, tends to be irrelevant. We talk about Jack and we talk about Frank. We talk about Jane and Rosemary, who have little or nothing to do with us. When I'm in the audience, I always wish the play could have done more for me not only as a human being but as an Indian living in Bombay.

In my production of *Kabaret* (as in the German kabaret political café theatre of the 1930s), I saw very clear parallels between the rise of Hitler's fascism and the rise of fundamentalist fascism in India, and I took liberties with the costuming. Instead of Hitler's Brownshirts, my characters wore saffron shirts, and I used projected slogans between scenes. These slogans everyone assumed were Hitler's, such as, 'The only place for minorities is outside our borders or inside our prisons.' But at the end of the play, the last projected slide said, 'We would like to give credit to our local politicians for the slogans that we have projected during the play.' Here again, the original New York production would have had a minimal immediacy if we had not given it an Indian relevance. In the light of the Bombay riots which occurred five years later, did this production, too, have a hint of prophecy about it?

In this way I like to tease, provoke the audience into thinking beyond just the play. I like them to feel the play as timeless and eternal and very human. So the audience thinks, 'Hey, wait a minute. In the social/political context in which we live, this damn play makes a lot more sense than when I read it.' I think if a production can't add anything to the relevance of the play, let it remain on the printed page. Let people enjoy reading it, full stop. I believe that the director and the actors always bring something to a play when they produce it on stage. They bring a point of view. And the audience may agree or disagree with their version, but one hopes they will not remain uninvolved.

If a production can't add relevance to the play, let it remain on the printed page.

In 1963, I did Arthur Miller's *The Crucible*. At that time we had a big scare in India. In 1961 the Pakistanis were threatening to bomb Bombay. We had skirmishes in Kashmir and the papers were full of news that war was likely to break out between India and Pakistan. There were also other alarming items in the newspapers. About how anyone with a beard on the streets of Delhi was being manhandled and beaten up because he was a Muslim and since he was a Muslim he might have Pakistani leanings. There was a kind of a witch-hunt going on.

It struck me that the witch-hunt happening in India was akin to what Senator McCarthy did in the 1950s to loyal Americans who happened to be communists but owed no allegiance to Russia. We premiered in New Delhi before Prime Minister Jawaharlal Nehru (with Indira Gandhi sitting right by his side, looking so sweet and innocent before her reign as India's Maha Kali).

The morning after the play, some friends of mine who'd had dinner with Mr Nehru the previous night told me, 'He talked about nothing else but the parallels between the play and what is happening in India. People are getting hysterical and violent.' But most of the sophisticated audience missed the parallel. Many of them said to me, 'What rubbish, Alyque, what allusions are there?' Even in *Kabaret,* a lot of people missed it. When I asked them, 'Did you read the slide about the local politicians?' they replied, 'Yes. We were wondering what that meant.'

This upset me and I said, 'From now on, when I do a play where I want to put across a point of view, I am going to underline it and not just imply it. I am going to spell it out.' But I'm often caught on the horns of a dilemma. On the one hand my worry is that if I over-explain, the audience will say, 'Listen, we're not babies! We don't need to be spoonfed.' And on the other hand, if I don't explain, the audience very often misses the point. But whatever happens, it is vital to speak to the public in a way they understand.

When we were stuck on Surf and went to Unilever and told them, 'Look, we are being beaten hands down by Nirma,' they replied, 'Well, we have an international campaign, why don't you try that?' They told us to stress the superiority of the washing power and safety of Surf over the cheaper competitor.

This had worked for Unilever in other markets. Our gut feel told us the Indian consumer would not appreciate or understand this sort of logic.

In addition, Levers had never faced a situation where Surf was three times as expensive as the competition. Elsewhere in the world, there had been situations where Surf was marked up twenty-five per cent to fifty per cent, but never 300 per cent. So Nirma detergent sales went from 1,000 tonnes to 250,000 tonnes, while Surf fell from 45,000 tonnes to 35,000 tonnes. Obviously we were in danger of losing the detergent market almost entirely.

Hindustan Lever insisted that we use their international approach which stressed whiteness and the powerful action of Surf that gets right into the thread of the garment and removes the dirt. Justifying the fact that even if you are paying a little more, it seems well worth it. Our new campaign demonstrated that half a kilo of Surf could wash as much as one kilo of Nirma and was therefore economical. We showed school children running out of a bus with white uniforms and we counted them as they got out. While only twenty-five children got out of the Nirma bus, fifty got out of the Surf bus.

But this didn't work. It was all too rational. I believe that unless you can emotionally convince your audience about something, they'll nod with their heads but not with their hearts.

Unless you can emotionally convince your audience, all they'll do is nod with their heads but not with their hearts.

So we were caught in a bind. We were losing market share badly. That is when we put our Indian heads together and came out with a uniquely *desi* approach. This was based on the Indian need for getting a damn good bargain.

But how can you sell a bargain which is three times more expensive than what you are bargaining against? So we invented Lalitaji. She was a hardheaded bargain hunting housewife, who demanded value for money and not just a cheap price.

Consumers' faith in Surf was restored, not just because she offered a rational argument (we still featured the two jar comparison showing how half a kilo of Surf was equivalent to one kilo of Nirma). The real reason Lalitaji was believed is because she was trusted by the Indian housewife to get them a good bargain. We showed her bargaining with the vegetable vendor about good tomatoes and bad tomatoes. She was willing to buy good tomatoes at a higher price because they were better value for money. As she said wisely, '*Sasti cheez or achchi cheez me farak hota hai, bhai saab.*' (There is a difference between buying cheap stuff and good stuff, my dear man.) Thanks to the force of her personality, she convinced consumers that buying Surf made good sense (*Surf ki kharidari mein samajdari hai*). It only goes to prove that a rational but radical point of view needs an emotional spokesman (in this case spokeswoman) to convince the audience. Think of John F Kennedy's radical request to the American people: 'Ask not what your country can do for you. Ask what you can do for your country.' JFK's charisma made this palatable. Like it or not, charisma sells better than logic.

Charisma sells better than logic.

Indian businesses should not slavishly follow what are called global strategies. For example, if you're bringing power tools into India, easy-to-use is not the platform. Because in India there is no Do-It-Yourself culture. The guy who buys it is never going to use it himself. His servant is going to use it. Or the carpenter. The buyer doesn't give a damn whether it is easy to use or not. He wants to know if it is strong enough to withstand the rough handling his carpenter will subject it to.

Right from 1958 when we launched Surf up to 1993, I played the role of key strategist for Levers in Lintas. In the early years, about ninety per cent of my time was spent working only on Levers accounts. Later on, this came down to about fifty per cent. I was involved in every major Levers strategy for more than thirty years. And in all that time, I can't remember a single Levers brand that utilised an international approach. None of them seemed to work in the Indian context.

For example, in the late 1950s-early 1960s, almost all over the world Levers was using the body odour platform to sell Lifebuoy. And there was a lot of pressure on us in India to go with this same strategy. But I said, 'In India, body odour is not a problem,' to which they replied, 'Yeah, but it wasn't a problem in the West either. We made people conscious of the problem.' I said, 'Yes. But you live in closed apartments and offices in Europe. And particularly in winter, you become conscious of people's body odour (furthermore, bathing is less frequent when the weather is cold). In our tropical climate, most of the time people live with their windows open and a lot of fresh air circulating around. Besides, strong odours are more acceptable in India because all our food has a pungent aroma. Therefore I don't think body odour is going to cut much ice. I strongly feel that the old but now disused health appeal of Lifebuoy will grab the Indian consumer. And we can reinforce it with "washes away the germs in dirt and leaves you with that healthy feeling of freshness".'

We got no opposition from Levers when we came up with the memorable line, *'Lifebuoy hain jahan, tandurusti hain wahan.'* (Where there's Lifebuoy, there's health). It was a line penned by our brilliant Hindi copywriter Shanti Narayan, a tiny man with horn-rimmed glasses and a formidable intellect which was sometimes incapacitated by a weakness for the bottle. I was Films Chief at the time, and I developed with him the long running Lifebuoy ad films featuring sports like hockey, football or kabaddi in which our hero falls to the ground... and is then shown having a healthy bath with Lifebuoy which washes away the germs in dirt. Instead of a boring voice-over commentary, we preferred a jingle which kept repeating the phrase 'Where there's Lifebuoy, there's health.' The tune for this jingle was composed by the renowned Hindi voicer Brij Bhushan. Incredibly, the same tune with different orchestrations is still running more than thirty years after it was created.

Today, Lifebuoy has almost completely died out in the West. But in India, it is still the biggest soap brand, with sales of almost 150,000 tonnes per annum. In fact, Lifebuoy India is the largest selling soap in the whole world. You can go against a global strategy if you can prove that a global strategy won't work in your country.

You can go against a global strategy if you can prove that a global strategy won't work in your country.

A lot of global marketeers feel that a brand must have the same appeal all over the world. Especially since many consumers travel frequently and are exposed to brand advertising in different parts of the world. So when someone picks up a Coke in India, they feel it must have the same image, same advertising, same appeal as it does in the US.

I don't think that is strictly necessary, because I don't think that Coke itself tastes exactly the same or should taste exactly the same as in the US. There may be certain nuances in tastes that need to be adapted. In India, we have a very strong sweet tooth, whereas in the US they may prefer it a little less sweet.

When I was in Beijing a few years ago, as a speaker at the Third World Advertising Congress, we were invited to a grand seventeen-course meal. All the Indian delegates were aghast at the food. Chinese food as eaten by the Chinese in China is nothing like the Chinese food we Indians were used to in India. Ours is spicy, theirs is bland. When we asked the host, 'Why don't you give us prawns in hot garlic sauce?' he replied, 'We eat prawns, but never in hot garlic sauce. Hot garlic sauce is Italian. How can you call it Chinese?'

So I think steamrollering everyone into accepting a standardised global taste or global advertising platform could be courting disaster. In fact, if anything, I feel that niche marketing is what is going to really take off in the years to come. 'I don't want to be like my neighbour. I want to be different. I don't want to wear exactly the same brand of jeans.' Variety is the spice of globalisation.

MNC stands for Misreading National Culture.

GANDHI AND THE
GANDHIJI EXPERIENCE

*T*here was a tremendous furore when it was announced that an Englishman, Sir Richard Attenborough, was going to make a film on the Father of the Indian Nation, Mahatma Gandhi. Why allow a foreigner to portray our greatest leader was the cry. Wouldn't he give it a British Raj slant? However, Attenborough proved the doomsayers wrong. His *Gandhi* is an affectionate but perceptive view of the man and his times, and became a worldwide phenomenon.

In fact, 'Of course I know you. You're Mr Jinnah!' is how I'm often greeted around the world. From London to New York to Berlin to Brussels to Brazil and even to Honolulu. *Gandhi* has had such a global impact — not only as a movie, but also as a human experience — that people still remember me for my portrayal of the founder of Pakistan, even years and years after the film was released.

It was a fascinating experience playing Mohammed Ali Jinnah in an international film being directed by one of my boyhood heroes, Richard Attenborough. My thoughts go back many years to a cocktail party in Bombay, given for Sir Richard. There were quite a few theatre people around and the legendary director and I spent about five minutes or so together. At first glance, Attenborough strikes you as a stocky, affable banker, but you soon appreciate his intellectual vitality the minute he begins to speak. We discussed *Death of a Salesman,* which was the play I was performing in at the time.

The next morning my telephone rang. 'Is that Mr Aleek Padamsee?'

'Yes', I replied.

'Richard Attenborough here.'

'Good morning, Mr Attenborough.'

'Mr Padamsee, I was wondering whether you would care to be my Jinnah in the film *Gandhi,* which as you know I'm directing.'

'Really? You want me? I mean, you want me to come for a screen test, right?'

'No, no. I want you to play Jinnah.'

'Without any screen test? I've never been in the movies.'

'I know you are a theatre actor and I have great faith in stage experience. I cut my teeth in the theatre myself. I've cast Ben Kingsley as Gandhi. And he's a theatre actor, not a film actor. I've cast Roshan Seth as Nehru. He, too, is from the stage. I'm about to cast Rohini Hattangady as Kasturba Gandhi and Saeed Jaffrey as Sardar Patel, and they've both been on the boards, so why not you? Movie actors are fine, but I have more faith in actors from the theatre.'

So I said, 'Why yes! I'll be honoured. I hope there'll be some money in it.' He replied, 'Well, not much. This is an art film.' Now Richard Attenborough is a smart man. The film went on to make $200 million, and he paid us as if it were an art film. But still, no regrets. It was an honour.

Then he said to me, 'Is it possible for you to go to London next week? I'll send you the ticket, of course. I want you measured out for Mr Jinnah's clothes, because they've got to be very special.' I replied, 'Yes, marvellous. I'd love a trip to London.' And before I knew it, I was playing a role in what later turned out to be one of the greatest epic films ever made.

I later asked Attenborough, 'Richard, you cast me as Jinnah, when you had only met me at a cocktail party. But how did you know that I would be right for the part?' And he replied, 'You know, Aleek (which is how he pronounced my name), I have a sixth sense about these things. I meet someone and "click" it goes. I know at once that this is the person who's perfect. It was your personality that convinced me that you were right for the part.'

'Really?' I said. 'What was that?'

'Well, Jinnah was an autocratic man. And I see in you all those same signs.'

'I don't know whether to be flattered or insulted.'

'Yes, well, besides that, you are also tall and slim, which is what Jinnah was, and you have this air of being able to command people. You raise your eyebrow and people immediately get nervous. Which is what Jinnah was known for.'

Before we started shooting I did a lot of research. I went to several people, including my friend, Mr Rustom Gagrat, who at one time used to work for Jinnah. Gagrat, a small-built, gracious Parsi gentleman of the old school, was most helpful. I asked him, 'Can you tell me any stories about the great man? I've read books and I've seen him in a few newsreels and heard some radio speeches, but I haven't yet got a feel of him.'

He recounted this anecdote for me: 'I remember the day it was announced in the papers that Mr Jinnah wanted to set up Pakistan for the Muslims. I felt very bad being a Parsi. I thought that all the minority communities should stick together. So with a great deal of courage, I knocked on Mr Jinnah's cabin door and he called for me to enter, in his typical authoritative voice. So I opened the door and peeped in, and he said, "No, no. Come right in." With my knees trembling, I went in. "Yes, Gagrat. What can I do for you?" he asked. Still trembling, I said to him, "Sir, I'm very disappointed. I thought all the minorities like the Parsis and the Christians and the Sikhs and the Muslims would stand together. But you have declared Pakistan for the Muslims." Mr Jinnah arose from his chair to his full height of six feet, adjusted his monocle, looked down at me and in a tone that was unmistakable, said, "Mr Gagrat, the Muslims are not a minority. They are a nation."

'Boom! The whole world collapsed around me. And like one does for royalty, I backed to the door, found the handle with trembling hands and went home for the rest of the day, because I was so badly shaken. Mr Jinnah had this two-nation idea very clear in his head. "We won't share the same nation. We'll have our own nation." As far as he was concerned, all true Muslims would side with him and cross over to Pakistan.'

One of India's outstanding legal minds, H M Seervai, was another person who gave me an excellent insight into the kind of man that Jinnah was. He told me, 'Mr Jinnah had been called to the Governor's house, here in Bombay. I think Sir Roger Lumley was the Governor at the time. Mr Jinnah's wife, Rati, a flamboyant Parsi lady, was wearing an off-the-shoulder gown, and was sitting next to the Governor, talking nineteen to the dozen. The Governor's wife was seated on the other side. She looked pointedly at Rati's off-shoulder gown and remarked, "Isn't it a bit chilly this evening? Shouldn't we all dress for the occasion? It is winter after all."

'In an instant, Mr Jinnah was up from the table and said to the Governor, "Your Excellency, I request your leave to take my wife and depart." The Governor was surprised, "Mr Jinnah, what's the matter?" "I would prefer not to discuss it, sir. My wife and myself request permission to leave your banquet."

Now this could have been taken as a great insult. Even though the British Raj could be pretty mild at times, they were very uptight about protocol. You could actually be slapped in prison for that sort of thing. But Jinnah didn't care. His wife had been insulted by the Governor's wife. And he was no less a person than the Governor. Sir Roger reluctantly nodded his head in assent, looked rather sternly at his own wife and said, "Yes, Mr Jinnah. You have my permission to withdraw." And swoosh, he was out of there.'

Jinnah was the kind of man who wasn't cowed down by anyone. Not even the British. He was a very learned man, a barrister, in fact, who had got his degree in London. He was also something of a snob, and didn't like to mix with people who he felt were intellectually inferior, whether they were English or Indian or Martian. Very well read, very cosmopolitan. He even married outside the community, and he spoke little or no Urdu. He was from Gujarat like me. Interestingly, Ben Kingsley and I, who played Gandhi and Jinnah respectively, both come from villages not more than hundred miles apart from those of the original Gandhi and Jinnah.

Another aspect of Jinnah was his sartorial elegance. He was considered one of the ten best-dressed men in the British Empire. So when I went to London to be fitted for my wardrobe, the clothes had to be cut in the style of the famous Saville Row suits that Jinnah favoured. Made from alpaca material, a fine cotton, the kind that never creases.

However, before I went to London, I explained to Attenborough that I would do the film on the condition that I could only shoot on weekends, so as not to interrupt my regular job as head of one of India's largest advertising agencies. Surprisingly, he agreed. 'I'm glad you told me well in advance.

Now I can arrange my schedules accordingly.' It was only later that I found out how strictly Attenborough stuck to his schedules.

For my first shoot, I travelled to Delhi and stayed at the Ashoka Hotel. The night I arrived, a one-page schedule called the 'call-sheet' was slipped under my door. The call-sheet for 'Mr Jinnah' read:

5.30 a.m. : Wake-up call.

6.00 a.m. : Breakfast served in the room.

6.30 a.m. : Make-up in the cafeteria downstairs.

7.00 a.m. : Report in the lobby for the car to take you to location.

Sure enough, I got my wake-up call at 5.30 a.m. and breakfast was served at 6.00 a.m. At 6.30 a.m., I was in the make-up room, where I met Saeed Jaffrey, whom I hadn't seen for at least a year. Saeed is a jovial raconteur who can keep you spellbound for hours. Since we used to be in the theatre together, we chatted away about old times. Suddenly I looked at my watch and said, 'I'd better rush for my car.' I raced to the lobby and went to the Car Scheduler, an Englishman. (I couldn't believe that Attenborough had brought a guy all the way from England, just to schedule cars. I soon learnt why.)

I walked up to him. 'Mr Johnson, is my car ready?'

'You are Mr Jinnah, sir?'

'Yes.'

'What time was your car called for?'

'7 o'clock.'

'Sir, the car has gone.'

'What do you mean, it's gone?'

'Well sir, it's getting on to two minutes past seven and the car has gone. It's taken the other actors who were also assigned that car to the location.'

'Oh my God! What do I do?'

'Sir, what you do is be on time. Every time.'

'I'm sorry. But I'm only two minutes late.'

'Sir, two minutes is a lot of money.'

'Anyway, how do I get out of this jam?'

'Sir, I believe Mr Saeed Jaffrey is due to leave at 7.15 a.m. Maybe we can try and squeeze you in with him and the others.'

Saeed was there at 7.14, and when we got into the car, I asked him, 'Saeed, what is this crazy business? I mean two minutes past seven is hardly late.' And he replied, '*Alyque, aap nahin jaante. Woh paagal hai timing ke liye. Indian time nahin chalega. Elastic time jo hota hain India mein, bilkul nahin chalega.* You've got to be absolutely punctual.'

When we reached the location, I went up to Attenborough. 'Good morning, Richard.' He looked at me and said, 'Aleek, you are very late.'

'I'm sorry, Richard, I missed the car by two minutes.'

'Aleek, let me explain one thing since this is your first day of shooting. This film is costing us £1,000 a minute. So two minutes is £2,000 down the drain.'

Considering the fact that I was getting less than £2,000 for my role in the entire movie, I had spent it all before I had given my first take! 'I'm sorry, Richard. It won't happen again.' 'I sincerely hope not,' he replied, and we got down to shooting.

It just shows how thorough Richard Attenborough is. And that's the difference between an amateur and a professional.

A professional does his homework. An amateur waits for inspiration.

A professional does his homework. An amateur waits for inspiration.

I was simply amazed by the professionalism and thoughtfulness Attenborough exhibited on the sets. The first scene I had was Jinnah addressing the 1916 Congress convention. At that time Jinnah was President of the Congress party. Gandhi had just arrived from South Africa and was relatively nobody in the Congress. Jinnah's speech ends with him saying that the British had promised India Home Rule if the Indians helped them in the First World War. 'We were promised Home Rule. We demand Home Rule.'

It's a stirring speech and after I had delivered it, Attenborough said, 'Excellent. Cut. Cut. Cut.' I asked him, 'How was it, Richard?' and he replied, 'First class. Absolutely excellent. Let's do one more.' Then he came up and whispered in my ear, 'Aleek dear boy, do you think you could throw it away this time?' Now the theatre expression 'throw it away' means you underplay it. Don't punch it. So I said, 'I'll try.' This was the marvellous thing about Attenborough. He didn't shout out in public, 'Rubbish! What are you doing, hamming it up?' He came quietly and whispered in my ear, subtly asking me to play it down.

So I climbed up again to the dais and did what I thought was 'throwing it away'. And he said, 'Excellent. Cut. We'll do just one more.' Then he came up to me and said, 'Aleek, I told you to throw it away.' I said, 'But Richard, I am trying to throw it away.' He said, 'No, I'll explain. I too am a theatre actor and the first lesson I learnt in films is you never act the lines. You just think them and because you are a trained actor, your face and body automatically respond to the camera — which magnifies everything anyway — so it will come across without effort. Remember, it's in the eyes. Film actors act with their eyes. They are the windows of emotion. You just need to feel it. And if you are a good actor, it will transmit through your eyes. With very little of the facial contortions that we use on the stage.'

So I went before the camera once more and gave what I thought was a rather dull rendition of the speech. But this time he said, 'Perfect. Perfect. That's it. Print it.' Which meant that it was an 'OK Take' and not an 'NG' (No Good) like the others. When I see the film today, I realise he was so damn right. Instead of my eyes bugging out of my head and my hands waving about as I would do on the stage, the scene comes across with a tremendous intensity that the camera has caught in the close-up of the eyes.

Gandhi was the first time I was acting in a movie. I had been acting in the theatre for thirty years. I had directed a lot of ad films and documentaries, but I had never been on the other side of the camera before. And I learnt from Attenborough that a film director's job is not to direct the actors at all, but just to nudge them in the right direction. He placed a lot of faith in us. He'd make all the characters in the scene run through their lines, and when he was satisfied, he'd say, 'Fine.'

Then he got busy with his work. Where should the camera be placed? How should the light hit each actor's face? Is Jinnah's suit looking a little crushed? Perhaps I should take my jacket off and have it pressed. Was Gandhi's make-up okay? A little too chubby, maybe. Could the make-up people put a few more shadows in his cheeks? He took care of every detail. But the actors were left to work out their own details for themselves. At first, I found that a very unnerving experience.

On the stage, as director, I'm always worried about my actors. Here, he seemed to be only worried about the technical things. Then, as soon as he was satisfied with the technicalities, he'd say, 'Okay, let's do the master shot. Roll the camera.' Then we'd do the scene and he'd say, 'Cut. Fine, gentlemen. We'll do one more for safety.' And after the next take, 'Okay, that was perfect. Print it. Now, we'll do close-ups.'

Attenborough took no chances. After the master shot he'd shoot close-ups of each and every actor going through all their lines. This gave him plenty of options when it came to editing. (The amount of film stock this method used up would give an Indian movie producer double heart failure.)

An interesting incident occurred while we were shooting close-ups one day. It again demonstrated to me how much of a stickler for perfection Attenborough is. It was a scene outside the Lok Sabha in Delhi, where Attenborough had miraculously got permission to shoot, thanks to his co-producer Rani Dubey. I'm speaking to Gandhi, and as the scene opens, I've got an unlit cigarette in my mouth. I'm supposed to raise the lighter, light the cigarette and then take the cigarette out of my mouth, before I deliver my lines.

So, on 'Action', I raised the lighter to light my cigarette, when I suddenly heard, 'Cut. Cut.' I said, 'I'm sorry, Richard. Did I do something wrong?'

'No, no, dear boy. Not you Aleek. It's this wretched jacket!'

'Oh?'

'When you lift your hands up, the coat is riding up here, like this, and the collar is riding up your neck, which looks very strange in close-up. You're beginning to look like Father Christmas.'

'What can I do?'

'I'll tell you what we'll do. We'll bring in the costume lady.'

He called her in and said, 'Look, can you do something about this jacket?' She stitched the inside of the jacket to my shirt, so that it wouldn't ride up. 'Okay, Take 2. Action!' Again, I raised my hand to light my cigarette, when I heard a terrible tearing noise as the jacket tore away from the stitches, tearing the shirt too, in the bargain. Attenborough wearily said, 'Cut. Cut.'

'What do we do now, Richard?'

'Well, I have an idea. It's a little uncomfortable I think, but I hope you don't mind. Let's tuck in all that torn bit of shirt, so we can't see it. We don't have time to get a new shirt.'

Then he turned to the costume lady. 'Come here my dear. Will you kneel down and hang on to Mr Padamsee's coat-tails for dear life? Let's see if it works that way.'

So I said, 'Okay, Richard. Always willing to try anything.'

'Fine, action!'

I tried to lift the lighter to my lips and I found that I was almost paralysed and couldn't move my arms because the costume lady was hanging on to my coat-tails so tightly.

'Cut. Cut. Gosh, this is terrible. Just a simple thing like lighting a cigarette. By Jove, I'm wondering whether I should change the move.'

Just then the assistant director came up. 'No, no. I'm sure we can handle it, sir.' He asked the costume lady to step aside, and he went behind me and said, 'Look Mr Padamsee, when you raise your hands, I will gradually relax my hold, so that you'll be able to light your cigarette.'

Attenborough piped in, 'I hope to goodness it works. Third time lucky, and all that!'

'Richard, I think we're on the seventh take now.'

'Jolly good, seven is my lucky number. Okay, roll. Lights. Sound. Camera. And action!'

I raised my hands and lo and behold, the coat did not ride up. I lit the cigarette, and by this time my state of mind was such that I was more worried about the lines of my coat than the lines of my script! I took the cigarette out of my mouth as nonchalantly as I could and got back into the mood of Jinnah, just in time to deliver my dialogue. Everything was riding on my coat-tails.

'Marvellous! Cut.' And everyone gave a round of applause. Not for me, but for the invisible performance of the assistant director. When you see the film, you'll know why Jinnah looks so tense in this scene!

I am often caught quoting the dictum, 'God is in the details'. Pre-production meetings are the stepping stones to success. In the theatre, I insist on half a dozen technical rehearsals, a good month before opening night. But even a martinet of 'Check and Double Check' like me had something to learn from a professional like Attenborough.

'God is in the details.' Pre-production meetings are the stepping stones to success.

One day, when I received my call-sheet, I noticed an asterisk at the bottom of the page. 'Special note to cleaning staff: Today we'll be doing some helicopter shots. Please ensure that not a scrap of food is left outside the food tents. Hire extra sweepers.' We used to be served food in tents set up on location, and people had a habit of taking their food and sitting outside the tent to enjoy the Delhi winter. The reason for this special note to the cleaning staff was that if food was left outside the tents, it could attract birds which would prove hazardous to the helicopters being used in that day's shoot. Talk about attention to detail!

It was during the filming of *Gandhi* that I wrote the most successful ad of my career. Attenborough came to me one day and said, 'Aleek, we have a problem. We need to shoot Gandhi's funeral and I can't assemble extras of that magnitude. We need something like 500,000 people. So I've decided we'll shoot on Mahatma Gandhi's death anniversary and invite all of Delhi to come and see and be a part of the film. You're an advertising man. Will you write me an ad?'

The ad I worked on was released in *Hindustan Times* on 30 January 1981 and it simply said, 'On 31 January, history will be re-created. Will you be there?' (We had to move the shooting by a day to the 31st, which was a Saturday, so that working people could join in on their day off.)

When we got to the location in the morning, there were hardly about five people who had responded to the ad. Then ten people came. Then five hundred. Then five thousand. And eventually the whole of Rajpath was full. Attenborough shot for the entire day with about eight cameras and he provided all those who turned up with packed lunches. No one got paid, of course. But the movie shot of thousands and thousands of people on Rajpath is awesome.

As expected, in a film called *Gandhi,* Jinnah's role was minuscule. As were the parts of Subhash Chandra Bose, Sarojini Naidu and many other historic figures. Consequently, I only had to shoot for a total of seven weekends. After my last shoot, I went up to Attenborough and said, 'Well Richard, I'm off now. I guess I won't be seeing you for a while. I hope you don't mind, but I've had my eye on something I'd like to keep, which you won't need any more, now that Jinnah's role is over.'

'Anything you want, dear boy. Just ask for it and it's yours, Aleek. You've been frightfully cooperative.'

'Well, you know the suits I've been wearing, which I had fitted out in London. There are six of them and I was wondering whether I could have one of them as a memento. They're so elegant.'

'Dear boy, I'm dreadfully sorry. I'd love to give you one of those suits. But do you know how much they cost? Each one's about £5,000.'

'£5,000?'

'Yes, and in any case, I can't give away any of them, because they don't belong to me. They belong to Berman and Nathan. They are the costumiers for this film. The suits will go back into their stock to hire out for future productions.'

'I thought that because I'm such an odd size, tall and thin, no one else would be able to use them.'

'Oh, they have extra material in there. Don't you worry. They'll lengthen them. They'll be able to fit a short man, fat man, anyone they like.'

'I see.'

He could see the disappointment writ large on my face, so he said, 'I'll tell you what. I can't give you a £5,000 suit, but you can have Mr Jinnah's monocle that you've been wearing throughout the film and mind you, that costs a good ten quid. That's a present from me to you, Aleek. How does that strike you?' And till today, I treasure my monocle from my role as Jinnah. It's one of my heirlooms which will be passed on in my family, I hope, for generations.

Attenborough's *Gandhi* went on to become a major success. Not only at the box office, but also at that year's Academy

Awards, where it picked up as many as eight Oscars, including the major ones like Best Director, Best Actor, and Best Picture. And most importantly, the film managed to touch a responsive chord all around the world.

My friend, Gerson da Cunha, a man of tremendous dimensions, both physically and intellectually, was with UNICEF in Brazil when *Gandhi* was released there. He told me the queues outside the cinema were phenomenally long. I said, 'But Gerson, the film is in English, and the people there speak Portuguese.' And he replied, 'But the public still want to see it because they've heard it's a very moving film. Besides, it has Portuguese subtitles.'

And when I went to Brussels, the Creative Director of Lintas: Brussels, Rene Geneaux, told me with his lively eyes twinkling behind his rimless glasses, 'Alyque, you've created a sensation here. The movie you've acted in. You should see the queues!' I repeated, 'But it's in English.'

'Yes! But with French subtitles.'

Even in Nairobi, where I had accompanied my wife Sharon, who was doing a two-week stint with a club over there, I was amazed by the response to the film. When they heard I was there, the local newspaper ran a feature, '"Mr Jinnah" in Town.'

When the film was released in Bombay, I said to my teenage daughter Raell, 'Darling, are you going to see *Gandhi*? It's running at the Regal cinema. I can get passes for you.'

'Dad, do I have to see it?'

'What?'

'Well Dad, we learnt about Gandhi in college and it was very boring. I don't want to see a documentary on...'

'Number one, it's not a documentary. And number two, your father's in it. Shouldn't you see it at least because of me?'

'Well, if you put it that way.'

'Okay, here are four tickets for this afternoon's show. I'm picking up you and your friends and dropping you all off at the cinema. Then after the movie, we'll go have tea and talk about it.'

So dutifully, Raell's friends turned up saying, 'Oh, this bloody Raell and her father. Forcing us to go see this horribly boring film.' They went in grumbling. The last thing I recall saying to them before they disappeared into the dark cavern of the cinema was, 'Remember, he's the Father of the Nation.' And they jointly raised their eyebrows to heaven, as if to say, 'So what? Tell us another.'

After the movie, they came streaming towards the car. As they jumped in, I asked them, 'Well, what did you think?' And Raell said to me, 'Dad, you never told me that Mahatma Gandhi was such a wonderful man.'

'I think I've been telling you that since you were two years old!'

'No, no. I heard all that Satyagraha and Swadeshi mumbo-jumbo and they made no sense to me. They were all boring. How he lay down on the railway tracks and all that. I always suspected he was a bit, you know, weak in the head. But now Gandhiji is a hero for me. For the first time in my life, I'm proud to be Indian. This was a man who really meant something.'

And all her friends agreed, 'Yes Uncle, she's absolutely right. We went in thinking we would be bored. But after seeing the movie, we can't talk of anything else. We've discussed the scenes. And the man who played Gandhiji. We're all in love with him.' I said, 'I must tell Ben Kingsley about it.' And sure enough I wrote to Ben telling him about his young female fan club in Bombay!

That's the impact vivid communication makes. After that film was released, the whole world treated India with new respect. The entire tourism industry received a great fillip. People who had seen the film wanted to go to all the places they had seen on screen. So they visited spots like Rajpath in Delhi and the Sabarmati Ashram in Gujarat where an entire 'Dandi' tour was organised for them.

It will seem like heresy if I say that Mahatma Gandhi was the greatest communications guru who ever lived, but it's true.

Even if the media is not on your side, you can use word of mouth to swing public opinion in your favour.

It is from Gandhiji that I learnt that even if the media is not on your side, you can use word of mouth to swing public opinion in your favour. In his day, the British controlled all the newspapers, radio and newsreels. There was no television, and certainly no internet. And they wouldn't publish anything about Gandhi unless it was negative.

So he had to rely on staging events. Maybe he did it subconsciously. But as far as I'm concerned, he was one of the greatest Event Marketing people the world has ever seen. I think even Martin Luther King Jr learnt a lot from him and his march on Washington owes a lot to Gandhiji's Dandi salt march. It was this event that really galvanised India into realising that the British were cruel taskmasters for imposing the draconian salt tax.

Gandhiji decided to defy it, but he didn't do it instantly. He let it all build up, and in that, he was the master of Hitchcockian suspense. He sent out word that on a certain day, he would be picking up a handful of salt on the deserted beach at Dandi. And he let this message percolate.

His second brilliant innovation was interactivity. He could easily have taken a train to Dandi, walked a few furlongs and got to the beach. Instead, he announced that he would start from Sabarmati Ashram. This meant that it would take him several days to reach Dandi. And as he walked from village to village, the word spread that Gandhiji was approaching. *'Mahatma aa rahe hain. Mahatma aa rahe hain.'* And as Gandhiji walked through each village, most of the villagers would join in the march. This transformed an act of defiance by an individual to a people's participatory movement.

Then the press got wind of it, and reporters and photographers came from all over India and abroad to see who this frail man was, ready to defy the might of the British Empire. Pretty soon, the entire country was talking about Gandhiji and his *padayatra*. The suspense was building up. Would he reach Dandi? Or would the British prevent him from getting to the beach?

And when I studied this, my personal interpretation was, 'My God! Imagine any of us creating an Event and marketing it as successfully as Gandhiji did with the Dandi march. You have people literally hungry for your event before you even reach them.' Gandhiji also had this incredible knack of speaking in homilies or one-liners. Like 'An eye for an eye only succeeds in making the whole world blind,' is a marvellous summation of non-violence. In my opinion, one of the greatest slogans ever coined in our country is 'Quit India.' In just two words, it gave all Indians a nationalistic rallying point. A good slogan emotionalizes the message. It acts as a guiding star.

And don't forget the lessons we can learn from Gandhiji in the field of imaging. He taught us that if a leader wants to empathise with the people, he must live like them, dress like them, be like them. Unlike Jinnah who never gave up his western dress and his fine Saville Row suits. The first time Jinnah was seen in public in full Muslim regalia was on 14 August 1947, Pakistan's Independence Day.

If a leader wants to empathise with the people, he must live like them, dress like them, be like them.

When Gandhiji returned to India from South Africa, he decided to switch to Indian clothes on the boat itself. So, as he came off the boat, he sported a Gujarati pagdi. And because he wasn't used to wearing one, he looked quite sheepish in fact. But after that, he even adopted the traditional dhoti as to the manor born.

He was a master at handling sentiment. When he did his Bharat Darshan, he travelled the length and breadth of India by train. Because he realised that it was poverty and a very basic lifestyle that would make the masses empathise with him.

And take his very title, 'Mahatma.' In advertising, the importance of naming a brand correctly can never be stressed enough. When he first heard the title, *Maha Atma*, meaning Great Soul, he said, 'This is wrong. Nobody should be putting me on a pedestal.' But eventually he learnt to live with it, and it helped his charisma tremendously. When anyone talks about the Mahatma, we know who they are talking about. Only one person.

Not since Jesus Christ has a man preached the kind of things that Gandhiji stood for. Albert Einstein paid tribute to the 'great soul' by remarking that it was amazing that a man such as this ever walked the earth. Personally, I also salute Gandhiji as a great Mahatma. More importantly, I salute him as a great motivator who understood that real communication is emotional communication. He knew that you can change more people's attitudes through warm human sentiment than with cold rationality. The Mahatma relied on emotion. The British applied reason and they lost their jewel in the crown.

When you impact the emotional retina,
you create an indelible impression on the memory.

TOTAL IMMERSION
AND THE ART OF ZEN

G etting totally immersed in what you do is an out-of body experience that is like nothing else on earth. It is very Zen. I have always been influenced by the book *Zen and the Art of Archery*. The pupil, after missing the target several times, asks the master, 'What is the secret?' And the master replies, 'As you stretch the bow, you must become the arrow. This way you will hit the bullseye every time.' Nike says 'Just do it'. Zen believes 'Just be it'. In late 1974, I started on a Zen journey called *Jesus Christ Superstar,* which was to occupy my waking and sleeping hours for almost two years.

I was introduced to *Jesus Christ Superstar* by my brother-in-law, Deryck Jeffereis. He arranged for the recording to be played in the Gothic confines of the splendid Afghan Church in Colaba (South Bombay). I must say it was an awe-inspiring evening. Just hearing the music. At the time, I was reasonably attracted to rock music, but not really into it. Listening to the recording of *Superstar,* it suddenly dawned on me that rock music had enormous possibilities as a kind of release of emotional imagination. Rock as a kind of sexual experience. And even as an apostolic experience. None of these insights had ever occurred to me before.

Rock music had enormous possibilities as a kind of release of emotional imagination. Rock as a kind of sexual experience. And even as an apostolic experience.

I also saw the impact on the audience. Who ranged from grey-haired veterans to bouncy teenagers. The veterans took it all in their stride, but were a little shocked by the fact that the story of Christ was being retold in a rather irreverent manner. Christians, and even those of us who have been brought up in Christian schools, have a certain reverence for Jesus. Not the kind of reverence which requires that we should kneel. Rather, we should respect him as an extraordinary man. A saint. And to believers, he is more than a saint. He is God. And you don't look at God with a jaundiced eye, do you?

I feel the beauty of Tim Rice's work is that he looks at Christ in a stark contemporary way and yet retains the greatness of Jesus. The lyrics are just brilliant. More than the music, it was the lyrics that hit me. 'Jesus, tell me you're no fool. Walk across my swimming pool.' The lines hold both a challenge as well as mockery. A hint of 'I hope it comes true and that you can walk on water.'

But the jazzy way in which it was put, with reference to a swimming pool, really grabbed me. In *Superstar,* there is this constant vibration between the present day and the historical, religious myth. And the multiplicity of levels on which JCS operates fascinated me.

Quite a few of the plays I've done are about mythological figures. Whether it's Gurcharan Das's *Mira,* about Mirabai, or Girish Karnad's *Tughlaq* or even *Evita* (which is not the real life of Evita, but Tim Rice's imagined life of Evita). Don Quixote in *Man of La Mancha, Hamlet, Othello* (which I have done more than once), *Julius Caesar* (which I have done at least three times). I like to give an off-spin to these characters. Scratch below the surface, and see what you find. Try and discover an insight that was relevant then and is relevant even today.

Like in *Hamlet,* when I tried to re-experience Hamlet seeing the Ghost. The only experience I have known of ghosts was in the 1950s, when we indulged in table rapping, trying to summon up spirits through a glass that moved around an ouija board. As I imagined it, Hamlet's father's ghost does not 'appear.' Instead, it enters Hamlet, who becomes the medium through which his father speaks. So in my production, the Ghost was never seen, but only heard as a voice emanating from Hamlet's mouth. And as in a séance, Hamlet falls into a trance while the Ghost possesses his body. This became a contemporary experience for the audience of today which is unable to relate to ghosts in the old-fashioned sense.

Looking back, I realise that in 1974, which is when I decided to do *Jesus Christ Superstar,* I was in a very creative phase of my life. I had just staged Harold Pinter's *The Birthday Party* in my mother's drawing room and before that I had done Gurcharan Das's *Mira,* which was a great artistic success. Besides the play itself, people who saw it were struck by the way it was produced.

Little did I know that from the day I heard the recording of *Jesus Christ Superstar* in Afghan Church, the songs and the tunes would enter my bloodstream. I began to eat, breathe, sleep, dream *Superstar.* I was taken back to my school days when I used to win the scripture prize for religious knowledge. I have always been obsessed with Christ. And though I am not a Christian, I am half a Christian, in the sense that I know more about Jesus than about any other religious head.

Questions were racing around my brain. Who was Jesus? Why did Jesus appear in that particular era? I always write a director's note before doing a play. Why am I doing this play? Do I want to spend at least six months in rehearsal on this particular project? And then, depending on its success, 'x' number of months or years, performing the play again and again. I write this note in order to justify to myself why I'm getting involved in this nightmare of work, work, work. With no pay, pay, pay.

So *JCS* began to take over my life. Not just the music and the lyrics, but the characters. I began to see similarities between British Raj India and Roman Raj Jerusalem.

I always write a director's note before doing a play in order to justify to myself why I'm getting involved in this nightmare of work, work, work. With no pay, pay, pay.

A foreign military ruler dominating the local population who were looking for a messiah to lead them to deliverance. Initially there's nobody on the scene, and then suddenly this Gandhi-like figure emerges, who proclaims, 'I will save you.'

Everyone clusters around him thinking he is going to preach some kind of rebellion. Instead he says, 'Love thy neighbour as thyself.' And 'If thy neighbour slaps thee on one cheek, turn to him the other also.' I suppose the first reaction to this must have been, 'This guy is crazy.' And I thought to myself, 'This is exactly what they said about Gandhi.' Instead of Gandhi telling the people to chuck the British out and blow up railway trains and the sort of things that Subhas Chandra Bose was advocating, he told them exactly the opposite. The only way to redemption was through non-violence, not violence.

I thought, 'My God! Here is a parallel. Let us see whether it carries through to the end. How did Christ die? He died on the Cross. And what did he die for? He died for other people's sins. How did Gandhiji die? He died by an assassin's bullet. What did he die for? Other people's sins. And they are both inspiring examples to us.' I was convinced that there were indeed many parallels between the frail old man in his late seventies, and this young man of thirty-odd years.

This began to work on me and I began to work on my production. As we started off, I realised that in Bombay, nobody had really done a musical on this scale before. Is bigger better? Not necessarily. But for the audience, it's always more fun. The sheer magnitude of size often makes an indelible impact. *Gone with the Wind* has more memorability than *Brief Encounter*, which is one of the most touching love stories I have seen. A half-page magazine ad can't hope to compete with a double-page colour spread, or better still, a 60' x 30' hoarding. Godzilla is right. Size does matter. And that's why I decided to do *Superstar* on a massive scale. (Instead I could have done an intimate production at the Prithvi Theatre.)

Coincidentally, my former wife, Pearl, was at that very time preparing another musical, *Godspell*, which also was on the life of Jesus. For a moment I thought that maybe I should abandon my project, because it would be absurd to have two musical plays on Jesus Christ running simultaneously.

But by then, I was so obsessed by *JCS,* that it wouldn't let go of me and I couldn't let go of it. As it turned out, Pearl (God bless her) was quicker off the mark than me, and to her fell the distinction of producing Bombay's first full blown musical. I am a very slow producer/director. I can't rush into a play. I have to live it out. I have to feel the characters. I have to experiment with all sorts of things. All this takes time and more time. So we were trundling along, and actually at that point, I didn't even have a cast.

I was facing a dilemma which confronts anyone who dares to do a musical in the amateur theatre. There are next to no professional singer-cum-actors. There are singers and there are actors. But rarely do you find people with both talents. I needed help. First, I picked Noel Godin to be my song director. With thinning hair and tremendous eyes, Noel has a resonant voice that tremors through listeners when he speaks. When he sings, you are wafted away into wonderland. Noel said to me, 'Alyque, of the two, I think it's more difficult to teach an actor to sing than a singer to act.' I agreed, and we decided to cast singers.

We started searching around in the discothèques. There were quite a few in Bombay at that time. Not the yuppie disco-pubs there are today with theme décor and wisecracking DJs. The discos of the 1970s catered to the flower children. You entered into a sweet smelling haze of hash smoke to the sounds of a live band belting out songs of rebellion by groups like The Doors. The wonderful thing about rebellion is that it breeds innovation and shakes off the

The wonderful thing about rebellion is that it breeds innovation and shakes off the dead hand of tradition.

dead hand of tradition. Each disco was a mini-Woodstock festival in itself which ended only when there was no one left standing up. A quarter of a century later, our 'Moral Police' want to turn back the hands of the clock to eleven p.m.

Mercifully, back then the Moral Police were non-existent. It was the heyday of the late Indira Gandhi as the Empress of India, basking in her victory for Bangladesh, and everyone was riding high. (Little did we know that the following year she would clamp down the Emergency.)

Searching for our Jesus, we landed up in the very seedy disco, Slip Disc, which was notorious as a pick-up joint for sailors. In there, we found a tall, dark, gangly youth called

Madhukar Chandra Dhas. We approached him and he seemed interested.

'Any acting experience?'

'No.'

'Singing?'

'Yeah, mainly in discos, but I've sung in the church choir as well.'

Chandra Dhas was from Madras, in Tamil Nadu, and his family were quite religious. So we said, 'Okay, Madhukar. It looks like you could possibly be our Jesus.' We had him sing a few songs and he sang like an angel. Unfortunately, his diction was much like anyone else's from South India. A heavily accented English with very strong consonant sounds coming through. I said to Noel, 'Well, it will be a lot of hard work, but I think it will be worth it, because he really sings magnificently.'

So we had a tall dark Jesus Christ, and because of his colour, a lot of people were surprised. They said, 'Why did you cast him? Christ was fair.' And I replied, 'Rubbish. You've been fed on all those European versions of Christ with blue eyes and golden hair. He was actually a Semite, from the Middle East.'

Then, for Judas, we picked the scrawny, long-haired Nandu Bhende, who came from the illustrious thespian family of Atmaram Bhende, a leading light of the Marathi theatre. Nandu has since gone on to become the most famous Indian rock singer of his generation. Both Madhukar and Nandu were young boys, just out of college, who had formed their own rock groups then. Madhukar's was called Atomic Forest, and Nandu's was Savage Encounter.

We had found Jesus and Judas. Now came the search for the third main character, Mary Magdalene. Without the right Mary, there was no show. The great master song of *JCS, I don't know how to love him,* is sung by her. So Noel and I, joined by Rex Lobo, who was also Pearl's music director for *Godspell,* began the hunt. The bespectacled Rex with his hawk-like features and his courteous demeanour reminded me of an Ivy League professor.

The three of us were also on the lookout for the twelve apostles, as well as the other singing roles. There were two characters whom I didn't have to look for. One was Herod. I was very clear in my mind that I wanted Keith Stevenson, who is both singer and actor. He had worked with me in *Hamlet* and other productions. Keith is a broad bulky man and his forte is comedy. He was just perfect for the comic role of King Herod.

The second was Pontius Pilate. A role in which I saw a man with tremendous character and personality. And who better than my good friend, Gerson da Cunha? Gerson is not really a singer, but being Goan he has a good ear for music, and he plays the piano. So I said, 'I don't care whether he is a singer or not. He knows what melody is and he knows what rhythm is.' I wasn't aware that he didn't know what timing is.

We only found out about that later, and it was quite amusing. When you're singing, you've got to be able to come in on the beat and sometimes, on the off-beat. This is something that needs to be developed. My wife, Sharon, tells me that there's no easy way to learn the bar count. And so while Gerson was concentrating on his lines and words (which were always difficult for Gerson to remember), and on the melody (which he was reasonably good at), the bar count used to sometimes fox him.

So we had two singers and two actors. I realised that for Caiaphus, we needed a bass profundo. And I couldn't think of anyone in the rock field who had that kind of voice. Then I had a stroke of revelation. I thought, 'Why not have an opera singer?' I had heard of only one who would fit the bill. I knew him casually as a member of the Opera Society of Bombay. So I approached Conal Almeida, a man of medium height, with grey eyes and of course, the deepest voice I had ever heard. Conal said to me, 'Are you mad, Alyque? Do you think I would ever sing rock? I hate it. My son plays it every day at home and I tell him to keep his wretched door shut. I can't stand this kind of music. I am an opera singer.'

'Conal, trust me. You are the right man to portray Caiaphus, the high priest.'

I played him the track.

'Yes. It is certainly my kind of bass voice. But I have never sung rock.'

'Give it a try. Come with us. Trust me, and let's see how it goes. After a month, if you want to back out, no problem.'

And so Conal came to rehearsals.

At first he was appalled at what he saw. We had a very young cast. Except for Gerson, Keith and Conal himself, the others were in their twenties, many even under eighteen. Here was this very way-out cast at rehearsals, lying around and taking deep drags from hand-rolled joints. And unlike the US President Bill Clinton in his college days, they did inhale. My mother's drawing room, which is a sacred place for the Theatre Group, because it was born there and flourished there, was full of reefer smoke. I tried to stop them at first, but there was no way of knowing what was going on behind your back.

Throw one *chillum* out, and another joint would appear from somewhere else. But mind you, when the music started, they became very disciplined. After the music was over, they'd go back to their lackadaisical ways.

Conal was shocked. He said, 'What's this? I've come into a den of inequity. This is a cesspool of vice.' And used other biblical terms like 'This is Sodom and Gomorrah.'

After every rehearsal we would have a spontaneous party. Someone would bring a guitar. Someone would start drumming and suddenly we'd break into a Beatles song. Every night was party night. These kids would never go home. At four o'clock in the morning, they would still be there, hashing out, singing. After about two weeks of this indoctrination, Conal, a very orthodox man, started to relax. He began to actually enjoy singing with the young people, and their company. Until eventually, the passive smoking got into his lungs and it was as if he had been waiting for a 'fix' all his life.

Without ever lifting a joint to his lips, he was revelling in it. And the best thing I heard about this experience was that he finally opened his son's bedroom door and opened his heart to rock music.

Without my willing it, I began to be sucked into a world I had read about only in way-out magazines. Yes, I was a bit of a hedonist. Not so much in my lifestyle, as in my approach to life. I had been to Greenwich Village in New York and even to Haight-Ashbury in San Francisco, which was a hippie hangout, and I was very enamoured by the flower power culture and a great believer in 'Make love not war'.

And this to me is what Jesus is all about. Be loving-like rather than warlike. Pretty soon, we all discovered this. Noel Godin, who's younger than me, but who was much older than the cast. Rex Lobo, who was quite young, but had an old man's approach because he's a very serious musician. The three of us, who ran *JCS,* got sucked into this happy-go-lucky youth culture. The same happened to Keith Stevenson, and to a certain extent to Gerson and Conal as well. Mixing continuously with the young people of *JCS* was

Mixing continuously with young people is like bathing in the Fountain of Youth. Attitudes morph from fuddy-duddy to cool and hip.

like bathing in the Fountain of Youth. Our attitudes morphed from fuddy-duddy to cool and hip.

Any amount of flings went on. And I'm happy to say, a couple of marriages. And, I'm not happy to say, a couple of unwanted pregnancies. Which I didn't find out about till much later. Noel Godin was like a father figure to everyone. He was the priest in the cast, to whom you could go and confess. Everyone was swinging except me. I was biting my fingernails because we still hadn't found our Mary Magdalene.

A strikingly beautiful young girl, Devika Rajbans (now Bhojwani) was very keen to play the role, but we felt that although she was a fine singer, her quality of voice would not suit Mary Magdalene. What we were looking for was an absolutely angelic pure soprano voice. With no tricks and without any of the bad vocal habits of commercial singers who switch octaves mid-word and drag notes unnecessarily.

So we continued with auditions. We put up posters on all the church notice boards in Bandra, Mahim, Santa Cruz and wherever else there was a Catholic community, because we knew there were a lot of excellent choirs there.

We must have had auditions non-stop for at least two or three months. We would gather at Noel's house in Bandra and people would be called in. In those days, the most popular audition song was *I'm leaving on a jet plane*. Every second person — man, woman or dog — sang that song. Then Noel, Rex and myself would confer after each candidate had finished their piece. Some of them we chose to play other female roles, but try as we might, we just couldn't find a Mary Magdalene.

Devika would come to me and say, 'Look Alyque, you're wasting your time. Why don't you just take me?' And I would reply, 'Yes, Devika, I am going to create a role for you in the play, as promised, but it cannot be as Magdalene. Your voice is not right for her.'

So we went on auditioning, till we finally ran out of people. After the umpteenth audition, Noel, Rex and myself, as well as Madhukar and Nandu were sitting around feeling quite morose. Out of the blue, Nandu piped up.

'Well, if you haven't got anyone, do you want to try out my sister?'

'Your sister sings?'

'Well, she has done a little singing and she's been on the Marathi stage.'

'You mean Marathi singing?'

'No, no. She sings English pop also.'

'Has she done any professional singing?'

'No. No professional singing.'

I looked at Noel and he looked at me and we both looked at Rex and we all said, 'Okay, let's give it a try.' We were down to zero anyway. So Nandu brought his sister, who was a vulnerable looking Maharashtrian girl with extremely expressive eyes. Rex got on to the piano and started to play as he always did, and she began to sing, *I don't know how to love him.*

My God! You could have knocked me over with a feather. She sang like an angel. Pure soprano, beautiful voice, clear as a bell. Hit each note absolutely dead-on, no wavering, no wobbling, no sliding, no glissandos. Nothing but clean pitch. It was just mind-blowing. She had beautiful breath control. She was able to hit each note perfectly, and if it was a long stretch, her voice would be strong and unwavering, right till the very end.

When she finished, I looked at Noel and he looked at me and we both looked at Rex and we all said, 'Eureka! We've found her.' And we just clapped and clapped and clapped. Which quite embarrassed her, as she was a shy girl. Her name was Poornima Bhende. Affectionately known as Nima. I turned to her brother, Nandu.

'For three months we wasted our time and here was your sister, right under our noses. Why didn't you tell us about her before?'

'I didn't think she was the kind of person you were looking for.'

'You're crazy, man! Anyway, enough. That's it. She's in.'

And believe me when I say, throughout the rehearsals — and we rehearsed for six months — whenever Nima was called to sing, she sang almost exactly the same as she had on the day of the audition. I only had to work a little on her diction. In fact almost all the singers we had were so good musically, that all we had to do was to help them with their pronunciation and their acting.

Ghosts, 1953 (AP and Ebrahim Alkazi)

The Taming of the Shrew, 1954
(Pearl Padamsee and Gerson da Cunha)

Shishon Ke Khilone, 1957
(Shaukatji, Shabana Azmi's mother, on right)

The Zoo Story, 1962
(Cavas Amrolliwalla and Bubbles Padamsee)

Hamlet, 1964
(Zul Vellani as Hamlet)

Bed Room, 1967
(Shireen Chagla and Pervin Mandviwalla)

Oh Dad, Poor Dad..., 1968
(Pearl Padamsee)

Marat/Sade, 1969
(AP in bathtub, Bubbles on ramp and Gerson at lectern)

Marat/Sade, 1969
(AP as Jean-Paul Marat)

Mira, 1972
(Nirmala Mathan as Mira)

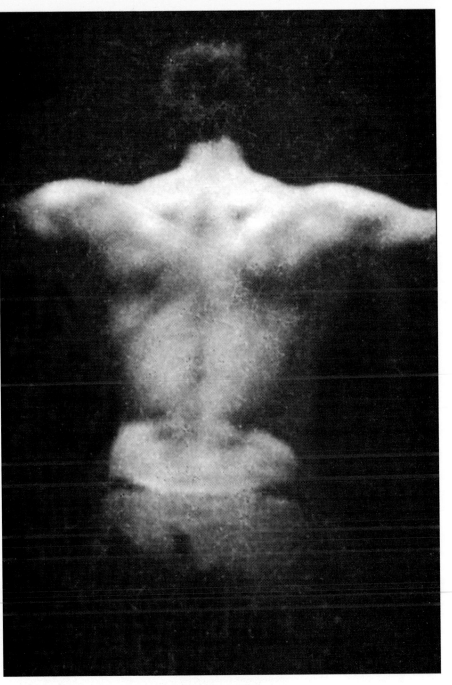

Tughlaq, 1970
(Kabir Bedi in prologue)

Jesus Christ Superstar, 1974
(Madhu Chandra Dhas as Jesus)

Jesus Christ Superstar, 1974
(Madhu Chandra Dhas)

The Birthday Party, 1973
(Vijay Crishna, Bomi Kapadia and Homi Daruvala)

Pagal Khana, 1981
(Kavita Chowdhry as Charlotte Corday)

Man of La Mancha, 1977
(Noel Godin and Darius Shroff)

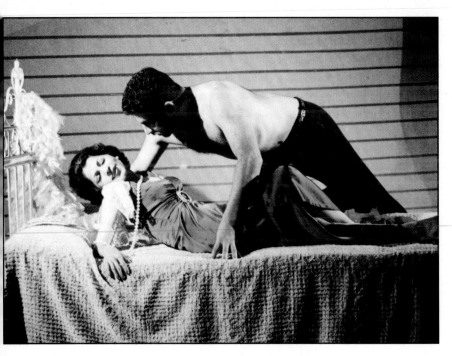

A Streetcar Named Desire, 1980
(Sabira Merchant and Dalip Tahil)

Evita, 1983
(Sharon as Eva Peron)

Death of a Salesman, 1981
(AP as Willy Loman)

Othello, 1990
(Vijay Crishna and Kabir Bedi)

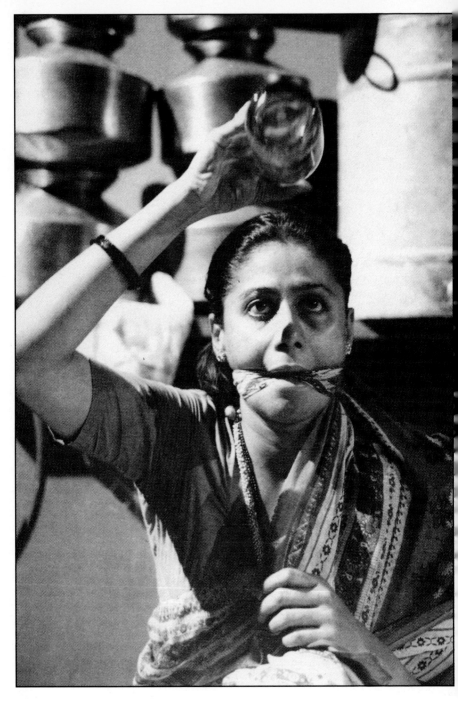

Aap Ki Farmaish, 1986
(Smita Patil)

Tarantula Tanzi, 1986
(Karla Singh and Shiamak Davar)

Final Solutions, 1992
(Vivin Mathews, Gayatri Iyer, Kartik Chandrashekhar, Francois Castellino and Anirban Roy)

Begum Sumroo, 1997
(Gerson da Cunha, Tara Deshpande and Aly Khan)

Opening Ceremony of Asian Track and Field Games, 1989
(Sharon Prabhakar singing the theme song, 50 feet up)

Even before we found our Mary Magdalene, as we started our rehearsals, we ran into another kind of problem. *JCS* had opened in New York, and Catholics there were *gheraoing* the theatre, saying that it was anti-Christ. This fed back to Bombay, and I began to get negative vibes from the Catholic community. In the end I had to go to the Archbishop of Bombay, and convince him that I was not doing a sacrilegious *Jesus Christ Superstar.* I explained that it was going to be something of a quasi-religious experience. How he bought this, I don't know. Perhaps it had something to do with the fact that I had a reputation as a straight shooter.

But convincing him wasn't enough. I then ran into opposition from quite another quarter altogether. Cossy Rosario, who at that time was the Copy Chief at Lintas, had recently become a sort of born-again Christian. He used to go for these charismatic sessions and he was dead against us doing the play. He said, 'No! I get bad vibrations. This is going to be a sacrilegious play.'

So in one of my best democratic moments (and I don't have them very often), I thought I'd try and convince Cossy. Not that I really needed his blessings, but I thought he might have a point. I didn't want to be going up the wrong street. So Cossy and I had many discussions and then I said, 'Cossy, I'd like to come to one of your charismatic meetings.' Noel Godin at that time was also very influenced by Cossy's religious fervour, and was beginning to waver. I knew without Noel, I couldn't do *Superstar.* So maybe I had an ulterior motive in convincing Cossy.

Together, we went off to one of these meetings where they all hold hands and pray and speak in different tongues. It was strange but exciting, and I am all for new experiences. It was totally unlike anything I've seen in a church. I told Cossy that just as the charismatic way of approaching Christ was different, so was *JCS*. Cossy disagreed and this contentious dialogue went on for about two months.

He kept telling me, 'Look, the play is obviously showing Christ doubting his own divinity.'

'No, Cossy. Christ is not doubting his divinity. The character as written by Tim Rice is asking each man to find the Christ in himself. Do you believe there is Christ in every man, Cossy?'

'Yes.'

'Then let each man question the God in himself, until he's convinced. Because in today's rational world, faith by itself is not enough. So what Tim Rice's Jesus is questioning in the Garden of Gethsemane, is why he has to go through this terrible torture of being crucified.'

Cossy was still not convinced.

'But in the end, Christ was divine. He rose from the dead after three days. Why don't you show the Resurrection?'

'Hold on a minute. That's going a bit too far. I think it's more a Resurrection of the spirit rather than the flesh. We don't really want to show Christ rising up out of the cave. One thing there will be, which is not in the original play, is the *Our Father* where Jesus asks God to forgive man for all his sins before he dies. And I can tell you, that will be a very Catholic moment.'

'Yes, that's a good addition, but where's the Resurrection?'

By this time, the rehearsals had become too big for the drawing room at Kulsum Terrace. So we shifted them to the top terrace. The problem was getting the piano up there since the staircase was too narrow. So Noel, whose family ran a music business, stepped in and said, 'Don't worry. I'll get Godin & Co to bring a hoist and pulley to transport it up.'

So the next day, in my usual style I was directing the entire operation, and as always, Cossy was harassing me.

'But you see, Christ rose from the dead in three days.'

'You'll rise from the dead in the next three minutes, if you don't get out of the way, because the piano's going to come crashing down on your head.'

So of course, he stepped aside.

'Listen, can we talk about the Resurrection some other time? Right now I'm trying to raise a piano twenty feet. Is that okay by you?'

In the end, I think Cossy was only half convinced. Noel was reasonably convinced and he came in whole-heartedly and trained the singers. The first thing I said was, we have to get everyone to be crystal clear. We can't have all this slurred diction and Americanisation that happens in rock music. You cannot deliver *Heaven on Their Minds* with people not understanding the words. So I worked on their pronunciation first. I gave them little exercises in speech, like 'Peter Piper picked a peck of pickled peppers,' and other similar drills to improve their consonants and vowel sounds, which tended to be all over the place.

Then I did something that audiences never noticed (only Noel, Rex and I knew about it). I slowed down the entire music track. If you hear our track and if you hear the original record, you'll realise that on ours, the tempo is at a slightly slower pace than the original. That's why the clarity. The words come through. I feel that in a musical it's futile to sing at a fast tempo. People miss the meaning of the words and get confused about the story line.

We also added two songs which were not in the original. The first is when Devika Rajbans as the Virgin Mary sings the prologue, *My Son, My Son, My Son*, in her beautiful contralto voice. This is a song that Noel and I wrote to set out the theme for our production. The other one is the *Our Father* sung by Jesus kneeling while the soldiers, on the high platform, are hammering the cross together.

The next thing I did with my singers was to teach them how to emote in a song. Not just sing the song with full-throated passion, but to really mean the song. And to me, acting is meaning with emotion. You must mean the words, in order to give them an emotional force. My singers initially had emotion but no meaning.

Acting is meaning with emotion. You must mean the words, in order to give them an emotional force.

The Garden of Gethsemane is a very moving piece, but unless you understand what Jesus is saying to his Father, it doesn't make much sense. And if the diction is awful, you will never understand what he is saying. And even if you do comprehend the words, but there is no meaning in them, all you will get is empty emotion. In this song, it is not just Jesus pleading with his Father to spare him the agony. There's more to it than that. There is a lot of very introspective monologue.

Similarly, even *I Don't Know How to Love Him* has to have a lot of meaning in its delivery. When Mary Magdalene sings, 'He's a man, just a man…', there is a certain meaning in that 'just.' And even in the phrasing. As Frank Sinatra taught all of us, phrasing to bring out meaning is key to the impact of the song.

So we worked on all these aspects for six months. We selected people like Joe Alvares who, though on the short side with a bushy moustache, has a fantastically powerful voice, for the role of Simon Zealottes. He was the only one who didn't need a mike. His voice is so strong. In those days, he was a young stud from the boondocks of Bandra. All power and no meaning. So we had to turn him into an actor. And each singer, in turn, gradually began to shape up.

I suddenly realised that I didn't have a choreographer. So we brought in Salome Roy Kapoor, whom I've known since she was a little girl. Salome has an open innocent face and a personality to match. She and her brother Edwin used to dance and act under the excellent tutelage of their father, Sam Aaron, who ran a ballroom dancing school. She had now grown up and had become a dance teacher herself. Not ballet so much as modern dance, or at any rate, what modern dance was in those days. She worked on choreographing the movements of the disciples.

Then we inducted Coomi Wadia, conductress of the Paranjoti Chorus. Coomi carries herself with authority and has a quiet but formidable personality. She, too, like Conal Almeida, was initially reluctant to get involved in a 'rock show', but we managed to persuade her. She went to work on the chorus, and I must say she did some wonderful things with my cast. Above all, she brought in disciplined singing.

What was unusual about our version of *JCS* was that it started off in Roman times, delineated through costumes, with the guards wearing Roman helmets and armour and lances, and the multitude wearing biblical robes. But as the play progresses, the guards gradually change to modern helmets, khaki uniforms and riot gear. And the mob switches to jeans and T-shirts.

In the scene where he is arrested in the Garden of Eden, Jesus is handcuffed, just like a modern-day arrest, and the guards no longer have lances. They have lathis. And when all the sceptics surround him and start screaming at him, I had them as reporters with notebooks and cameras. So suddenly you are in a contemporary world. You've moved from 2,000 years ago to today.

The play opens with the strumming of a lone guitar. The intro is *Ave Maria* which then merges into the Virgin Mary's song. In the background, we had an audio-visual going. Slides dissolving one into the other. My friend, Joseph St Anne, had got me this incredible book on Christ in different manifestations. Christ of Africa. Christ of Latin America. Christ of the Renaissance. A wooden Christ. A stone Christ. We got all these images on to slides and created a mind-blowing audio-visual, put together by Renan Jeffereis and his father, Deryck.

The climax is a cathartic moment. When the soldiers drag Jesus and nail him to the cross, it was very realistic. Deryck had worked out how the soldiers could actually hammer huge nails into Jesus' hands and feet, in front of the whole audience, and how the blood would drip out. I love this 'magic' of the theatre.

A lot of people actually began to cry. And at that time, quite a few of the nuns and priests who came to see the play took out their rosaries and began to pray. You could hear a murmur of prayer move through the audience.

When I think back now to all the challenges I undertook in this production, I'm sure I must have been insane. First I designed this crazy set. Well, most of it was simple enough. Just an altar-like platform on the stage with steps leading up to it from all sides, set against a cyclorama. But in addition, we had a giant cross that went over the seats, down the aisle and way into the auditorium. We had to adapt the seating plan of the Birla Matushri Sabhaghar auditorium, which is an underground theatre in the basement of the Bombay Hospital. It must be over 150 feet long, with seating capacity of about 1,200. To accommodate our cross, we had to cancel over 200 seats.

Then came the task of lighting this cross. We had to put up a special lighting bar at the far end of the auditorium, so that we could light up actors coming forward on the cross which acted as a ramp. (Later on, this lighting bar was very helpful for models on the ramp in fashion shows.)

We used the cross constantly for the movements of the cast. We used it for Jesus coming into Bethlehem on Palm Sunday. Jesus being led in chains from the Garden of Gethsemane with the reporters harassing him. For the merchants and moneylenders in the temple, who were driven out by Jesus for selling their wares to the audience around them. So the audience was in fact surrounded by the stage. The cross both divided them and linked them.

But the problem was the mikes. Until that time, nobody had ever used hand-held mikes before. Everyone was used to standing mikes. Remember this was long before the days of cordless mikes. But I did not want a static production. I wanted my characters to move freely about the stage and auditorium while they were singing. So I decided to have hand-held mikes.

Because the cast had to walk down this long ramp of the cross, the hand-held mikes needed to have long cables. About a hundred feet long! Which meant that an actor had to carry all this cable in his hand plus sing into the mike (which itself is quite difficult when you have never used a hand-held mike before), keep perfect pitch, keep the bar count, give expression and meaning, have clear diction and walk without looking down!

As each actor walked towards the stage, he had to pay out the cable with his left hand and hold the mike to his mouth with his right, without tripping over the wires. Letting out the cable was easy enough. The tough part was picking up the cable, on his way back.

It's frightening to think that we had only three mikes, which I had specially bought on a trip to London. That was it! Those three mikes had to be shared by some fifteen singers. So as each singer left the stage, he had to put the mike down on a little cushion near the footlights, so that the next singer could pick it up and sing. We colour-coded the mikes red, yellow and green, so everyone had to make sure they used the right colour at the right time. For instance, Judas could be singing with the red mike in one scene, but because it was left in another part of the stage, he would have to pick up the yellow mike on his next entry. And we had entries from every conceivable corner of the hall. So the actors had to be very colour conscious.

Everything was monstrously difficult. The music tempo in the play is relentless. There are no spoken words, so you can't buy time by asking actors to speak slowly in one scene, so that their fellow actors would have time to change costume. Everyone had to come in on cue. The live band would just strike up. And bang! You were on. You had to enter on that exact bar and be precisely on cue, visually and audially.

I was facing defeat on a hundred fronts. We had singers who we had only just turned into actors. And then we had a live band on stage, who had never played with each other before! There was the long-haired Gussie Rikh, a classical guitarist who was playing rock for the first time. Rex Lobo, who was a genius on the piano, but again, a classical musician. The maverick Steve Sequeira on drums, in full view of the audience. And we had a young acolyte, Verona Fernandes, helping on keyboards. At one stage we flirted with the idea of using a Moog synthesiser, which was all the rage in music circles at the time. But the owner of the only one in town refused to let us move it out of his studio, and instead offered to stage *JCS* in his premises, which measured all of twenty feet by fifteen feet.

Because of the nerve-racking risk factor, I didn't want to go before the public until I was sure that everything was a hundred per cent. So we had a preview, which turned out to be disastrous. The sound system was awful. Because of the length of cable, we had to boost the volume which caused it to feed back into the speakers.

At that time, the drama critic for *The Times of India* was the acerbic M V Matthew. He held this position for many many harrowing years. I say harrowing because he usually slammed all my plays. He was a purist and I belonged to the avant-garde. So I used to have *battles royale* with him through Letters to the Editor. The day after the Preview (to which he came uninvited) he wrote a piece in *The Times of India's* sister publication, *Evening News of India* (since defunct), under the headline, 'Jesus Christ Superstar: Cacophony of Noise.'

For a change, he was right. The sound was so bad that it distorted the words. Mind you, the friends of the cast who were invited to the preview loved it, because they knew all the lyrics by heart. So they didn't need to pay attention to the words.

Immediately, we had a crisis meeting. Keith Stevenson, who knew a lot about sound, Dolly Thakore, who was with me as production executive, and myself. We went to a restaurant where we were joined by the quiet Tyeb Tyabji and the irrepressible Debu Datta, who were the great sound experts at that time. This was before Roger Drego entered the scene. So we sat down and had this pow-wow, and tried to work out how we could overcome the business of feedback and what kind of speakers we could get and this, that and the other. It was a three-hour long meeting. When we came out, poor Keith Stevenson's car had been towed away because it was in a 'no-parking' zone. So although we had solved our crisis, Keith now had one of his own.

Since there weren't many good sound systems available on hire in those days, we had to depend on personal contacts and favours. One of the members of Madhukar's band, Atomic Forest, was Keith Kanga. Keith had a rich aunt who had left him a lot of money, with which he had bought tonnes of expensive sound equipment. He agreed to allow us to use it for our shows, and because he was a great fan of *Superstar*, he never charged us a rupee. But the logistics were a nightmare.

On Friday night, after the Slip Disc closed in the wee hours of the morning, we would take a tempo and load all Keith's huge JVC speakers and amplifiers into it, and haul it all to the Birla. Then it would take the entire day to set up, because we had to rig up wiring, plug in the mikes, check the sound balance and so on. We'd barely get it all ready before the curtain went up at 6.30 p.m. Then as soon as the curtain came down, we'd unrig it all and haul it back to the Slip Disc, just before the disco opened for the night. And then when it closed again on Saturday night, repeat the entire process for our show on Sunday.

After another series of previews, we managed to get the sound system right. Finally when we were good and ready, we opened to the public. And by this time, there was tremendous — not hype, because I think hype is empty — there was tremendous expectation for *Superstar*. Firstly, it has such well-known music. Secondly, there were mini-legends associated with it. We had people like India's top classical music composer, Vanraj Bhatia, sit in on rehearsals. Coomi Wadia was talking about it in opera circles. Salome Roy Kapoor was talking about it in her dance community. And the cast itself, numbering about seventy, were telling all their hundreds of friends about it.

When we finally opened at the Birla, there were hordes of people queuing up to buy tickets. I had never before seen such crowds outside the box office, except perhaps for *Tughlaq*, where fans queued up to see Kabir Bedi in the 'nude'. And the average age of the audience dropped. Until then, most of the theatre-going audiences in Bombay were in their forties. Suddenly we had a public as young as twelve and thirteen. I know people today, who say they saw *Superstar* when they were four years old. 'I didn't know we allowed four-year-olds,' I remark, and they reply, 'But my Daddy took me.'

Then there was the middle-aged Goody Seervai, the great bandleader with a chubby smiling face, who used to play at all the Parsi functions. I noticed Goody coming to see the play again and again and again. I went up to him.

'Goody, why are you coming to see the play so many times?'

'Alyque, this is the first time I am hearing rock music, and it is fantastic. I'm going to come to every show.'

'Goody, here is a golden pass. You be my guest from now on.'

And he was there. He saw every single show of *Superstar*. Never missed one. He sent his son to conduct the weddings and *navjotes*. And there were lots of other people who saw the play six times, eight times, ten times. They just couldn't get enough of it.

As the audience began to settle in their seats, the house-lights went down and the Virgin Mary was spotlit on stage.

Behind her the giant audio-visual was projected. It was as if a trance had fallen over the theatre. They had come, not to scoff, but to pray. They had come to be moved. Through the lyrics that Noel and I wrote for *My Son, My Son, My Son,* we tried to portray Jesus not just as a Christian icon, but a universal symbol who has influenced thinkers great and small. From Thoreau to Gandhi to Martin Luther King Jr.

As the beautiful slow melody of the opening song fades, behind it, the audience hears the ominous 'thunk' of a bass guitar, and suddenly Judas bursts on stage wearing very biblical robes but singing this very modern rock song. The impact was fantastic. You could feel the electricity in the audience, with heaven on their minds, as scene after scene unfolded.

In the triumph of Jesus coming into Jerusalem on Palm Sunday, Madhukar enters from the back of the hall, on the shoulders of his disciples, down the long ramp of the cross on to the stage. Madhukar's voice rings out clear and strong, 'Sing out for you are blessed.' Then, marvel of marvels, the audience responds, 'Christ, you know I love you. Did you see I waved? I believe in you and God, so tell me that I'm saved.' This scene was set to a terrific rock dance, with Jesus leading the swaying of bodies and his disciples dancing away.

What I had actually done was plant about fifty of my own 'actors' in the audience to start singing with the chorus. This prompted many others in the audience, who knew the songs by heart, to sing along too, and·it became a kind of communal experience. No prizes for guessing where this idea came to me from. The church. When the priest proclaims something, the audience responds with the right refrain.

Then we did a very daring thing. Jesus turns to the audience and says, 'You know I love you. Come join me.' And then, amazingly, one figure in jeans jumps up from his seat, on to the ramp-cross and joins the disciples dancing on the stage. And soon another one joins him, and another and another, till finally, all fifty of my own 'planted' people, dressed in everyday street clothes, join Jesus and his disciples dressed in biblical clothes. Until the entire stage is really rocking. You could feel the vibes. It was absolutely thrilling.

At one show, there was an amusing incident. As usual, I was watching the play from my own vantage point, when I observed that an actor at the corner of the stage was dancing out of step. When the others would go left, he'd go right and vice versa. He looked like he was having a great time though. Probably hashed out of his head.

So I went backstage to Keith Stevenson.

'Keith, watch this guy. Is he one of our cast?'

By this time, our cast had grown so big, I couldn't recognise everyone.

'No, he's not one of ours.'

'What do you mean?'

'He just came on stage from the audience.'

'But he's buggering up the show. This is a "rehearsed" spontaneous event. Not a spontaneous spontaneous event.'

Meanwhile, our new 'disciple' was enjoying himself in his corner of the stage. So I tried to catch his attention by waving to him from the wings. When his head turned, he saw me waving and waved back! Then I tried making gestures with my hand to signal him. He still thought I was waving to him, and continued to wave back. Finally, I crooked my finger and beckoned him towards me. So he came, probably thinking that I was going to congratulate him.

As he came off stage, Keith and I picked him up under the arms, lifted him off the floor, frog marched him out of the auditorium, right down the courtyard and on to the road, and flung him away. 'Don't dare come back to my show again.' I was furious. He turned to me, 'But sir, you see, my friend Josie asked me to come and see the play. But I told him that I don't have any money. So Josie said not to worry. There are many seats kept free for the chorus.' So he had quietly sat with Josie and the rest. And when Josie had gone on stage, he just followed Josie… and almost ruined the show. After that we relaxed the rule and allowed audience members to dance with the cast if they were so inclined.

The *Superstar* experience went on for almost two years, if you count rehearsals as well as shows. Why did we stop? We used to have long queues outside the box office. I had never seen anything like it. We ran from the beginning of February till the end of November. Two shows a week. Every Saturday and Sunday at the Birla was booked for *Superstar.*

By mid-year, our production of *Jesus Christ Superstar* was being talked about all over India, and even abroad. It was being compared to the Broadway and West End productions. People were saying, '*Superstar* in India is in some ways more exciting and more memorable than the ones abroad. And the singing is of very high calibre.' Every city in India wanted us to stage performances for them.

In November, we fixed a date to take the production to Calcutta. I worked out the logistics and the elaborate schedules and everything. Then I started getting dropouts. First it was the band.

'We've got jobs here in Bombay. In nightclubs, and film studios. You'll have to get another band.'

'Oh God! I can't do that.'

'We're truly sorry but how can we cope? They hire us on contracts for three to six months. And pay us good money. We'll lose all that if we have to go to Calcutta.'

Only three people were absolute rocks. Madhukar, Nandu and Nima. Even though Madhukar too was in a nightclub band, he was willing to give it up for *Superstar*. He said, 'I don't care. I will come. This is more important to me.' So I tried to get another band. Without success. Then Keith, too, said that he couldn't make it. And by this time I was worn to shreds anyway. Because I was replacing singers and dancers almost every fortnight (either someone was getting married or someone had a job transfer). This is the curse of the amateur theatre which has no contracts with its actors.

So in spite of packed houses, I had to close the show. 'Guys, we need a rest. Let's take a break for six months and then re-open again.' But in the amateur theatre, it never works out like that. To get all the energy back again and then reconstruct the cross in the auditorium and get all the sound equipment from Slip Disc was too terrifying a thought. To top it all, the money you earn is niggardly after deducting costs. So eventually you say, 'Why continue?'

But *Jesus Christ Superstar* was the experience of not just a lifetime, but ten lifetimes. It was crazy. It was inventive. In many ways, *JCS* has been my most innovative production. We said, 'Let's go for broke. If we fail... let's not think about it. We must not fail.' If Zen is the art of becoming what you do, *JCS* was even more Zen than the art of motorcycle maintenance. Ours was the excitement of singing, dancing, living, and if it had been a flop, dying... in a total immersion experience called *Jesus Christ Superstar*.

Why settle for brilliant when you can try for superb?

PERSPIRATION WITHOUT INSPIRATION
IS A WET BLANKET

*T*here have been a few people who have put me in a sweat, in order to extract the best from me. But more than just make me perspire, they have proved to be great sources of inspiration. One of them was the late Ravi Mammen. He was the young son of the South Indian patriarch Mr Mammen Mapillai, who had decided that Lintas was the agency for him, although it was situated in Bombay and he was based in Madras. He ran MRF (Madras Rubber Factory), which at that time was allied to the American tyre company, Mansfield Tyre USA.

Now Ravi was what you might call a bit of a playboy. Lean and wiry, he was crazy about fast cars. Of course, he used to race on MRF tyres, and we did a lot of publicity about that. But when he took over I thought, 'Oh God, here we have a spoilt playboy who doesn't really know what advertising is all about.'

But as time went on, I began to see that Ravi had an incredible gut feel for what excited the public, and I think that is very important. Not just *Not just what convinces* what convinces the public, but *but what excites.* what excites them. Too much advertising all over the world believes we have to convince the consumer that ours is the best product, and that's all.

Ravi had a knack of dreaming up crazy ideas. I remember the day he told me this absolutely way-out gimmick. 'You know Reliance is sponsoring the cricket World Cup and wants to sell advertising space on the field. I'd like to advertise on the drinks trolley which goes out during the break.' I said, 'Yes, but I don't know how much mileage you'll get out of it, because a drinks trolley is very small and the TV cameras may not pick up your logo.' He replied, 'No, no, Alyque. I have decided that instead of a drinks trolley, I am going to design an MRF car with giant soft tyres which won't spoil the outfield. When it's driven out and the players gather around it, the MRF sign will be big enough to be seen by the TV audience. Furthermore, the novelty of having a car instead of a drinks trolley will create a *hungama*.' I looked at him incredulously. 'Ravi, where are you getting this car from?' And he replied, 'I am building it.'

'You are building a car just to use it for one day?' 'Why not!' he replied. 'Besides I can use the car as a drinks trolley for other sporting events for the next ten years.' 'How much are you paying for all this?' I asked. He mentioned an astronomical sum which I realised was half our annual advertising budget gone in one blow.

'Have you got Reliance to agree?'

'Yes. I have told them that I will handle the drinks trolley. I just have not told them what the drinks trolley is.'

'Well, best of luck then!'

And by God, Ravi did it. He made the car.

It was built on the chassis of a Standard Herald. It was done up to look like a Formula One car, but with even bigger tyres, and had MRF displayed prominently. It created a sensation. Next day there were headlines everywhere. In fact Reliance got very upset because everyone was talking about MRF and not Reliance. I remember they got into a hassle with MRF and refused to allow Ravi to bring out the car for the next match. MRF threatened to sue them for breach of contract.

So Ravi got his way. The amount of publicity that gimmick created was just mind-boggling.

Today you have to be noticed. You may be noticed in a negative way, and I dare say Benetton is noticed negatively, but it is talked about. If you are noticed, you are remembered. (For instance, all Padmini Kolhapure's performances on the screen have been forgotten, but the one she performed in real life, kissing Prince Charles when he visited her shooting, is burned into our emotional retina.)

If you are noticed, you are remembered.

The best brief I have ever come across in advertising was given by Ravi. Two BBC documentary film makers came to shoot the Sholavaram rally, and after they finished, Ravi took them aside and said, 'Listen, what about shooting an ad film for me while you are here. I will pay you handsomely and throw in a free trip to Goa.' They agreed and asked for the brief. So he scratched his head and said, 'I want you to make a film on the Romance of Tyres.'

'What is that?'

'I have absolutely no idea! You are the creative guys. You dream up something.'

They went away and came back about a week later, having lived the life of Riley in five-star hotels, drunk gallons of scotch and Goan feni. They returned with an absolutely brilliant film which had only music and no commentary. There was not a word about the Romance of Tyres in the film. They did not even mention MRF. They just had the Muscleman appearing at the end of the film with a caption: 'MRF. Tyres with muscle.'

I can remember this ninety-second film vividly even twenty years later. Breathtaking shots, brilliant cinematography of cars racing down the beach, tyres being rolled across the Sholavaram race track, a few mechanics in MRF uniforms, and the red banner which you see at rallies fluttering in the wind. Once this commercial was aired, everybody wanted to see it again and again. There were requests to Doordarshan to show it. Like your favourite piece of music which you can hear over and over because it gives you pleasure each time, this MRF film never wears out its welcome. Often the less you say, the more the impact.

Often the less you say, the more the impact.

However, Ravi could be very aggravating. Sometimes he never made up his mind as to what his brief was. So you dreaded and loved working with that man. He was young enough to be my son, and yet he drove us extremely hard to do great work.

The next memorable occasion with Ravi was when he saw the film we made for MRF Zigma Radial tyres to his brief: It should be space age. It turned out to be one of the most outstanding commercials that had been made in India at the time. Wherever in the world I have shown it, they ask, 'How the hell did you make that in India?' This is the one with the flying saucer. It opens with these Maruti cars beeping and blinking their lights as if appealing for a saviour. Then this giant flying saucer comes down from the sky and zaps them all. The Marutis are now without tyres, and suddenly with a flash of blinding light, the Zigma tyres are lasered on to the Marutis. The film was a minute and a half long. The brilliant Vanraj Bhatia provided the music once again, and the idea was originated by Cedric Serpes, Creative Director of Lintas: Madras.

We showed it to the client in Delhi because MRF were having their board meeting there. Therefore all the bigwigs of MRF were present. For the first time in my life I saw the entire client group absolutely astounded. Even Kama Sutra and Liril didn't get such a unanimous response. Here, the whole board stood up in the auditorium and began to applaud. They were just knocked over.

I turned to Ravi and said, 'Well, any revisions?' He replied, 'Alyque, not even half a revision. It's perfect as it is. What's more, it is so damn good I am going to double the media budget.' Now that's what I call a great client. Because no matter how much good work you put in, if the client wants itty-bitty trivial revisions, you won't get much sparkle in your advertising.

But Ravi could sometimes be quite rude and blunt too. Once, I remember, Lintas had made an ad film. Not a very good film, a documentary. It was supposed to be about ten minutes long, on the Sholavaram rally. The producer let us down badly and the footage was not up to the mark. Ravi took one look at it and turned to me, 'Is that really your standard?' I was in an embarrassing position. It wasn't my standard, but I was representing the agency, and so I said diplomatically, 'Well, Ravi, what's wrong with it?' And he shot back, 'What's right with it?'

So we went back and revised the whole damn thing. We re-did the music, we re-edited, took out the bad shots and replaced them with whatever stock shots we could lay our hands on. We went back to him with something juiced up and he accepted it, but with a very sour expression. God bless him. He was young enough to show his likes and dislikes very openly. Something you learnt to appreciate. There are too many diplomats in our business, and Ravi was certainly not one of them. He didn't just call a spade a spade – he called it a shovel.

Another great client I can remember is the late Bobby Kooka, one of the first ever marketing heads I worked for when I started my advertising career. He not only created the Air-India Maharaja mascot, but the unique Air-India personality. He was a dapper man. Very well dressed: blazer, scarf, white shirt, sometimes white flannel trousers. He was a stickler when it came to dress.

In all aspects, Bobby always had to get it just right. There is something to be said for this Parsi attitude — finicky about detail and getting it perfect. As a junior you cursed Bobby, and both dreaded and loved to write copy for him. Bobby himself was a brilliant copywriter, and he knew every nuance of the language, so he could rip your copy to shreds when he didn't think it was up to his very demanding standards.

But when your copy was up to the mark, he had no hesitation in saying, 'This is damn good, old boy.' He even sent you a personal letter. 'I thought your ad on so and so was tops.' He did not pull punches. Neither in praise, nor in criticism. You got it straight between the eyes, both ways.

I remember one sales letter I wrote. It was a fairly corny old thing, something about the Emperor Shahjahan weeping for Mumtaz Mahal. And as his teardrop falls to the ground, he sees in it a vision of the Taj Mahal. (This was all made up by me. It was one of those fanciful stories which copywriters dream up, but it was nicely written.) Bobby saw it and said, 'My word, this is prize-winning stuff.' And sure enough, he entered it in an international airlines contest, and it won the prize for the best sales letter of any airline, anywhere in the world. I was really proud. I treasured the trophy for a long long time. Bobby had that ability to both inspire you and make you perspire.

Bobby rarely wrote himself. But he would re-write. Especially the Air-India hoardings. Like very often, he would say, 'Why don't you do one on the Queen? She's pregnant.' Or, 'Why don't you do one on our jumbo jets?' Bobby would always get it written by one of us. Then he would tidy it up. He was more of a tidy-upper and inspirer than he was an actual copywriter.

And he was a shockmaster. If the Queen was expecting, he would show her bulging tummy, knitting, typical mother-to-be. Then he would show the Air-India Maharaja with a similar bulging tummy saying, 'There is another one on the way', hinting that Air-India was about to 'deliver' a new jumbo jet. This cheeky attitude got Bobby hauled over the coals regularly. Not by his chairman, the venerable J R D Tata, but by Members of Parliament, who, as is well known, notoriously lack a sense of humour. They lack a lot of other things as well, but I won't go into those right now!

Another thing Bobby did to get the best out of the agency was to set deadlines that were impossible. I was in JWT in those days and Nuru Swaminathan was Air-India's Account Supervisor. He would call in Nuru and say, 'Look, I want an ad in tomorrow morning's paper.' This was at 9.30 in the morning, say on a Friday, and he wanted the ad in the newspaper on Saturday, announcing three flights a week to Nairobi or wherever. Today it doesn't sound difficult but this was long before computer-generated artworks were invented.

Nuru would come flying back to the agency and sit down with our creative team. In those days, the lean and angular, and very English, Josephine Tuor (who I was half in love with) was the Copy Chief. I was number two and Liz Sinha, a plump but ravishing beauty, was number three. (Incidentally, Indra Sinha, the renowned former Creative Director of the legendary British Agency CDP is her son.) The three of us would put our heads together, and then each of us would rush to our typewriters and start typing furiously the very first thing that came to our minds. Literally. So very often, the first thing was the worst thing. But sometimes, very occasionally, it was the best thing. The ideas just flowed. Why? Because of the adrenalin of the deadline. It had to be on Nuru's desk by two o'clock, straight after lunch. And she would whisk it off to the brilliant Waghulkar who was the Air-India art director, and he would draw a marvellous illustration without any reference to us. And without us even seeing how our work had been treated visually, she'd trot off to Bobby in the afternoon. He would usually brush up the copy, but rarely touch Waghulkar's drawings.

Nuru would hurtle back (we still had not seen it), rush into the studio and get the art work done. (In those days, we had to manufacture blocks and matrices.) The art department would be up all night. Then Nuru's assistant would dash off to the press usually after the deadline. They would close the ad pages at eleven p.m. and we would sometimes get there around midnight. But we'd get it in by hook or by crook. The next morning, bright and early at seven a.m., I would open the newspaper with trepidation to find our ad. I say 'our' because there was very little of 'me' left in it.

You felt proud to be a copywriter working on the Air-India account. When anyone praised the Air-India ads (and in those days almost everyone did) I would shamelessly say, 'All my own work!' (I hope Bobby is not eavesdropping from his heavenly abode!)

Bobby had the ability to make the public sit up, especially with his Air-India hoardings. He was the one who invented the idea of a weekly change which Amul Butter has adopted extremely well. The Air-India site on the India House building at Kemps Corner was looked forward to...as much as my dear friend Nana Chudasama's banner at Talk of the Town, in South Bombay.

Now Shunu Sen, the Marketing Chief of Hindustan Lever at that time, was the total opposite of both Bobby and Ravi. The round, jovial Shunu rarely made you perspire. He is always smiling, always looking at the better side of things. But when it came to his standards, he was also very exacting. However, instead of cutting you down, he'd say, 'Well, this is good, but from Lintas I want excellent.'

He had a way of motivating people to do better. I remember when the Lalitaji idea was shot, Shunu was out of town. His Product Manager, Dhariwal, approved the film. This was the one about Lalitaji buying tomatoes. It was a super idea and a lovely script. The petite Usha Bhandarkar was Creative Director and the experienced Pooh Sayani shot it. However, when Dhari (as he was nicknamed) showed the film to his boss, who was an Englishman from London, he bounced it. Therefore, I had to enter the picture as head of the ad agency. I explained the rationale of why Lalitaji had to be a tough, almost unpleasant housewife. Then I showed them the commercial again.

There was a Levers chorus of 'Oh! This is terrible. The woman is so rude. It will be a disservice to the Lever image. Surf is known as the housewife's friend and this lady is so damned insulting.' I tried to explain that that was the whole point. She had to be a person who took no nonsense from anyone including the vegetable vendor. But they didn't buy it. 'The commercial is so bad that we are not going to pay for it. You'll have to re-shoot a new film at Lintas' expense.' Dhari bravely fought a rearguard action but was overruled.

I then did something I rarely do. I waited till Shunu came back and I met him. 'Your boys have rejected the film. I would

like you to see it and give me your candid opinion. If you
think it is as lousy as they say, we will can it. Whether we pay
for it or not, we can debate. But give me your view straight
from the shoulder.' Shunu had

Remember that clients
enjoy getting
involved in the
ad making process.

a look at the film at my home
on my VHS VCR. I was able to
run it for him several times and
freeze the frame whenever we
wanted to study Lalitaji's
expression. (We agency people
have to remember that clients enjoy getting involved in the ad
making process.) At the end of it, in his diplomatic way, Shunu
said, 'Look Alyque, it is not up to the mark. But I don't think
that it's so bad that we should junk it.' I said, 'I personally
was not at the shooting but I like the film visually. I love the
character of Lalitaji. I selected the model after auditioning
two or three dozen actresses. She looks just right but her voice
is too mild. I'll redub her and put some sarcasm into it which
will give it a slightly humorous edge.'

Off I went. I didn't have much time since I was to leave for
a Lintas international conference. But I personally supervised
the redubbing so that we got a nice rapport going between
Lalitaji and the male commentator. With sarcasm that I rightly
borrowed from my mother's intonation. Typical up-ending of
lines, like *'Ravi betaa!'* meaning 'You better watch your step'.
And also when Lalitaji says, *'Bhaisaab'*, in an exasperated
way. Finally we finished at about four o'clock in the morning
and I said, 'That sounds fine.'

I took the film and after I grabbed a couple of hours'
shuteye, I rang up Shunu. 'I've got it ready. Can you come
over to my house? I don't want to take it to the office. I want
your frank opinion.' After seeing our revised version, he said,
'This is a real improvement. It makes me sit up and say, "This

interesting woman who has solid commonsense and yet she buys Surf even though it is not cheap." Lalitaji makes the point: Listen, it is not expensive — *Achchi cheez aur sasti cheez mein farak hota hai.* (There is a difference between buying good stuff and cheap stuff.)' Shunu continued, 'In any case, I've got to get a Surf film on air because I've bought time on the Olympics' telecast. I'll tell you what, Alyque. I want to be fair to you and to my boys. We will run the Lalitaji commercial during the Olympics and do an advertising recall test. If the film bombs we will can it. If it scores high, we'll continue to back it.'

Well, I'm happy to say that Lalitaji scored a bullseye. The telephones were buzzing. 'Who made this marvellous Surf film? Who is this Lalitaji?' The Chairman of Levers, Ashok Ganguly, saw it and rang up Shunu. 'Both my wife and I saw the Surf film. It's quite remarkable. So unadvertising like. I think it will make our customers rethink the value of Surf. This Lalitaji convinces us that a low price is not everything.'

When the advertising test results came in, we weren't surprised that Lalitaji scored higher than any other commercial on the box. On noticeability and memorability. After that, they just ran Lalitaji for the rest of the Olympics, and for the next seven years. She was talked about in advertising magazines and even the general press as an advertising icon. In a sense, Lalitaji rescued Surf.

Earlier, Shunu worked with me on Liril. There again he was an inspiring person. He invited me to a presentation by Hindustan Lever market research on an image study of various soaps. After a while, I scribbled a note to Shunu during the meeting. 'I find there is a gap in the positioning between Lifebuoy and Hamam. I think we should have a brand in that gap, which would say freshness rather than health. Not a healthy feeling of freshness, and not fresh and glowing which is what Hamam is saying, but just fresh fresh. A lively sort of freshness.'

And from that remark, Liril was born. But it was not an easy birth. The next step after the soap image study, was to get Levers market research into the Indian housewife's bathroom, believe it or not. I had a theory that the only occasion the harried middle-class housewife had any time to herself was in her bath. The rest of the day she was cooking, cleaning, shopping, getting the kids ready for school and her husband off to work, and other endless chores. Through the miracle of projective techniques, the researchers came back with some amazing revelations. It seems that when the woman of the house latches the bathroom door... she begins to daydream. In her fantasy world, she imagines a film hero carrying her off on his white horse. She fantasises about her escape from boring household responsibilities. Her secret desire is to be *bindaas*. Live a carefree life without onerous duties.

This set me thinking. Could we imbue freshness with a quality of feeling free? And this insight was the springboard for the creative expression of the nymph in the waterfall. The name Liril had been registered by Hindustan Lever from a list sent to them by Unilever in London. Levers were very keen that the soap have striations, wiggly stripes of a different colour running across the tablet. I recommended the tablet be blue (because a waterfall is blue) with white striations. Hindustan Lever were very excited and produced 1,000 tablets for testing.

At this point Derek Wooller, the Marketing Controller of Hindustan Lever's soaps division, stepped in and suggested we add the freshness of limes to our story. He strongly felt that though the waterfall had tremendous emotional appeal, Liril needed a rational ingredient to clinch the sale. I was not averse to this but suggested we do an 'As Marketed' test: Blue

Liril versus Green Liril with limes. I was wrong and Wooller was right. The rest is history.

Actually, from the time I was very young I never had to look far to draw inspiration from motivating individuals. There was one in my very own home. My brother, Sultan 'Bobby' Padamsee. He was ten years my senior, so when I was ten, he was twenty already. I have heard from all the people who worked with him that he was a man who inspired you by saying, 'I know you have got it in you and I know that you are going to be able to achieve it.' He was a bit of a genius. When a genius believes in you when you are losing faith in yourself, you suddenly get re-motivated. You get pepped up and begin to deliver your best.

He had a knack of saying, 'Ah, you have tried it this way. There are three more, but I know only one.' Then he'd give you his option and get you to look around for the two other ways. And even if you did not find the other two ways, you could go with what he said and it usually worked out.

My brother-in-law Deryck Jeffereis was a great admirer of Bobby and was one of his disciples. In a sense, Bobby's *shishya*. (And later, I became an apprentice of Deryck.) When he first met Bobby, Deryck was an engineering student with little or no interest in the arts. He was of Anglo-Indian parentage, very fair but also very overweight and self-conscious... which may have accounted for his stammering while speaking. Gradually, through Bobby's kindness and patience, by encouraging him and giving him tasks that he knew Deryck could do well, Bobby built up his confidence. After a while, Deryck's stammer began to disappear.

If Deryck had an idea, Bobby would always find the time in his busy day to sit down and say, 'I know you have been trying to talk to me since morning. It is now evening and it's time to really get into the idea.' And he would listen patiently. Bobby would really listen to you. He was not just flattering you. He would get totally engrossed in the idea and they would bounce it around.

Bobby could be arrogant at times. If he read a review, a know-nothing review, he would sit down and dash off a fiery letter, full of witticisms, poking fun at the reviewer's lack of knowledge. He could be quite cutting in that sense. But whatever Bobby did, he did with style and charm. This is something I realised I lacked when I was a young man.

If you want to grow as a person, like an actor you must study other people. I was aware when I took over Lintas that though I had most of the qualities one needs to be a good Chief Executive — vision, drive, organisational ability, money sense, and creativity, I lacked the charm and the understanding of human weakness that my predecessor had. So I decided to modify my own hard-driving personality and cultivate a more fatherly side. The finest Chief Executive is a Chief Motivator.

The finest Chief Executive is a Chief Motivator.

In the advertising business, people need a military commander and I tended to behave like one. When I took over Lintas, people thought, 'Oh my God. This army dictator is going to ruin the family spirit.' They were in for a surprise. All the things I've described in the chapter *Having fun on the way to number one* were really inspired by people like Bobby and later by Gerson.

Developing the 'people touch' is important. It is not patronising to put your arm around a peon. I had an excellent senior peon, the tall and dignified George Daniels, who worked with me for fourteen years. Putting my arm around him and saying, 'George, that was a great idea of yours, telling the person on the phone that AP is speaking to London. It really saved my life', was a thoughtful way of appreciating George. Acknowledging someone's contribution helps motivate the person. Up to that time, I was pretty self-centred and not outer-directed.

One of the things the managing directorship of Lintas taught me was: You have to think of each of your staff and you should make time for all of them. People knew that after six p.m. my door was open. You could come in, have a cup of tea and pour out your heart. You could say, 'I don't know what to do. My husband and I are not getting on.' Or 'I really want to study abroad, but the money at Lintas means too much to me. What's your advice, Alyque?' The best thing about being a father figure is you begin to enjoy it.

I found I was built for this role. It was deep inside me but I had neglected it. To bring out from yourself, from the inner recesses, some qualities that are there, helps you develop. I began to do a lot more listening as MD, than talking. Though people have said it for years, 'Be a good listener, rather than a good talker', we often pay lip service to these things. But once you start the process and it begins to work, you say, 'Why the hell didn't I do this before?'

When I say 'begins to work', I don't just mean that people get better motivated, and you build a better team. I mean that you personally enjoy listening to other people. Unless you *enjoy* something, you won't do it for long. *Unless you enjoy something, you won't do it for long.* An attitude change occurred, and I began to open my ears and shut my mouth. What other people say, and even what other people do, can lead to new insights, if you are observant.

Orson Welles is one of the greatest inspirations I ever had in my life. He was a man who always took a different and radical approach to anything that he did. He didn't give a fig for the traditional. He was a great improviser. While shooting for *Othello,* he ran out of money. All his actors were assembled in Venice but the costumes had not arrived because he had not paid the bills. He had to shoot the killing of Roderigo. The production manager said, 'Sir, I am sorry we can't shoot.' And Orson replied, 'I have an idea. We will do it in a Turkish bath. Can you get a number of large white sheets and towels?'

It was brilliant. All he needed was a couple of steam-makers. He placed Roderigo under the Turkish bath slats with steam rising through the slats. Iago, above him, is calling out to Roderigo. And then he spies him below. He shouts to Cassio's friends that he has discovered the assailant. Iago draws his sword and begins to stab at Roderigo through these slats. The poor man runs like a rat, hither and thither until one of Iago's sword thrusts runs him through. This innovative piece of improvisation by Orson has inspired me to use my imagination whenever I am in a tight corner.

I love this sense of being able to come up with a trump card when cornered. However, it's a dangerous thing if you start trusting your instincts only and forget that pre-planning is the key to disciplined success. The other thing I love is Orson's complete lack of inhibition in tackling the text. Even if it meant putting it back to front or changing the lines of the author, including Shakespeare. But Orson's masterstroke was frightening the whole world with his realistic radio broadcast of H G Wells' (no relative) *War of the Worlds.* It was so true to life that Americans began vacating cities in the belief that real aliens had landed in New York. Orson's Negro *Macbeth* was another first. It was full of voodoo and black magic. I believe it was set in Haiti with witch doctors instead of witches.

Unfortunately our critics are very myopic about the way they approach anything which is more than fifty years old. Suddenly it becomes a classic, even a modern classic. I much prefer the free and easy attitude of MTV and Channel [V]. It is so irreverent and yet it's so human. It is for U, it is for We, it is for V. I don't say all of it is terrific, but it never stops being creative and innovative. I think Channel [V] is the most outstanding piece of consumer communication in the world.

I enjoy Orson Welles' freewheeling imagination, and when he hits it right, by God, he wins with a bang. And when he gets it wrong, so what? I hate people who just don't even want to try something new. One of the things I find stifling about Satyajit Ray is that his work tends to be strait-jacketed. Everything has to be very studied, beautifully executed, beautifully thought out, very high intellectual quality but no surprises, no off-the-wall stuff. Give me the New Wave break-the-rules cinema of Jean Luc Godard any day. Caution preserves the past. Innovation invents the future.

Caution preserves the past. Innovation invents the future.

When you are good at something, you tend to continue to do it and stop experimenting. You get creative arthritis. Personally, I like to change and venture into an area which is different. I love Sir Laurence Olivier for that reason. Always experimenting. The world's greatest actor and risk-taker. I admire that part of him. Olivier took enormous risks with the roles he played. For instance, when he did *Othello,* he and director John Dexter decided that he would play a really black Othello. Black at that time in England was West Indian. So he gave Shakespeare's blank verse a slight West Indian lilt and he came on to the stage as a typical swivel-hipped Black, almost nude. He trained his stiff British body to adopt the swagger of a smooth ball bearing-jointed kind of Black. Now this was in the early 1970s. Olivier came on with a big smile, or what used to be known then as the 'watermelon' grin, twinkling eyes and a mischievous roguish expression. Anything but the stately Shakespearean general you were used to seeing. When he made love to Desdemona, by God, we knew he was turning her on. He took a terrific risk when he had to say, 'Oh! Oh! Oh!' which most English actors find very difficult to do. So he used to do three 'Oh's' in a row. Olivier had decided that they were very very Black 'Oh's.' And it was one enormous groan of pain.

Even when Sir Laurence played Shylock, he did it with daring. I remember the scene in which Portia gives the judgement against him and indicates that Shylock can cut off a pound of flesh, but no blood, no muscle. And if he failed, then all Shylock's lands would be forfeited. Olivier looked at Portia, and then he looked down. Suddenly he stiffened up his spine and walked straight out of the court. There was a second of silence after his exit. Then from the wings Olivier gave this terrifying howl of pain. The whole audience was chilled to witness a man totally humiliated. With every role Olivier took enormous chances. But because of the brilliance of his acting and his intensity, he just carried the audience with him.

Again, when Olivier was playing Iago and Ralph Richardson was playing Othello, with Tyrone Guthrie as director. Guthrie and Olivier plotted together that the motivation for Iago was that he was secretly in love with Othello. They decided to give the Iago-Othello relationship a homo-erotic spin. But of course, they didn't tell Richardson who would have objected strongly. Whenever Iago stood behind Othello, one could see a kind of passion Iago had for this big black animal.

Only when the critics wrote, 'What on earth is going on with Shakespeare?', did Richardson realise what was going on behind his back. He confronted Olivier who confessed the truth. This subterfuge almost brought their friendship to an end.

That's the kind of exciting insight that is inspiring. I enjoy it. But I will say that the excitement or the originality of the approach should not overshadow the work itself. I always try and work from an insight. 'Why really does this man hate this woman?' In Mahesh Dattani's play about the riots, *Final Solutions,* we tried to discover what is the root cause of prejudice. We brought in a psychoanalyst who had worked with me earlier in *Marat/Sade,* Udayan Patel. He came to rehearsals and probed with my actors: What is the meaning of prejudice? Where does it come from?

We did a lot of improvisations on each of our personal experiences in the riots, and the approach evolved. Many directors have a clear idea, right at the beginning, of how they will present the play. I don't. I am only clear about what the play should mean to the audience. But I am very fuzzy about how to create that impact. The main things I do know are (a) trust the work, and (b) trust your actors. It's the same thing with advertising: trust the product and trust your creative people. Gradually, if your instincts are right, you will evolve something that will be powerful enough to motivate an audience to tears or laughter or which motivates a brand preference.

Bill Bernbach was a great one for inspiring consumer insight. I learnt that from Bernbach, though he never used the term. He would examine the product and find a reason why people should get involved with that product. He took an ugly car like the Volkswagen Beetle, and asked, 'Why would people love this car? Since it's so damned ugly, there must be something else that's good about it. It is a car dedicated to performance, not looks. An engine that never fails you. It never gets overheated. It's totally weatherproof.' He kept looking for the hidden pluses of the Beetle. It was that kind of consumer insight that enabled his agency to create the breakthrough advertising they did. Bernbach was the master of turning a negative into a positive. Look at his pathbreaking Avis Rent-a-car campaign. How number two is better than number one because 'We try harder'.

'Come at it differently,' he used to say. The creativity of the paradox. How ugly can become beautiful. How something as expensive as Chivas Regal could be treated in a miserly manner. Because it was so expensive, you needed to conserve it. He showed how people would pour other whiskeys into the Chivas Regal bottle to augment their stocks. Or he would show you a Chivas Regal bottle and recall to mind the famous phrase, 'Is it half-full or half-empty?' The host looks at it with a sad heart as half-empty while the guest joyously sees it as half-full. It's such a human approach.

He was always looking for the unusual angle from which to view the product. Like the famous 'Lemon' ad for Volkswagen. Imagine mentioning that the Volkswagen factory could occasionally produce a lousy piece. He did that. He was very bold. The other ad I love is the 'Garage' one. The one with two cars. In a two-garage home, the huge one is empty and the small one has a Beetle in it. The line goes something like this: 'It does all the work, but on Saturday night, guess who goes to the party.'

Lovely sense of humour, making fun of yourself. Bernbach from that point of view is my favourite adman of all times. More than even Jerry Della Femina, whose irreverence I love. More than Mary Wells' gimmicky ideas like painting Brainff planes in all sorts of colours, and doing the 'I Love New York' campaign. More than Ogilvy with all his status conscious, image building brands. The only one in my opinion who comes close to Bernbach is Saatchi & Saatchi, who again combine irreverence with an unusual product point.

Now, on the opposite side of the spectrum of terrific clients like the ones I've described, is the client who is just plain pigheaded, who only makes you perspire and never inspires you. Without naming names, I can tell you I worked with at least two of them. Sad to say, I sacked both of them shortly after I became Managing Director of Lintas. I tolerated them for many years as Creative Director with gritted teeth, but I didn't have the authority to fire them. It was my ambition that they would both bite the dust even if it meant us losing valuable billing.

The incident that caused me to part company with our third largest client became something of a cause celebré in the advertising world. The Chairman of this company was constantly bullying our client service and creative people. He was a short squat bulldog of a man with tremendous stamina and formidable intellectual capacities. His idea was to pay the agency to listen to him pontificate. He was a very bright man (no two ways about it), but he had fallen in love with his own intellect, and worse, with his own voice. So a meeting would begin at nine o'clock in the morning and could end at twelve midnight without even a pause. Neither for 'the pause that refreshes', nor for a pause in his monologue to enable us to get a word in edgewise. This was a sermon not from the mount but from the non-stop fount!

He was obstinate about his own opinion. He was always saying, 'Now, what do you think?' And after you had said what you thought, he'd say, 'That's a very good argument, but let me show you that I have six reasons why I should not take it. One...' And the first one would take one hour. The second one would take two hours, and so on. Eventually it would be midnight and we would all be falling asleep in our seats. To

To bore or bully an agency is to deplete its creative fire power.

bore or bully an agency is to deplete its creative fire power.

Furthermore, he was extra miserly and penny pinching. Always telling the agency that they were taking him for a ride. Why shouldn't the agency pay for all the free space they took for their key number, where you put 'Lintas' or just 'Lin' or 'L'? He would say, 'Wait. I have measured the last ten ads and I find you have used up my space to the tune of seven column centimetres. And at the current ad rates, you owe me 'x' amount of rupees.' I mean, how cheap can you get!

Year after year, he would browbeat our team during his six- and eight-hour meetings, leading to demoralisation and frequent resignations. He would demand that the agency work on several propositions and creative approaches simultaneously. A wasteful practice in my opinion. I insisted we select the most appropriate proposition first, and then create as many approaches as he wanted. We crossed swords.

I had our accountant do me a *hisab* before this historic *Kurukshetra*. In spite of large billings, this client was showing negative profitability in terms of man hours spent and umpteen revisions not paid for. Armed with this key factor, I sailed into battle. He wanted it his way since, as he trumpeted, 'I am the client and I am paying the bills.' On a matter of principle I informed him that the agency would not budge regarding multiple propositions. (Was it my imagination or did I hear a silent cheer run through the room?) The client rose from his chair. So did I. (It's useful to be six foot two.) He looked up at me. 'So that's it?' And I replied, 'Yes. That's it.' And that was it!.

a double life

Legend has it that the servicing team distributed ladoos that afternoon in celebration. If they did, all I can say is, 'Naughty! Naughty!'

The other bully boy was from a big multinational company. And he was not even the Managing Director. At least in the other case, the fellow was the proprietor. This chap was supposed to be a Marketing Manager who had grown out of the advertising ranks. So he should have known how an advertising agency works. He was extremely blunt and rude, whereas at least the other bully had style in his cutting jibes. This man was just a bumpkin. He was not only pigheaded, but full of ham!

His brand had a good budget and we were doing brilliant work for him. We repositioned his brand which was dying, gave it a whole new lease of life. But he showed little or no appreciation, and was always whining, 'Why can't you get special positions from TOI (*The Times of India*) without paying for them? After all, I have such a big budget and I think I deserve this and I think I deserve that.'

I remember speaking about this impossible situation to Bagu Ochani, a solid rock of a man and my very trusted lieutenant. Bagu was of Sindhi-Sardarji parentage and although his surname is typically Sindhi, he maintained a full beard and turban.

'Bagu, I am going to sack this chap.'

'No, no. He is too important to us. One, because it is a prestigious multinational, and secondly because we have grown this account from tiny beginnings to a giant brand leader. It will make a huge dent in our billings.'

'Well, only on one condition. You handle it yourself Bagu.'

'Okay, I accept the challenge, but please retain the client.'

So Bagu handled it for over a year until one day he came into my office, red in the face. I've rarely seen Bagu thrown, absolutely livid, and he said, 'Alyque, I have to say for once I was wrong. Completely wrong. The man is a cannibal. He eats his own flesh and blood alive. We must sack him.' I said, 'Well Bagu, it has taken you a year. I admire your patience, in fact your masochism, for having tolerated this man for so long. Tell me the reason you now want me to fire him. I will do it anyway because I'm happy to. But tell me why. I'm intrigued.'

In a voice quivering with rage, he told me that after our senior media planner had presented the media plan, this gentleman just flipped through it, slammed it down on the desk and gave it a shove to send it flying to the floor. 'That is what I think of your media plan!' At that point, Bagu said though he wanted to punch him, he got up and said, 'Excuse me Mr X, but I think my agency and I would like to leave right now. You are entitled to keep the plan and use it as you think best, but we cannot tolerate this behaviour.'

The media planner was in tears. Bagu helped him up and exasperated they left. He drove straight to Express Towers, stormed into my room and related the entire incident to me. I telephoned the MD of the company and said, 'I am sorry but we will have to part ways. I don't think my agency can stand any more demoralisation by your Marketing Manager.' And so we called it quits.

Inflated egos are a mask for an inferiority complex.

Both these gentlemen were suffering from terribly inflated egos, and inflated egos are always a cover, a mask, for an inferiority complex. Somewhere early in life, these unfortunate people have been given a raw deal by someone and have been belittled. So they have to make up by humiliating other people. They enjoy making their suppliers perspire.

There are all sorts of clients. There was this Marwari client of mine with a small company. He had done very well because our ads had made them a national brand. But he was always finding fault, nit-picking. He spoke in Hindi, 'Padamsee *saheb, aap bade advertising genius hain. Hum to chota mota aadmi hain, magar main kehta hoon ke yeh advertising...*' and his voice would trail off. What he meant was, 'Listen, I think I can get a better deal with an agency that has offered me a discount.' What clients don't realise is that asking for a discount is like asking for a favour. You now owe the agency one.

Now, our Calcutta office was not doing all that well. So I used to humour him a bit. 'You know *saheb,* it is true that you can get a discount, but in the end you know, it is our name that appears on your ad. *Prestige hota hai, multinational naam hai.*' Fortunately, he realised our Lintas name was worth more than a cheapo discount agency. A lot of Indian clients are very keen to get a multinational agency key number attached to their ads. In complete contrast to the other bully who wanted us to pay him for using our logo in his ad, here was I telling a client that he should be happy to pay us for using our logo. Credit lines would open: 'Oh, Lintas does your advertising. HTA does your advertising. O&M does your advertising. If they trust you, we'll be happy to lend you money.' That's an interesting aspect of small clients. How much they value a big name.

Talking about client attitudes, there was another small manufacturer in Coimbatore with a brand of underwear called Crystal. Very enthusiastic, and nothing was too good for the agency. He had a budget of just twenty lakh rupees. I told him, 'Well, you know, twenty lakhs won't get you anywhere.

Tell you what. I've got such a fine campaign, why don't you take this year's and next year's budget and spend it all this year. Let's spend forty lakh rupees now.' And he said, 'Padamsee *saheb,* if you say so, let's do it.' And he did.

We produced some brilliant advertising for Crystal underwear. Our two bright sparks in Lintas were Neville and Josie — Neville D'Souza and Josie Paul. They are a terrific team. And they came up with a fabulous campaign. I don't think I've seen advertising like that for underwear, anywhere in the world. However, we found it very difficult to collect our overdues, but it didn't matter. We loved the campaign and were very proud of it.

We got a lot of favourable comments from the press. But above all, we got respect. If a client wants to get the best out of his agency, the first thing the agency wants is respect. Even more than money, they want *izzat.* They want to be treated as professionals. Secondly, they need to have exciting briefs. Not boring, rational, full-stop and comma pieces of paper. No, what they want is what I call the 'three dots and a dash' brief. Like Ravi Mammen's 'The Romance of Tyres'.

If a client wants to get the best out of his agency, the first thing the agency wants is **izzat.**

I think if you've got these two things: a client that respects the agency and a brief that allows creative imagination to soar, then the client has a right to expect outstanding advertising from you. Advertising that will shake up the consumer, not just get him nodding in agreement until he nods off to sleep!

Today, you have some pretty knowledgeable MBAs working as clients. I have only one thing against them. An MBA client is sometimes a pain in the ass. Not always, but often. Because he wants to prove that he knows more than the agency. I found that many MBAs, maybe because of their rapid rise up the corporate ladder, switching jobs to get another promotion… arrive at the Peter Principle. They are promoted to their level of incompetence.

I'm not saying all of them. Some of them are in fact brilliant, bright and pleasant. But when you want to get the best out of anyone, whether it is to get your son to do his homework, or your boss to give you a raise, you've got to motivate. You can't just browbeat. Browbeating works once, twice, then it is up against the law of diminishing returns. If you want results, enthuse, don't enforce. (This is why Indira Gandhi's Emergency failed.)

MBA doesn't mean Master of Boring Administration. MBAs have got to wake up to the fact that you hire an agency because you have faith in its ability. You inspire them. They will perspire for you.

When you hire an agency write down why you hired them. Put it in a locked drawer. And when you want to sack the agency, pull it out and say, 'This is what I hired them for. So why am I sacking them for the wrong reasons? Maybe I should keep them on because they are still delivering on all the reasons I hired them for.' I think that is a good rule of thumb for clients to assess their agency.

The shortest distance to boredom is a straight line.

Chapter 9

HAVING FUN ON THE
WAY TO NUMBER ONE

*T*he Lintas I joined in 1957 was basically a rather fuddy-duddy Levers agency. It was run on rule-ridden lines. But at the same time, it was an unusual place because it had a lot of madcap Englishmen around. And so the agency had a certain playboy atmosphere about it.

When I joined, Razmi Ahmed had recently been appointed the head. And though he himself was anything but a playboy, at the same time he was not strict in a martinet type of way. But there were people like Rex Berry, a senior copywriter, who was a bit of a wild man. Then there was Hugh Atkinson, a brilliant creative man. He was Australian, and legend has it that on the flight from Sydney to Bombay, while the plane was over Port Darwin, he said to the pilot, 'Oh my God! I can see my girlfriend's house. Well, bye now. I'll see you later.' And he jumped out of the plane, pulled the parachute ripcord and landed, if you believe this far out story, in his girlfriend's front lawn.

So there was a certain vibrancy about the agency. Unfortunately, by the time I joined, most of the expats, except one or two, had left. Below Razmi Ahmed — the head of the agency — was the Copy Chief, a chap called John Walton. John was a pipe-smoking individual. Very slow-talking. Very thoughtful. He had this incredible knack, which people with a pipe seem to have, which is to listen, listen, listen. Finally they'll say, 'That's very interesting,' and then be silent for another half hour before saying, 'Yes, I think it'll work.' And that is about all their contribution to the brainstorm. Not all silence is golden.

Opposite him was an Art Director, an Australian called Roy Delgarno. He was an artist, and by that I mean a painter of fine art. He used to have exhibitions and stuff. Roy was the opposite of John. He was fast talking, he had a little goatee beard, loved boozing and he generally lived the bohemian life. Give me a garrulous Australian to a phlegmatic Englishman, any day.

These were the two creative heads of Lintas. The agency itself was located in a building called Khaitan Bhavan, near Churchgate. It had the usual cabin spaces and a little bit of open-plan seating for the secretaries and so on. And the agency seemed to work at a very leisurely pace because campaigns did not necessarily change every year. It was only much later when Rediffusion came on to the scene, mothered by Kersy Katrak's MCM, that they began to sell clients the idea of a six-ad campaign that you changed every six months. It was marvellous because, as someone told me, you make your money not so much on the agency commission, but on the markup on the artworks. So the more the artworks, the more profitable the agency.

But Lintas in the 1950s was a sleepy Levers-run agency. Ads ran unchanged for many many years. In a campaign you might have two or three ads maximum. Six was unheard of and was considered extravagant. What was good about Lintas was that it was marketing-oriented, which was quite natural, being the house agency of Levers. And in spite of that, it still had accreditation. If I recall correctly, at that time you had to have fifteen per cent of your billings from clients other than your main one. Or five clients in addition to the main one. And I think Lintas just about fulfilled those requirements. So it was accredited to what was known in those days as the IENS (Indian & Eastern Newspapers Society), now called the INS (Indian Newspaper Society).

Creative-wise, it was a laidback agency. Its reputation was zero. You did what you were told, because you were a house agency and the Brand Manager told you what sort of advertising he wanted. And since he travelled the length and breadth of India, he was supposed to know what would go down well with the target audience. Remember, in those days, and even till today, Levers had an unparalleled distribution system, reaching down to 500,000 villages. You can find mini-Lux soap in almost any village in India. Or even Lifebuoy for that matter.

Levers was a fantastic organisation, and Lintas was really just an appendage. It was more like an advertising department. Originally, we even used to sit in their office till the agency moved to its own space in Khaitan Bhavan.

Their people were straightforward. Which I've always admired. But being straightforward, they tended to think vertically. There was no lateral pattern to their thinking. They didn't jump from this to that. So there was very little cross-fertilisation. You had a rulebook and you followed it. I remember in the 1960s Unilever Worldwide said, 'This advertising business is very disorganised. It's all hunch and gut feel and fly-by-the-seat-of-your-pants kind of thing. There must be a rulebook for advertising like there is for everything else in the Unilever world.' They were always trying to prove that they could better the percentages of Lord Lever Hulme's famous dictum, 'I realise fifty per cent of my advertising money is wasted. But I don't know which fifty per cent!'

So they got together a number of brilliant advertising people. I think David Ogilvy was one. Rosser Reeves was another. And they put them in a hotel room in New York, locked them up for a week, paid all their bills, and said, 'Now come out with a blueprint for good advertising. It will be called the "Unilever Principles for Good Advertising (UPGA)."'

And so UPGA came to be the bane of the creative department. It was the sword of Damocles that brand managers dangled over Lintas people. 'You know, you haven't followed the ten UPGA rules.' So there was a kind of love-hate relationship I've always had with Levers. I love their straightforwardness and their professionalism. I hate the fact that they think much too linear and can very rarely be creative.

I had joined Lintas from Thompsons, which had always been the number one agency. At that time Lintas was not even in the race and its reputation was based mainly on its remuneration package. It was felt that it was a great retirement agency. Join Lintas and you were set for life. Nobody ever sacked you and they gave you perks that were unheard of in those days. Like House Rent Allowance. And medical expenses for you and your family. And they gave you five weeks leave annually. So it seemed a very safe agency to join.

Of course, at that time Lintas was subsidised by Levers. And they were quite happy doing it because they felt that if they had their own advertising agency they didn't mind paying handsome salaries and so what if the agency didn't make a profit. Heck, Levers was making huge amounts of profits. Therefore they decided to treat it as a loss-making division. An important wing just like research which doesn't make any profit. Just an expense centre and not a profit centre.

Then in 1969, the FERA Act was passed which stated that all non-core companies would have to come down to forty per cent foreign ownership. Now, Lintas is an acronym for 'Levers International Advertising Service', and was owned 100 per cent by Lintas: London which in turn was owned by Unilever. The new FERA Law meant that Lintas: London could hold only forty per cent, while sixty per cent had to be owned by Indians. But Unilever did not want to get into this kind of arrangement. Around the same time, Levers decided that they would divest themselves of Lintas: Worldwide on a gradual basis, because they didn't want to be in the advertising business any more.

So we became Lintas: India Limited and as soon as we did that, we became a little more open to taking on other business. Mind you, there was no pressure from Unilever, but we took on clients like Tik-20. And I remember writing copy such as 'How to get away from mosquitoes' showing a man sleeping on the roof of his house, and another sleeping underwater. Not very creative, but quite an amusing series. I kept the ads for many years. I was very proud of them because at least they had a sense of humour which Levers advertising always avoided.

Levers thought humorous advertising was frivolous. In other words, it frivolised your brand. And they had this dreadful

Humorous advertising, whatever else it does, is very memorable.

worry that people would laugh, not at the ad, but at the brand. And therefore consumers would think less of the brand and its status would go down, resulting in falling sales, and so on. Which I think is a bit far-fetched. I believe humorous advertising, whatever else it does, is very memorable and can add status to the brand. (Amul Butter is a good example.Take the one where the Amul cartoon mascot is holding up her finger full of butter and saying 'Goldfinger' – which was a take-off on the smash hit James Bond movie.)

Now, also in 1969-70, Gerson da Cunha took over as head of Lintas from Razmi Ahmed. I was Copy and Films Chief until then, and moved up to being Creative Director. The bearded Hassan Taj, lean and elegant, was the Art Director of the agency. The fine aesthetic sense he displayed in his ads carried over to his personality and dress sense as well. Of course, in those days, there weren't ten creative directors in one agency. There was one person in charge of art, one for copy and one for films. And they had their teams working under them.

At the same time, we moved out of Hindustan Lever House (where we had moved to in the 1960s), and into our own premises at Express Towers at Nariman Point. I think that move was a very important one, because it signalled that we were independent. We were also told that we would have to pay our own way. Though Levers would subsidise us partly, they wouldn't pay 100 per cent of our shortfall. But even that didn't incentivise us to go on a real drive for other businesses.

Initially, we got a few clients like Sandoz and Pfizers, and then some more trickled in. But we didn't look for accounts. They came to us. It was very important that our status be maintained. Lintas never begged for business. When clients approached us, we examined their credentials to make sure they were in line with our image.

In the mid-1970s, I became Deputy General Manager and Creative Director, and finally in 1980, when Gerson left to join UNICEF in Brazil, I was appointed Chief Executive. At first I stoutly refused, but then my Regional Director, the Frenchman Jean Francois Lacour, said, 'Alyque, why don't you think of Lintas as a brand? Just as you have built up famous brands like Liril and Rin and Cherry Blossom.' That struck me as a revolutionary insight. I gave it a lot of thought and finally agreed. And that's how I began to build the Lintas Brand.

My goal was to make Lintas the number one agency in India. But I was determined to have a lot of fun on the way to number one. I wanted Lintas to be tops, not just in size, but in employee satisfaction as well. And in creative innovation. And to make our agency a place which people can't wait to get back to on Monday morning. That is presuming they've resisted the temptation to work through the weekend!

My managing committee and I decided that we would be a creative agency that concentrated on brand growth. And not just create campaigns simply to win awards. Our slogan was 'Win sales and win awards.' In that order. I think Liril, Kama Sutra, Cherry Charlie, Lalitaji, the MRF Muscleman, proved you could do both.

As soon as I took over as chief of Lintas I said, 'I want to revolutionise the agency. Let's go after new business with a vengeance. I want to un-Leverise the agency. Not non-Leverise it, but un-Leverise it. We should no longer be a clone of Levers. The only way to do it is to go after fresh accounts that don't have their way of thinking.' I set up a cell whose function was to do nothing but look for new business, new business, new business.

Gradually we began to grow. First, at the rate of about twenty per cent a year. Then thirty, and finally we ended up growing at the rate of forty-five per cent year after year. This was possible mainly because of the growth of non-Levers business. But significantly, even our Levers business grew. Liril, which had always hovered around the lakhs mark, suddenly went up to crores. So did Rin and many other brands.

In the early 1980s, any non-Levers brand that was accepted by Lintas had to agree to spend more than our minimum billing mark. I think we were the first agency in India to insert a minimum billing clause in our letter of contract.

Of course, once the company was Americanised in 1982 (when Levers sold its remaining stake to the Interpublic group), there was no question of slow growth. Interpublic, our holding company, had very clear growth goals. The minimum was fifteen per cent per annum. If you didn't achieve this, there was a real danger of being sacked. It was not like, 'Oh well, you better pull up your socks.' No, no. It was, 'Shape up or ship out.'

But even prior to that, I felt that growth was the name of the game. I had two priorities. One was growth and the other was profitability. I said, 'We don't just need growth. We need profitable growth. If we don't have money, we can't have an in-house TV-video facility. If we don't have money, we can't buy flats. And if we can't buy flats, we can't hire executives in Bombay city, where nobody is willing to rent us one. No executives. No growth.' I wanted to build, not just a bigger agency, but a better agency.

I also learned from the collapse of Kersy Katrak's MCM, how a big agency billings-wise, could be a loss making one. MCM was like a shooting star in the 1970s. Creative-wise and billings-wise. But they weren't careful about collections, and so they

Creativity is your showcase, but your bottom line is your bottom line.

were forced to close down becuase they could not pay salaries. Profit-making is the name of the game. Not just billings. Creativity is your showcase, but your bottom line is your bottom line.

So when I took over Lintas I said, 'Let me have a look at the collections.' And I found them dismal. So I set all sorts of targets and incentives for collecting money owed to us. I put it on the managing committee agenda as the first item of business, not the last. And once every week, for ten years or more, my committee met from ten in the morning to two in the afternoon, and fifty per cent of the time we spent discussing how we could improve our collections. This had me charging out of the room to the nearest phone, and ringing up various clients: 'Look, you know, we are short of money and we'll be grateful if you could somehow or the other expedite your cheques.'

I also learnt from Roger Neill, CEO of Lintas: Australia that they were collecting clients' dues early and paying suppliers late. They could then invest the fifteen- or twenty-day cash float they had on the short term money market and make a nice bit of interest. We adopted that system in India, with certain modifications to suit our situation. And lo and behold, every year, ten per cent of our profits came from this simple little device. (I suppose that's the Gujarati-Kutchi in me.)

I am always prepared to listen, but I have never been prepared to take orders if they go against the grain. Long before I took over, Lintas had a reputation of standing up to clients, especially when they wanted the ads to say something that the product could not deliver. We developed this attitude from Hindustan Lever, which insists that every ad should be checked for legal and technical accuracy. 'Truth Well Told' is the McCann Erickson Worldwide slogan. Long before I became a Creative Consultant to McCann, I knew this was the only way to go. Is it a coincidence that Lintas and McCann, the two agencies I worked with, share this vision?

But still, I wanted to un-Leverise the agency, not only in terms of our goals and ambitions, but also in our method of working. I particularly didn't like the red tape we had inherited. If you wanted a pencil from the stationery department, you had to fill up three forms which had to be countersigned by three people and all that sort of thing. I found this very frustrating and time-consuming.

I wanted to remove inhibiting rules and restrictions. I wanted Lintas to be more like the theatre where everyone is informal but effective. The first thing I did was to tell trainees to drop the 'Sir' when they addressed seniors. They were a little reluctant at first because there was a lot of 'Sir' culture we had inherited from Levers. But I insisted, 'No. That reminds me too much of the British Raj and of my school days.'

Funnily enough, I made the dress code more formal. Because at one time Lintas had become a kind of kurta-pyjama place. People coming in chappals and so on. So client servicing people were asked to wear a tie, and directors had to wear a tie and a jacket. Creative still came in kurta-pyjamas and chappals, but when they went to client meetings, they had to wear at least shirts, trousers and shoes.

One of the first guidelines I laid down was that no one could attend any meeting without a pad and pen. This is a legacy from the theatre. If you don't write a detailed list of properties required, the unfortunate actor can open a drawer to take out a revolver and find it empty. (A shooting does take place, but this is backstage after the show!)

This simple rule was later formalised into the AQT diary, which I helped to brainstorm together with the brilliant team, Josie Paul and Neville D'Souza. AQT (pronounced 'act') is an acronym for Action of Quality on Time. It is an easy system designed to prioritise your plan of action and move it from words into energy. It helps you not just talk the talk...but walk the talk. In its physical shape, we designed it as a planner which helped the user to focus his daily tasks and complete them.

The biggest enemy of the important is the emotionally urgent.

What a person normally does is tackle the job that is urgent rather than important. (I believe the biggest enemy of the important is the emotionally urgent.) This often results in key work getting delayed or being rushed through at the last minute, with a resultant fall in quality. In its essence, the AQT system helps you get a grip on the future and puts you in charge of your destiny.

At Lintas, we used the internationally prescribed technique of the Strategy Review Board (SRB) to position brands. Every Thursday, without fail, the SRB assembled in the boardroom. There was me of course, as the Chief Executive. Then there were the Executive Creative Director, Kersy Katrak, the Client Service Head, Prem Mehta, and the Research Director, Pranesh Mishra. These were the permanent members. By invitation, we sometimes included the Media Director, Helen Anchan, and a top gun or two from Client Servicing and Creative.

Presenting to the SRB was the brand team. The discipline of the SRB required you to conduct at least two Focus Groups with target users, to arrive at a consumer insight. You had to then posit two or more positionings based on this insight. If you wanted you could also present prototype executions to illustrate each positioning. The brand team was given only half an hour to complete their presentation. You were not allowed to ramble. By the time you came to the SRB, your thinking and your ideas had to be clearly focussed. Not only about the advertising positioning but also about the marketing positioning.

The members of the SRB would then debate whether the consumer insight was on the ball. And secondly, which of the alternative positionings made more sense. As CEO, I played the role of the referee. Sometimes, the debate would get very heated and it was my job to blow the whistle. Many brand teams tried to avoid the SRB and rely on the infamous 'gut feel'. But unless you have years and years of experience, gut feel, being subjective, can be just a shot in the dark. The discipline of the SRB forced you to justify your hunches.

An added plus of SRBs was that clients were assured that they were in the hands of advertising and marketing seniors.

Unless you have years of experience, gut feel can be just a shot in the dark.

Often, we invited a 'Doubting Thomas' client to one of our sessions...And he came out of it a 'Reassured Thomas'.

I also noticed a distinct lack of professionalism around the agency. So I introduced a new 'professionalism by example'. Whenever I had to make a presentation, young executives would see the 'Old Man' burning the midnight oil, going through his rehearsal again and again. And even on the day of the big presentation, they would notice the Chief Executive handing out checklists to each person involved. Not only to those who were going 'onstage', but even to those who were manning the slide projectors and room lights.

But I soon realised that observing personal example would not affect more than a couple of dozen people who happened to be around me at the time. Therefore I decided that if we wanted Lintas to be a truly professional agency, we needed to have clearly defined goals.

So for the first time I believe, anywhere in the Lintas world, we started the MBO system (Management By Objectives) for our top dozen executives. Our head office told me this would never work in an advertising agency. Here I was aided by Farrokh Mehta who was an expert in the field. Farrokh has been in the theatre with me ever since school days. His goatee and his commanding presence is a familiar sight in the boardrooms of marketing companies and advertising agencies. Over a period of time, Farrokh trained more than 150 of our executives on how to visionise and plan their future. This exercise became much talked about in Lintas international circles and resulted in Farrokh travelling all over Lintas in Asia to inculcate the MBO system.

Funnily enough, when my predecessor, Gerson, had on and off mentioned introducing MBOs into Lintas: India, as Creative Director, I resisted it stoutly. I thought MBOs were handcuffs that didn't allow creative options. I realised how wrong I was when Farrokh explained that even a creative person needs to have a yardstick to measure his creativity. For instance, a senior creative director at Lintas had the following MBOs one year:

1. Win at least two awards at next year's Advertising Club Awards.

2. Fifty per cent of the department's creative work should be okayed by the client first-off (without revisions).

3. Hire and train two trainee copywriters and two trainee visualisers, so that they can be promoted to the next rank at the end of the year.

Although the MBO system sounds frighteningly complex, actually it's as simple as putting down what you want to achieve in concrete terms during the coming year. For example, my MBOs for 1982 read as:

1. Establish Lintas as a highly creative agency by (this is the tough part) creating six talked about campaigns.

2. Establish superiority of our television product by setting up our own video studio.

3. Reduce our overdues from sixty days to forty-five days by starting every client meeting with the Overdues Statement. (Bringing it upfront, instead of sliding it in at the end in an embarrassed fashion.)

We started off by introducing the MBO system for the managing committee, which was about nine people. Then we spread it to our operations committee of about twenty people. Then to our senior managers, which covered a hundred people. This clear statement of objectives with a plan of action enabled us to focus on where we wanted Lintas to be by the end of the year. I read somewhere that 'MBOs are like dreams with deadlines.' But the best thing about MBOs is that it gives the executive a chance to write his own destiny. In fact, I encouraged the linking of MBO performance to year-end appraisals and promotions. Together with AQT, it becomes your karma. Your AQT and your MBO are in your hands. They bring a hot focus to bear on your priorities and make you a more efficient, action-oriented executive. If only all government bureaucrats followed this, we would have real accountability.

MBOs are like dreams with deadlines.

On the humorous side, I remember an anonymous note that was popped into our suggestion box one day: 'MBO stands for Murder By Organisation.'

When I was Creative Director, I had always felt that my best creative people were handcuffed by the Levers philosophy of 'Play it straight. Play it simple.' They were always champing at the bit, dying to do something that would win awards. Sure, Lintas turned out some outstanding creative work in the 1970s like Liril, Standard Batteries, Four Square Kings and Mafco. But we needed a change of philosophy, which I outlined as: Put the proposition in the head and not in the headline.

Put the proposition in the head and not in the headline.

I also worked out the philosophy of the Ziegarnic Effect along with Cossy Rosario, who was our Copy Chief. Basically, this meant, 'Pitch your message at the right level of difficulty', a phrase that Gerson had brought back from London.

The Ziegarnic Effect intrigues the reader so much that he must read on. For example, the campaign we did for the Britannia biscuit, Orange Delight, simply said, 'Unpeel an orange'. This ungrammatical headline caused a lot of distress among the purists and they wrote furious letters to the editor of *Solus* (the Bombay Ad Club magazine). But the Ziegarnic Effect was in play, because it got people talking about the advertising. This was linked to the plus point of the product which was the orange flavour. And then capped by the brilliant film, made by Mubi Pasricha (née Ismail) with Naseeruddin Shah (in his early avatar) sleepwalking and muttering, 'Britannia Delight. Britannia Delight.'

Pitch your message at the right level of difficulty.

Further kudos came to Lintas when we launched *The Telegraph* newspaper in Calcutta, with a campaign that featured a phrase that entered the language. 'Unputdownable', it said. And another for Luxol Silk Wall Paint: 'When the vase is Ming, the walls are Luxol Silk.' And yet another prize winning campaign for The Village restaurant: 'The only five-star restaurant with more than five stars.' This implied that The Village was Bombay's only open-air restaurant, where you sat out under the stars.

It was breakthrough campaigns like these that began to earn Lintas a creative reputation. Mind you, by this time, Rediffusion and other small agencies were firing on all cylinders, but Lintas was the only one among the big five that was wedded to a creative cutting edge.

What we were afraid of at that time was that because of our new razzle-dazzle reputation, Levers would move a large percentage of its billings to its other less flamboyant club agencies, Thompsons and O&M. My job was to keep the strong bond between Levers and Lintas going, without allowing Levers to dominate our philosophy.

In the end, we managed to retain eighty per cent of the entire Levers billings and at the same time, we were able to attract giant accounts like Bajaj Auto and ITC. We also grew our older accounts like MRF from a few lakhs to several crores of rupees. Even the conservative Reckitt & Coleman upped their budget for Cherry Blossom Shoe Polish from five lakh rupees to fifty lakh rupees, thanks to the Ziegarnic Effect of the Cherry Charlie campaign. All this new business changed the Levers share of our billings from seventy-five per cent to thirty-five per cent.

When I began to run Lintas, I realised I was not only Chief Executive but I was also the Creative Director. Which was ridiculous. I could not give enough time to either job, and I thought, 'Damn! If we want to break out of the umbrella of Levers and become an agency in our own right, with our own personality, our own charisma…then the first thing I need to do is replace myself as Creative Director.'

So I looked around, and at that time, just as luck would have it, I found Kersy Katrak. Actually, I think these things have a lot to do with karma. Mind you, you've got to keep your eyes open. Kersy with his manicured beard, manicured mind and rotund voice, had built one of the most creative agencies this country has ever seen — MCM (Mass Communications & Marketing) — but he was currently at a loose end. A few years before, he had gathered together an array of very exciting talent. Just to give you an idea, he hired Ravi Gupta, who went on to establish Trikaya. He had Arun

Nanda, who formed Rediffusion. He had Mohammed Khan, who started Enterprise. So, in a sense, Kersy gave birth to three agencies that were outstanding in the 1970s and 1980s. But I'm pleased that the father of them all, Kersy, got his early training at Lintas in the 1960s. So in an upside-down way, Lintas is the grandfather of them all!

Kersy was available because, unfortunately, his agency MCM had closed down due to poor management of funds. He had sort of retired to the hills, but when he came back to Bombay he met me. He was an old friend, and in some ways I was a father figure to him when he was doing dramatics at St Xavier's College and later at the Theatre Group of Bombay. He said to me, 'I'm looking around for some sort of money earning, bread winning opportunity.' I asked him, 'Kersy, can you run some courses for Lintas in creativity? I find my people are stuck. Stuck in a kind of proposition-oriented advertising. Boring stuff. You know, "Surf washes whitest", "Sunlight washes white and bright" and so on and so forth ad nauseam. I want us to get out of this.'

'But that's the kind of stuff Levers wants. They want it said upfront,' he replied. I said, 'I believe in communication that intrigues and provokes. Messages that state the obvious are rarely remembered. Can you help create ads that tease and tickle consumer participation?' 'You're on,' he said to me.

Kersy ran a dozen workshops or so. At that time, we had a transit flat in Colaba where the workshops were conducted. I realised that it would be no use doing it in the agency. Phones would be ringing. People would have to answer them. They would get distracted. So I decided that six or eight creative people at a time would go across to this flat and spend the whole day with Kersy, who would stimulate them into thinking themselves out of the strait-jacket that they were in.

Very soon I began to see results. Headlines were now implicit, instead of explicit, and people began to enjoy writing at Lintas. In those days, although our copy had a snap, crackle and pop, our art side seemed to be dragging their butt. Our visuals tended to be very mundane. They were like illustrations to the headline. The headline and the visual have to work in synergy to create a flashpoint. Of course, sometimes we'd have brilliant visuals, like Liril, but then we'd have lousy copy like 'Come alive with freshness'. A boring kind of line.

Kersy went on to have outstanding assignments for the next six months, conducting similar workshops for O&M and even HTA. So I said to myself, 'Since Kersy vibes so well with my guys, why the hell don't I take him on full-time' I made him an offer that I thought he couldn't refuse. But he said, 'Alyque, you know I've retired to the hills.' So we worked out a deal, where he would go off for two months every year, but the rest of the time, he would spend stimulating Lintas. He would be a Creative Director of stimulation. And of head hunting for creative talent.

Because I realised that though Kersy may not be 'creative' creative any more, he was a great magnet. Once people heard that Kersy Katrak was the Executive Creative Director of Lintas, we began to attract a very fine array of talent. Very lively people like Ryan Menezes and Sanjay Sipahimalani, Adi Pocha, Sonal Dabral and Prasoon Pandey (who both came to us from NID) and a whole bunch of others including Josie and Neville.

How do you go about selecting the right kind of people for advertising? I'd say there's one Golden Rule: Anyone who has imagination and ideas is good material for our business. Anyone who's an accountant and just wants to deal with facts and figures, forget about.

With this guideline behind our hiring policy, Lintas was soon filled with people from various backgrounds. Poets, painters, film makers, theatre people, sculptors. Each of them excited about dealing with emotion and fantasy. And once they were hired, they were encouraged to continue with their art forms. A painter of fine art continued to paint fine art. We always encouraged hobbies that people were passionate about. Because advertising is a very demanding profession, I knew they'd burn out if they didn't have something they enjoyed, to transfer their thoughts and ideas to from time to time. To get away from advertising for a while so that they could return to it the next day, refreshed and recharged.

HRD is just jargon. What it really means is, 'Do people love their workplace?'

I said, 'This whole business is about head hunting and retention. We get the best people who are at the top of the IIM list. But they tend to hop across where the grass is greener. How do we retain them? We don't really have an HRD policy. I mean, Human Resource Development is just jargon. What it really means is, 'Do people love their workplace?' Do they love to come to the office and start work in the morning? Or in some cases, the afternoon, especially when you're dealing with creative madcaps. Is there a burning desire, an urgency, to create ideas, to create brands?

So I started looking around for an HRD manager who knew the advertising business. And I found a guy who was very keen. He was in O&M Calcutta at the time. Sumit Roy wanted an opportunity to switch from client servicing, and I said to him, 'Come aboard.' That was my favourite expression, 'Come aboard'. (I got it from Humphrey Bogart in *The Caine Mutiny Court Martial.*) Of course, it's not as if everybody came aboard. Some did and some didn't. Mohammed Khan, for instance, was one who didn't. I knew Mohammed was unhappy at Contract, but I didn't realise that he was about to start his own agency.

Anyway, I said to Sumit, 'I don't want the usual HRD stuff. I want everyday to be a really stimulating day for our employees. A fun day.' We developed lunch time stimulation sessions, where we'd invite people like Satyadev Dubey from the theatre or Nissim Ezekiel on art and poetry. We would invite anyone from anywhere who had new ideas to feed into the group. It could be on economics. It could be on sex. It could be on philosophy, literature, anything.

Anyone could attend, but fifteen was the maximum number allowed. We'd be having sandwiches and a soft drink. Beer wasn't allowed. Beer was okay in the evenings, but not during office hours. Each session was a free-for-all. You could choose to agree or disagree with the speaker. Sumit would act as the facilitator. He guided the discussion if it went off track, and occasionally, if somebody went on and on, he'd say, 'Thank you very much. But we really must give someone else a chance.'

There were all kinds of things we did to build up solidarity. We decided to invest in a cricket team. And we had a damn good bunch. The first year we entered the CAG Shield, we won. We also encouraged our people to come to the field and cheer.

Another thing we did was to try and turn Lintas into a recreation club. So we put up a table-tennis table in the lift lobby. After office hours, if you were waiting for an artwork or whatever, you could play a fast paced game or two. We had darts competitions, and also a video club. Long before anyone really thought of it, we used to have video movies and discussions thereafter, with a little beer and chips. We even had a billiards table. Can you believe that? A billiards table in Lintas, occupying a sizeable piece of very expensive real estate! We had carrom and cards. But we had to stop cards, because it became a gambling den after a while! Above all, we believed that our people should be enjoying themselves physically and mentally at the Lintas club.

We did up the lobby so that it looked like it was an advertising agency, not a bank. In Express Towers, you sometimes had to wait helluva while for the lift to arrive. A lot of our clients used to say, 'Alyque, we hate to come and see you, because to get up and down takes ages.' So we put a VCR and TV set on the lift landing, playing all the latest commercials from abroad from Clio and Cannes festivals. People love to see foreign commercials. Remember, these were the days before the satellite TV boom. In fact, this worked so well, that when the lift arrived, I'd say, 'Don't you guys want to get in?' and they'd say, 'No, no. We must see the end of this terrific commercial.'

We encouraged people to do up their individual cabins. Put up posters, anything. Somebody wanted to hang up a doll. Fine. Somebody wanted to stick pins in the doll. That was also fine. We even had a graffiti board, where you could put up any damn thing you liked, write messages, sometimes rather rude in fact. So there was a certain devil-may-care atmosphere about the place.

Outsiders also began talking about our training methods. This was an area where Sumit was especially useful. I think one of the most rewarding statements ever made was by a young account executive. He came in as a trainee and after a couple of years, he wanted to leave us for a fine job abroad. Usually, Lintas people didn't leave to join other agencies. They either left to go to marketing companies or they went overseas. He said to me, 'I'm very sorry to leave Lintas.'

And I replied, 'Well, I'm flattered to hear that, but tell me what Lintas has done for you.' He said, 'AP, Lintas has increased my net worth, my market value.' 'In what way?' I asked. 'Before I came to Lintas, I *thought* I knew what advertising was. Now I'm sure I know. But more importantly, I'm a better presenter. I'm a better thinker. I'm a better listener. And I understand concepts better. And people around me say, "What a change in two or three years. You are now on the fast track."'

As MD, I realised I didn't really want an office. I wanted a drawing room. I think best in a drawing room or bedroom. It would have been a bit much having a bedroom in an ad agency, because the models who came for interviews may have got the wrong idea that it was the casting couch! So I created a drawing room with an armchair. I had a bad back, and I had heard that President Kennedy used a rocker for his back ailment. So I had a rocker made, and even today I sit on that same chair. Of course, the wags came up with 'AP is off his rocker. Watch out!' and corny quips like that.

But it was a different way of looking at an office environment. When we were renovating the office and spending quite a bomb, the first thing I wanted was a video workshop studio where we'd be able to shoot, edit, everything. So we bought expensive TV equipment, and were the only agency to set up full editing and shooting facilities in-house. I knew television was just round the corner, commercial TV that is. I was right, and by God, we got a head start. Every year, Lintas won five out of the top ten TV awards. Not so many press awards, but always for TV.

At the time we were renovating, I also felt that there was a lot of noise in the agency. So I said to Kersy, 'Listen, we must have a room where people can go and brainstorm in slience.' Every cabin or cubicle had three or six people talking at the top of their voices. 'Isn't there some kind of oasis that we can build? Especially now that we're making handsome profits and I have the budget.'

Kersy thought about it and he came back and said, 'What about a Zen room? A stark white room. People take off their shoes when they come in, and total silence is observed. There'll be mattresses to sit on, with cushions so that they'll be comfortable. But no other furnishings and everything is white. The walls are white, the mattresses and cushions are white. They just sit there and meditate. Think. Anything. Sexy thoughts, whatever. As long as they're silent.'

I bounced the idea around a few of my senior executives and they said, 'Kersy is crazy.' I said, 'Good. That's why I hired him. We will do it.' And we did. For many years, creative people who joined Lintas said, 'That white room. The meditation room. That's pure genius.' Later on, sad to say, with further renovation, it disappeared.

Another thing I realised as early as 1982 was that though we were making profits, we were paying most of it as tax. Believe it or not, we were paying ninety-three per cent tax on our profits. Now what's the point of working, you may well ask, when you get only seven rupees out of every hundred you earn? But those were the good old Indira Gandhi days, when you taxed everyone who was already paying up, but never taxed anyone who was really supposed to pay and never did.

So I went to my American shareholders.

'Listen, it's silly just making profits and paying so much tax. Why don't we invest the money instead? And when times are good, we'll reap rich rewards.'

'What do you want to do?'

'I want to buy flats. In Bombay nobody is willing to rent

you space, because of the iniquitous Bombay Rent Control Act. We're finding it difficult to hire good managers because we've got no place to house them.'

'Are you crazy?'

I've always been asked this question, 'Are you crazy?' The phrase has followed me throughout my life.

My Regional Director told me I was crazy and that our international bosses would never allow it.

'Advertising agencies are supposed to be in advertising, not in the real estate business.'

'Yeah, I want to stay in advertising. So I've got to have premises, otherwise I can't get good people. No good people means no new clients. No new clients means no growth. And soon we'll be out of the advertising business. QED.'

He understood this logic, and said, 'Okay, we'll give it a try.' We bought one flat in the first year, two in the second, three in the third. Thereafter, every year we aimed to buy at least two or three flats out of our profits. And by the time I left Lintas, I think we had bought about twenty flats. We bought them for two lakhs, four lakhs, six lakhs, the highest we went up to was ten lakhs. Today, those flats are worth crores of rupees. This was a good investment because we were able to hire excellent people and unlike any other agency, we could provide them accommodation.

I also realised that if you want to attract good people, you have to start winning awards. And if you wanted to be noticed in the marketplace too, you would have to start winning awards. But I was quite clear that we would do creative advertising as long as it sold the product.

So we began an award-winning drive. At first we only won awards where we had no demanding clients, like for public service advertising. But gradually, we began to win for product advertising as well. Our approach was, 'Don't tell it like it is. Tell it like it isn't.'

Don't tell it like it is. You didn't show a girl having a **Tell it like it isn't.** bath in the bathroom, which in the old days Levers would have insisted on. You showed her having a bath under a waterfall. Crazy. Absolutely crazy. Which middle-class housewife ever has a bath under a waterfall?

Gradually we began to get into what I call the provocative and entertaining area of advertising. Lots of Lintas commercials had a repeatability. You could watch them again and again. They had high emotional content independent of the story. So the 'wear-out factor' doesn't come into play. Many commercials are great on first viewing but become boring once you know the story. On repetition they wear out their welcome.

At that time, Lintas had a very small Calcutta operation, where we handled just a couple of brands. Reckitt & Coleman, British Paints and one or two small accounts. And we had a Madras office that handled Ponds and MRF. Bombay, of course, was huge, because Levers was here. And in the past we never felt the need to invest outside Bombay. I thought, 'There must be expansion. We can't be just a single city agency, with some post office kind of branches. They must be full service agencies.'

I started with Calcutta. We sent a Creative Director there, we sent servicing people, we made a lot of investments, and Calcutta began to show signs of growth. We did the same in Madras, and then we said, let's go after Delhi. We tried two or three times and failed, failed, failed. Finally we hit it right.

We sent this IIM graduate Atul Sharma to grow our shop in Delhi. He was followed by Jayant Bakshi. And they did a super job, so Delhi began to expand. One of the problems why Delhi didn't grow as fast as we would have liked is because clients kept saying, 'We don't want your small hole-in-the-wall agency with just one writer and a couple of art directors. We want the giant force that works on Levers. So we'll place our business with Lintas: Bombay, thank you very much.'

To change this attitude, I sent one of our top creative teams, Neville and Josie. (Kersy had picked them up from O&M, where they were languishing. They came to Lintas and they thrived.) I sent them to Delhi and told them, 'You show them what Lintas: Bombay creative is all about. You train them.' After three to four months, I began to see the Delhi work shine. I then did the same for Calcutta and Madras, and gradually clients began to say, 'Yes. The creative product of Lintas is pretty much tops all over.'

One of the problems we had was the 'Alyque Padamsee Syndrome'. Since I was so closely identified with Lintas: Bombay, people would say, 'Yeah, it's all very good. But you don't have Alyque here.' So I began to build up people. Atul Sharma, followed by Jayant Bakshi, who became stars in the Delhi advertising firmament. Stanley Pinto was already a Big Daddy in Calcutta. And after Stanley left, we built up Pranesh Mishra.

In Madras, we didn't get the equation right for a long time. We tried several experiments, all of them unsuccessful. Then we got Asit Mehra. And he gave Madras some clout. But hardly had we done that, than we realised that he was too valuable to expend on Madras, so we brought him to Bombay. And replaced him in Madras with Shavak Srivastava.

After that we decided to open an office in Bangalore because Lipton had moved from Calcutta and Britannia was about to do the same. Plus Levers' Animal Feeding Stuffs division moved there too. Now, I was always keen on smart office surroundings. When Bangalore was opened by Faizal Ahmed, it looked as good if not better than Lintas: Bombay. Then we started attracting all sorts of big clients. Brooke Bond, Timex Watches, and a number of others. Soon Bangalore became our second largest office.

But in spite of all this expansion, at the end of the day, Bombay is Bombay, just like Madison Avenue is Madison Avenue. Seventy-five per cent of the total advertising billing in the country is generated out of one town. So it was very important that in our expansion drive, we didn't forget Bombay. And one of the experiments we came out with was the idea of having a Bombay 1 and a Bombay 2.

This was based on the concept of 'Small is beautiful' because small is effective. Clients had started to complain, 'Lintas: Bombay is huge, and

Small is beautiful because small is effective.

if I want to meet the top man, I've got to wait for Alyque Padamsee to be free.' I decided to decentralise power. So I turned Lintas: Bombay into two agencies, Bombay 1 with its own MD and Bombay 2 with its own separate MD. And I gave each of them a Creative Director. So there was no need to refer all the time to me or to Kersy, who became the National Creative Director. This also gave people a chance to grow. Now there were two Creative Director positions you could aspire to in Bombay. Subsequently, I expanded this idea and added Bombay 3 and Bombay 4.

You must realise that in the 1980s Lintas: Bombay was so enormous that it was twice the size of HTA Bombay and had on its roster of clients practically every product category under the sun. That's why we needed to open Karishma, our second agency, to mop up any business where Lintas had a conflict. But I must admit Karishma never achieved the charisma of Big Brother Lintas. It remained a small agency. So I brainstormed with my able lieutenant Prem Mehta.

We realised that clients wanted the Lintas name and clout. They were not willing to go to Karishma because they didn't see it as a Lintas brand. So in the 1990s, we decided to set up yet another agency, this time called SSC&B-Lintas. (SSC&B was an earlier incarnation of Lintas: International.) This agency, unlike Karishma, had the advantage of the Lintas brand name. But an agency is only as good as its founder, in its early stages. We looked around within Lintas and discovered that the brightest brain we had, particularly in marketing and positioning, was the thoughtful, quiet Ajay Chandwani. He was heading Bombay 4 at the time.

What we did was break Bombay 4 away from Lintas: India into a completely new agency. We gave them a spanking new office in what was at that time a rather downmarket area of Bombay — Lower Parel. In order to make it sound appealing, I jokingly renamed it 'Upper Worli'. Which caused a wag in the press to quip, 'After Lintas has finished naming brands, they're now renaming localities of Bombay, in a bid to make them upmarket.'

Within a few years, SSC&B managed to carve a nice niche for itself. They have built up a formidable reputation among clients as well as advertising award juries around the world. They even compete with Big Brother Lintas for accounts. Clients are much more willing to call SSC&B Lintas for a pitch than to call in Karishma. So the strategy seems to be working.

Back in the 1980s, Lintas had begun to move up the ladder. From number five to number four to number three to number two and finally we were neck and neck with HTA for the number one slot. We had a look at our figures and realised that we were suddenly ahead of HTA in advertising billings. In fact, in the year 1987, *Advertising Age* put us at number one. So we came out with this ad which we thought would be good fun. It said, 'After turning so many of our clients into number one, we've finally joined them.' I enjoyed that hugely. But I don't think Mike Khanna enjoyed it half as much as I did.

Little did we realise that Mike and his team would react so strongly. They felt they were number one, and it was one of those mathematical things. They added up the billings of IMRB (Indian Market Research Bureau) to their HTA billings, which I thought was rather unfair. I said, 'Wait a minute. We're talking about advertising billings only, and our advertising billings are bigger than yours.' But they said, 'No, IMRB is a part of HTA.' I said, 'But IMRB is even handling conflicting clients to HTA. So you're talking about two different things. It's putting apples and oranges together and then saying, "We have more fruit than you." I am saying we have more advertising billings than you.'

The press, of course, had a field day. And for the first time, the media began to view advertising as an industry important enough to report on. Today, all business newspapers and magazines run at least one article or more on advertising. In fact, there are now even magazines wholly dedicated to the advertising profession like *A&M, The Brief* and supplements like *Brand Equity* and *Brand Wagon,* and others.

Two things resulted from this controversy. First, Lintas had never been seen as a number one or even a number two agency.

That immediately changed. We acquired a whole new status in the eyes of clients. We had repositioned ourselves. The second thing that happened was HTA woke up. It was forced on to the fast track and suddenly began to act like a number one agency. In fact, Mike Khanna later told me this jolt did HTA a world of good. (Obviously, what I didn't tell him was that though our billings were running neck and neck, our profits were running ahead of theirs by more than a 100 per cent!)

Another interesting factor was, on a paid up capital of only three lakh rupees, Lintas achieved a billing of Rs. 200 crores. That capital to turnover ratio was probably one of the best in the world. Certainly better than any Indian company, including marketing and manufacturing firms. Plus we had purchased twenty-one flats. What's more, we had achieved our Rs. 200 crores with just 600 people, whereas HTA had almost 1,100. So I felt that we were the Numero Uno in more ways than one.

In 1989, I was reminded that it was the fiftieth year of Lintas in India. So we decided that this was a good opportunity to fly the Lintas flag and further raise our image. We were tops creatively, our profits were up, and our morale was high. We needed to add a bit of vintage.

Going gold should be a sign of profit, not just age.

So we coined the slogan, 'Lintas goes Gold'. This was a double-edged slogan because it was also in tune with my intention of Lintas being the number one company in the country in terms of profits. Going gold should be a sign of profit, not just age.

So we had a lively string of celebrations. We took out a special supplement in *The Times of India,* covering all our achievements over the past fifty years. We spent several lakhs to create a campaign to raise the status of women, entitled the 'Second Freedom Movement'. We had a grand party at the

Oberoi Hotel, where there were lifesize cut-outs of our famous characters like Lalitaji, the Liril girl and Cherry Charlie, which you could put your head through and click a photograph. We even invited the entire Board of Directors of Lintas: Worldwide to hold their quarterly review meeting in India. And we held an International Symposium on Public Service Communications in Delhi with Prime Minister Rajiv Gandhi as the keynote speaker.

The climax of our Golden Jubilee celebration was getting the windows of Express Towers (the headquarters of our agency in Bombay) to light up with the letters:

'L-I-N-T-A-S G-O-E-S G-O-L-D.'

Dull ads (and dull ad agencies) finish last.

THERE IS NO FREE LUNCH

*W*hen Richard Nixon was President of the USA, he once said, 'There's no such thing as a free lunch.' Meaning that someone had to pay for the free lunches that were being given to children in American schools. And that someone was the American taxpayer. My interpretation of 'There's no free lunch' means that corporates who make a profit out of society must put a little of those profits back into society.

In that sense, the Tata Group is an excellent company. Always thinking of public welfare. Not by giving handouts, but by motivating people. Whether it's the Tata Institute of Fundamental Research, the Tata Institute of Social Sciences or the Dorabji Tata Trust. The Tatas always seem to be aware that they have certain responsibilities to society and they often take the lead.

There are other companies that also donate to charities in India. And the Birlas are famous for that. There are also companies like MRF. If today we have pace bowlers in this country, it's thanks to a man called Ravi Mammen. He felt that cricket was in the doldrums, and as a young tycoon inheriting a huge conglomerate, he decided he would establish a Pace Bowlers' Foundation. So he roped in one of the world's all-time fast bowlers, Dennis Lillee, to come to India and train our boys. And after a few years, it started turning out a whole slew of fast pace bowlers. Even Sri Lanka is grateful to the MRF Foundation. (But our Indian batsmen aren't!)

Britannia is another company that has always been at the forefront of public service activities. They started with the Britannia Children's Film Club, where they supported the

Children's Film Association of India by subsidising movie tickets for kids. They then went on to set up the Britannia-Amritraj Tennis Foundation to hone tennis talent in the country. (Say thank you, Leander Paes.)

But I often feel that not enough is done by our advertising fraternity. Since we have developed skills in mass communication, we should be at the forefront of changing attitudes. From awareness comes change, as we know. Why should we only motivate people to change from using charcoal to using toothpaste? We can use our skills to make people change their attitudes about other things as well. For instance, why can't we try to improve the status of women in India? Work with the *mahila mandals,* give them of our time, and our experience in the area of motivation.

This struck me very forcibly when I was the Chief Executive of Lintas. I realised that I now had the power to do something. I said to myself, 'How rewarding if I could convince our board of directors to pitch in a little money, a lot of talent and Lintas' time, energy, thought, ideas and execution to help public service organisations.'

Around that time, a circular came from UNESCO that announced that the International Year of the Child was coming up and they'd welcome any contribution in terms of ideas on communications. So I sat down one night and thought that our future belongs to our children. But what kind of future are we building for them? And slowly, a thirty-second script began to form in my mind.

The film opens on an egg in an eggcup, a hand enters the frame and attaches a long wire to the eggcup, and then unravels the wire and attaches it to a small detonator. The background music is children singing a popular song, 'All things bright and beautiful, all creatures great and small...' As it reaches a crescendo, a man's finger presses down the plunger on the detonator. Cut back to the egg, which is blasted to smithereens, blown all over the landscape. A voice-over says, 'Is this the future we want for our children? Think.'

A very simple film. This was the early 1980s, when the Cold War was at its peak. And there was talk of the cold war becoming a hot war, with nuclear holocaust about to descend upon us.

When I discussed the film and my idea of Lintas getting into public service with the board of directors, they agreed with me. After all, the company was doing quite well profits-wise. But were we contributing anything to public service? Yes, we did write a cheque to our favourite charities from time to time, but was that enough?

So I got the approval to shoot the film, and we arranged to have it telecast free of charge on Doordarshan. The response we got was encouraging. When the following year UNESCO declared the International Year of the Disabled, we felt that we must do another public service film.

We came up with a film called *The Story of Hope*. Once again, a very simple script. It opens on the hand of a little girl drawing on a slate with a piece of chalk. She draws a stick figure, complete with head, hands and legs, and says out loud, 'This is my Daddy.' Then she draws another similar figure and says, 'This is my Mummy.' She finally draws a slightly smaller figure and says, 'And this is me.' Then she thinks for a moment, wets her finger and erases one of the legs. 'No. *This* is me.' And the voice-over says, 'The disabled don't need your pity. They need your understanding.' This film was voted into the Clio Hall of Fame (the Oscars of world advertising). It was produced by Kailash Surendranath who also pioneered the Liril film.

The idea was based on a consumer insight that came from my habit of watching the way people behave. From childhood, I noticed that whenever a child was introduced as disabled, everyone would go, 'Tsk. Tsk Tsk.' It was horribly demeaning for the child on the receiving end. Pity is a humiliating experience. It destroys confidence.

Pity is a humiliating experience. It destroys confidence.

I realised that we needed to undermine this dreadful Indian pity or *bechara* syndrome. And this was the film that did it. More importantly, it opened people's eyes to the fact that they shouldn't take life just as they see it. But do a little more deep thinking.

This led to a whole series of public service films that we did at Lintas. There was one on family planning about tomatoes in a bottle. The film opens on an empty glass jar and a hand enters the frame and puts a tomato into it. Then a second tomato is put on top of the first and the jar is almost full. And then a third tomato is put on top of the second, but it won't fit. So the hand brings the lid and presses it down on to the tomatoes to force them into the jar. At this point, the camera zooms in to the tomatoes as they burst and splatter into a red gooey mess. The voice-over says, *'Ek ya do bas.'* (One or two. That's enough.) This thirty-second film was directed by Madhu Gadkari.

It makes a tremendous impact on the audience, because it's the last thing they expect to happen. Up until they end, they probably think it's a film for tomato ketchup or something like that. It's the Hitchcockian technique of an innocent object on screen being destroyed in a very brutal and shocking manner.

The film was researched with urban as well as rural audiences and returned with very positive results. Everyone got the message that it was indeed a film about family planning. Even the village folk responded that if you have too many children they would get damaged. It was also voted the most powerful public service film in Asia by the Japanese television authorities, and won Clios, awards at Cannes and elsewhere. It's interesting to note Lintas was winning international awards in the early 1980s, more than fifteen years ago.

But award-winning is not the name of the game. The name of the game is motivating people to change their attitudes. So when Lintas was celebrating its golden jubilee amidst parties and supplements in *The Times of India,* as I said earlier, we decided that we would set aside some money to improve the status of women, since our country is notorious for giving women short shrift.

The name of the game is motivating people to change their attitudes.

When we sat down to brainstorm, we asked ourselves, 'How can we get the general television public to examine how badly women are treated in India?' We came up with a series of four films.

The first one was aimed at the father of the bride. Where a father gets a guilt complex about his conduct: refusing to take his daughter back into his house when her in-laws are ill-treating her. The second one repositioned the 'traditional' *saas* or mother-in-law, who thinks that she is the benefactor of the *bahu.* The third examined a father's attitude towards his daughter getting a job. And the fourth showed how badly a husband treats his wife.

In each of these films, we used a consumer insight to illustrate the point we wanted to make. We were trying to tackle attitudinal problems by rethinking the premises they are based on. I've often said that there are no problems. There is only a lack of ideas in the solution area. What was needed was to take a fresh look at our value system.

There are no problems. There is only a lack of ideas in the solution area.

Communalism, for instance. One of the films we did had the camera panning on a number of newly born babies in a hospital. The accompanying voice-over says, 'Will your child grow up to be a Hindu?' The camera pans to the next baby. 'A Muslim?' The camera keeps panning. 'A Christian?', 'A Sikh?', until it stops at the last baby in the row. 'Or will your child grow up to be an Indian?' The film was accompanied by a hoarding with five or six newborn babies in the picture. The headline read, 'Don't open their eyes to differences they can't see.' This line was fashioned by Anita Sarkar who, with the contemplative Madhu Gadkari, formed a creative task force with me that produced fifty per cent of our award-winning ideas.

Then there was traffic safety. One of our trainees at that time, Adi Pocha (who now runs Script Shop), came up with a knockout idea. The film opens on two coconuts and two strong men holding hammers in their hands. A crash helmet is put over one of the coconuts. All of a sudden, wham! The hammers slam down on the coconuts. The first coconut immediately splits in two, while the hammer bounces harmlessly off the one that is protected by the helmet. The voice-over simply says, 'It's your head. Use it.'

After a while Lintas began to build up a reputation as an agency that was concerned about social issues. So one day the then Municipal Commissioner of Bombay, Jamshed Kanga, said to me, 'Alyque, we are having a terrible problem in the monsoons with sugarcane juice vendors. Because of the flies, this lovely cooling juice is leading to a large number of cases of dysentery, cholera, typhoid and jaundice. Can you ask the public to stop drinking sugarcane juice from street vendors?'

My first reaction was, 'Jamshed, why don't you get your municipal inspector to stop issuing licences?'

'These vendors are not licensed.'

'Then why aren't they behind bars for selling something that's injurious to the public?'

'Yes, that's what we intend to do, but we don't have the manpower yet. In the meantime, it would be helpful if you tell the public to stop drinking sugarcane juice.'

'I will not tell the public to stop doing anything. The government of India is full of messages saying, "Don't drink", "Don't fornicate", "Don't do this", "Don't do that". Nobody offers an alternative. As far as I'm concerned, I won't say "don't". Don't is a dirty word. But I will try and motivate the public so that they themselves will not feel like drinking sugarcane juice.'

We thought through the problem and came up with a simple documentary-type film. It opens on a sugarcane juice vendor with his trusty, rusty old machine, squeezing the sugarcane through the rollers. The camera zooms in for a close-up and in addition to the juice trickling down onto the galvanised plate, we see the rustiness of the whole thing and the dirt. We also hear the sound of flies buzzing. The buzzing gets louder and louder as the juice runs down into the glass which is being held by the vendor. He gives the glass to the customer who in turn takes out a rupee coin and hands it to him. (At that time, a glass of sugarcane juice cost just a rupee!) As the customer raises the glass to his lips, the frame freezes. And a voice says, 'For only one rupee a glass, you can buy jaundice, cholera, typhoid, dysentery.'

There was nothing about 'Don't do this' or 'Don't do that'. A lot of people said, 'Well, you know. It's a bit subtle and all that. Why don't you say "Sugarcane juice is dangerous to drink" or something like that.' But I was firm. 'No. I trust that people are intelligent enough to get the message.'

And this is one instance where I can say with hand on heart that our public service message worked hundred per cent. A couple of weeks after the film had been screened in all the cinema halls of Bombay (free of charge by Blaze Advertising), my secretary came running into my office shouting, 'AP, there's a morcha outside Lintas! They want to speak to you.'

'A morcha? What the hell is going on?' I asked.

I went out and the leader came up to me and said, in typical *Bambaiya* Hindi, 'I am the head of the Sugarcane Vendors' Association. You have destroyed our trade. Business is down by eighty per cent.' (I didn't believe him.) 'We want you to withdraw that film immediately.'

'I'm sorry. I can't.'

'What do you mean you can't? We'll *gherao* you till you do it.'

'It's not my film. It belongs to the Bombay Municipal Commissioner. You can *gherao* him all you like. I'll even tell you where his office is.'

So off they rushed. There must have been a hundred of them or so. And I believe they *gheraoed* my good friend,

Jamshed. And he called me up saying, 'Alyque, for God's sake, how do we stop that film?'

'Hey, wait a minute. You were the guys who wanted the film.'

'Yes, but I didn't want to ruin their trade. Besides, they're saying it's unfair. Why don't we talk about the *bhelpuriwallahs* and others?'

'Well, it's symbolic of consuming any open foodstuff.'

'Look, they don't understand all this symbolism. All they understand is that buisness is down and they're starving. So let's declare a temporary truce. Can you give instructions for the film to be suspended for the time being? I need to think this through and see when we can restart it.' Sometimes you can be too effective for your own good.

The fact that you're doing something for other people without any ulterior motive is in itself enriching.

Since we were doing so many public service films, year after year, we formalised Lintas' public service cell into SOMAC (Social Marketing Communications) run by the dedicated and personable Gulan Kripalani. And although it's been quite a few years since I left Lintas, SOMAC is still something that I hold very dear. I hope it goes on as long as Lintas goes on and even beyond. Because it is an idea in itself which is even bigger than advertising. It is communication for improving the quality of life. Not only materialistically, not only ecologically, but spiritually as well. Just the fact that you're doing something for other people without any ulterior motive is in itself enriching.

These days I find a lot of public service advertising that is not well thought out. It leads me to feel that perhaps the creators of these ads are not serious about their subject. Any advertising, even the public service kind, must have a unique consumer insight to motivate the target group into action. It cannot be something that you pull out of your hat. It's not enough to just shock the public in the hope of picking up an award at the annual ceremonies.

My first involvement with public service communication actually had nothing at all to do with Lintas. It was a famine in Bihar, many years ago. When Jayaprakash Narayan was very active with the Sarvodaya Mandal, and had asked the public to contribute funds. I read in a newspaper article that Bihar traders were sitting on mounds of rice and wheat, whereas the rural poor were reduced to eating the bark of trees. It brought tears to my eyes. And I said, 'My God! What's the good of tears if I can't turn them into some kind of action?' And that is how I first got the idea of using emotional triggers for social service action.

I checked with my friend B C Dutt, who's a wonderful human being and helps run the charitable Yusuf Meherally Centre at Tara village, seventy kilometres from Bombay. 'Is the Sarvodaya Mandal above board and will the money be well utilised?' He gave it a clean chit. Then I wrote an emotional appeal to a thousand of my friends and acquaintances, telling them that Jayaprakash Narayan was raising funds for famine victims in Bihar 'who were eating the bark of trees'. We managed to get together about two and a half lakh rupees, which at that time was a lot of money. Just through a simple letter. People have big hearts. You've got to know how to unlock them. Incidentally, the newspaper article that motivated me was written by a young cub reporter for the

Indian Express, Teesta Setalvad, who is now a well-known social activist and a very dear and dedicated friend.

And this enthused and motivated me to get involved with the drought in Rajasthan some years later. Even my wife Sharon got interested and together we sent out a circular to our friends. And again we got an excellent response. But before we sent the money, we first did our homework and identified two organisations run by very motivated and honest people, who were doing excellent work out of Udaipur.

If you have the will, there is no dearth of areas in which you can get involved in public service activities. An important need arose in 1992-93 during the Bombay riots following the demolition of the Babri Masjid. Bombay was literally set on fire. The minority community was attacked and many of them were left homeless. The police were unable or unwilling to do anything.

Fortunately twenty or thirty citizens' groups sprang up to offer relief to the victims. Among them were Titoo Ahluwalia's 'Citizens For Peace', the Governor's 'Peace Committee' and Shabana Azmi's 'Nivari Haq'.

Even high society ladies — I won't say in their silk saris and high heels, but certainly in their cotton saris and chappals — were actually delivering food and medicines to the injured, at great risk to their lives. This restored my faith in the westernised elite of the city who I always thought would never get involved in anything other than kitty parties. They could easily have rested safe and secure in their Malabar Hill mansions and pretended that nothing was going on, but they swung into action.

C Subramaniam, who was the Governor of Maharashtra at that time, took the initiative, and watchdog committees were formed to patrol the neighbourhoods to see that rioters didn't enter these areas. Call it self-protection, call it vigilante committees. But at least the upper class were down in the streets and not up in their air-conditioned bedrooms.

It was an example of public spiritedness in action. Not since the Chinese attacked India in 1962 had I seen such an attitude which transcended all castes, religions, and rich and poor barriers. People worked as one. And I do give some of the credit to the mass media, particularly the newspapers. They were wonderful in organising public opinion. Compared to television, which has usually done a very mediocre job.

Despite the tremendous influence that television has, it doesn't make its social voice heard loudly enough. It needs to speak up. We need more programmes on how people can help people. And particularly on how you can be a good neighbour. Good neighbourliness seems to be lacking in our society. Until there is a crisis like the Bombay riots or the Chinese invasion. Why can't it become a permanent part of our lives? Why can't we build it into our school curriculum, where we could encourage social service to become the highest form of human achievement?

During the riots, I served on the Governor's Peace Committee with other prominent Bombayites like Shabana Azmi, Kekoo Gandhi, Police Commissioner A S Samra, Cardinal Pimenta, the Sheriff, Mr Khorakiwalla, and many others. We put our heads together to try and figure out some way that we could send out a signal of hope to the minority community. Who was 'we'? We were the majority of citizens of Bombay who were not committed to communalism and certainly not to violence. How could we send out a sign that all of Bombay had not betrayed them?

Some suggested a peace march and a couple of us suggested forming some kind of a human chain. I said, 'Why don't we do a *Hands of Harmony* across Bombay? A human chain linked by hands, starting from Colaba (which is the southern most tip of Bombay) and going right up the island till Dahisar (which is about fifty kilometres away).' Everyone was enthusiastic but little did I know what I'd let myself in for.

As I've said earlier, an idea is only as good as its execution. So we got Dr Dhote who was the head of the Home Guards and other people like Maj. Gen. Eustace D'Souza to help us organise the whole event. We were keen on staging it on Republic Day, 26 January, 1993. But when we consulted with Dr P S Pasricha, who was the Commissioner of Police for Traffic, he advised us that it was too dangerous and said, 'If there's a violent incident, it will reflect badly on the Governor's Peace Committee. Can I ask you to postpone it by a fortnight?'

We decided that it would be best if we held it on a Sunday. Otherwise people at work might be unable to join in. We finally settled on Sunday, 14 February, 1993. The time was set for four o'clock in the afternoon. On the appointed day, we had thousands of volunteers wearing T-shirts bearing a *Hands of Harmony* logo, helping people form this winding human chain. Every hundred metres or so, we had a supervisor to help things go smoothly.

As planned, we started at the end of Colaba and went past R C Church, down to Regal cinema, Flora Fountain, Victoria Terminus, and from there onwards to Mohammed Ali Road. Now Mohammed Ali Road was one of the worst affected areas. Some people wanted to avoid it. But I was adamant. 'No, let us go into the areas where the minority community lives so that they know that someone else cares about them.'

So the chain went on and on and on, right up to Dahisar. Hindus, Muslims, Parsis, Sikhs, Christians, Buddhists, Jains, whoever. Total strangers holding hands just to show that Bombay was not dominated by only communalists and *goondas*. When the sirens blew, everyone linked hands and read out a pledge that we had prepared, and then sang the National Anthem together.

It was a most touching sight and it's a pity we didn't organise a helicopter to take aerial shots of the whole chain. When we went into the Muslim areas, we had ladies in burkhas coming down from their houses saying they hadn't been out in more than four weeks. Grown men had tears trickling down their cheeks, because somebody cared enough to risk his/her life to come out in the street and say, 'Listen, we are all brothers. We don't hate you.'

The following year, Mr Khorakiwalla came to me and said, 'What should we do to commemorate the *Hands of Harmony* Day?' And I said, 'Why don't we do a *Hands of Harmony Across India*?' Now this was a really tall order. Monstrously tall. But in my typical fashion I had shot off my mouth and now I had to live up to it.

So Mr Khorakiwalla and I literally travelled the length and breadth of India, trying to mobilise resources. We decided that we'd stage it only in the capital cities of each of the twenty-five states and union teritories, and we'd try and work through an organisation that already existed so that we didn't have to build an infrastructure. We hit upon the Lions Club of India, and Shirish Nadkarni from the Lions of Bombay helped us enormously. He wrote to the various Clubs in each of the cities and we sent them detailed instructions on how to organise the event.

We went to Delhi and met Sitaram Kesri who was in charge of Human Resource Development at the time. We met Arjun Singh, and we met Sonia Gandhi, who was most gracious and gave us a lakh of rupees from the Rajiv Gandhi Foundation to help stage the event. We met the Prime Minister, Narasimha Rao, who picked up the phone and spoke to Doordarshan and All India Radio to help us publicise the event. I got Lintas to make some films and press ads to mobilise people all over the country.

We selected 30 January, being the death anniversary of Mahatma Gandhi, as the appointed day for *Hands of Harmony Across India*. We didn't aim for an unbroken chain, because that would have been impossible; but we did get an excellent response from people in the twenty-five capital cities. An estimated one million citizens took part across the country. We also got wide media coverage and scores of sympathetic letters poured in from all over. Which just goes to show that with a good cause and good core group, you can organise almost anything. This is a country where if the motivation is right, people do come forward.

When Mr Ali Yavar Jung was the Governor of Maharashtra, his wife started the Clean Cities movement, which is still active today. She said, 'It's terrible that all our foreign dignitaries drive from the airport and the first thing they see and smell are the *jhopadpattis* (slums) alongside the Western Express Highway. There's a wall running along the highway, so why don't we get a paint company to donate the paint and why don't we just paint the wall all white? It will look rather nice.'

And I told her, 'Madam, it's a great idea to paint the wall but I think white is not a very practical colour because within two spits of a paan, the wall will soon be red.' She agreed. She also discussed getting drainage for the slum areas to help reduce the stench and disease.

A Gandhian by the name of Shantibhai Shah who was also on the committee spoke up and said, 'Look, if you want any development in the slums, why don't you let me go in there and live with them for a month to find out their views. Then I'll come back and report to you.' So after a month, Shantibhai returned and said, 'The slum-dwellers do want drainage but the problem is the huts are built so close together that there is no space for the drain. However, I convinced them that since this is in their best interest they should move their huts back, each by a foot, so that you get a two-foot alleyway. And if the Society for Clean Cities is willing to donate the materials, they will build the drains themselves. They don't want you to come in. They want it to be their own drains.'

I was very struck by this incredible insight. So when the time came to paint the walls, I said, 'Why don't we get the slum-dwellers to paint the wall themselves? In any way they want. Let them express themselves. Let it be a colourful mural.' Then we got the JJ School of Art students to help the slum-dwellers. The slum-dwellers would tell the art students, 'Well, I want the sun here. I want to be reminded of the village in Rajasthan where I come from.'

At the end of it all, we had a mural which should have been entered in the Guinness Book of Records. As far as I can tell, it was the longest mural in the world. It stretched for kilometre upon kilometre. This wall was painted with all these wonderful things of what the slum-dwellers wanted on the walls. Not what we from Malabar Hill wanted.

It really was a delightful sight, driving to the airport and looking at this mural of village dances and the sun rising and sunflowers and marigolds and all sorts of things in bright cheerful colours. Unfortunately, it was not preserved because the monsoons in Bombay are very vicious, and after a couple of years, the whole thing fell into disrepair. And shame on me for not having the energy with the Society for Clean Cities to repaint the wall.

Having worked on several public service projects, my conscience began to prick me even more. I thought to myself, 'Yes, it's all very well to be in the communication business and to help with making public service television commericals, but have I really physically gone out of my way to help someone in distress?'

While this was running through my mind, I read in the papers about a case in Rajasthan where some dreadful atrocities had been performed on a lower-caste woman called Prakash Kaur. Her crime was that her son had dared to steal some money from the local mandir. So she had been dragged out of her house, stripped naked, blackened with tar and paraded around the village on a donkey, without a single villager raising a voice in protest. She was then taken outside the mandir and made to beg for forgiveness of the deity, which she refused to do. They beat her and beat her and because she was a stubborn woman, she refused to do their bidding. Finally after many hours of being mercilessly thrashed, she succumbed.

The All India Women's Association had taken up the case, but were making little headway with it. So I rang them up in Delhi and the lady in charge, Brinda Karat, said that they were doing all that they could. I asked if it would be of any help if I went down to the village and spoke to the husband and children of the deceased woman. Maybe I could get them an audience with the Chief Minister of the State. She agreed. So I told Sharon, 'It's time I myself stopped talking the talk and begin to walk the talk.'

The walk led me to Delhi from where I took a car and I drove with my nephew, the social activist Feisal Alkazi, to this little village in Rajasthan. When we arrived, we found it difficult to get hold of any witnesses. The Brahmins who had perpetrated this heinous crime had a deathlike grip on the villagers. They were all scared and no one was willing to give evidence.

As I was standing outside the mandir, some burly men came up to me. In my broken Hindi, I struck up a conversation with them.

'Isn't this a terrible crime?'

'Yes, it is. Imagine this little boy robbing money from the mandir and then on top of that, knocking down the *diya*.'

'Are you talking about that crime? I'm talking about the crime where they murdered this woman!'

'Oh that! Yes, that too is a crime, I suppose.'

That made me see red and I was about to get into a fierce argument when Feisal put a restraining hand on my arm to prevent me from losing the infamous Padamsee temper.

I then went to see Prakash Kaur's husband. He told me that he had been away from the village when the incident had occurred. But from what he had gathered it was true that his five-year-old son had stolen money from the mandir. Somebody saw him and shouted. Frightened, he started to run and his hand knocked over the *diya,* which went out. He then fled home and hid under the bed. The angry Brahmins gathered around his house and shouted for his father who was not there.

So the boy's mother went out. Prakash Kaur was a fiery woman who was not going to take any nonsense from a bunch of Brahmins. She told them to get lost. This incensed them, and they dragged her out of the house…and beat her to death. All the time, the little boy and his ten-year-old sister were hiding under the bed in terror.

When the husband returned to the village, he went to the police station to lodge a complaint. Intsead of taking down an FIR (First Information Report), they began to beat him with their lathis, saying, 'How dare you complain about this? You know very well that your wife died of a heart attack. She wasn't beaten by anybody.'

Shocked, I asked him if he would like to accompany me to meet the Chief Minister who, according to press reports, denied that any crime had taken place. He readily agreed and so we bundled him and his daughter into the car and took off for Jaipur. His son was put in the care of some relatives in another village.

We got an audience with the Chief Minister of Rajasthan, Bhairoñ Singh Shekawat. I said to him, 'I hope we can have some justice for this man and his family. I've got the Chief Reporter of *Indian Express* waiting for me to report your views, after the meeting.'

Shekawat realised the seriousness of the situation and gave us a patient hearing. At the end of it, he asked us what we wanted him to do. So I put the same question to Prakash Kaur's husband. Besides the obvious demand that the Brahmins should be tried for murder, he said, 'Well, the police officer who beat me up should be dismissed.' Shekawat had a chat with his Chief of Police who informed him that they couldn't dismiss the man, but they could have him transferred to a remote region. This is generally considered to be heavy punishment in the Indian government service.

Shekawat then asked what else we wanted. 'The second demand,' the husband said, 'is that since my daughter is frightened of living in this village, she wants to enter the Government Girls' Hostel in the neighbouring town and study there.' The CM said that it could be arranged. The third request the husband made was for a piece of land since he was a landless labourer. The CM said he would look into it and if there was any surplus government land to spare, he would certainly be happy to provide it.

It seemed like most of our terms were more or less met, and I was impressed with Shekawat and his decisive air of authority. We went out and related the proceedings to the *Indian Express* who published the story the following day. I returned to Bombay while Feisal went back to Delhi. A fortnight later, I called the All India Women's Association to find out how the case was progressing. They said they were running into lots of problems since no one was willing to bear witness. So I waited another six weeks before I rang up again.

The news was more and more depressing. No witnesses. No witnesses. No witnesses. No one was willing to give evidence against the powerful Brahmins. Eventually, after almost a year of following up regularly, it nearly broke my heart when a social worker from that village informed me that the husband had recapitulated, withdrawn his objections and was no longer filing charges against the Brahmins.

'How did this happen?' I asked, and they replied, 'You are very naïve. You don't understand village politics.' Apparently the Brahmins went to the husband and told him that he had two options. If he continued to press on with the case and the Brahmins were found guilty, they would go to prison. But after that they would hunt him down. Not only him, but his son, daughter and every member of his family, his brothers, sisters and even his cousins. The other option was, if he dropped the case, they would give him two lakh rupees with which he could buy a piece of land that the Government had still not given him. He would be able to educate his son and daughter, and, they added, he could even buy himself a new wife.

Imagine my shock. But somewhere in the back of my head, I realised that in a country like ours, to have real social justice, you would need to change the entire system from top to bottom. The husband realised that it was better to run away and live to see another day.

An NGO that I've been involved with for a number of years is Akansha. A simple but brilliant idea dreamed up by a young St Xavier's College student some years ago. While at college, Shaheen Mistry, whose slight form belies her iron will, decided that the most important thing children in slums were deprived of, was not food, not shelter, not clothing, not even television which they have, but education. And so she got together with a number of her friends and started this society called Akansha (meaning aspirations) to take slum children to nearby unused school classrooms and teach them the 'three Rs'.

Dreams do come true as long as you have the energy and a plan of action.

They got permission from the priests at Holy Name School to use their classrooms in the evenings. They then went to a slum at nearby Cuffe Parade and asked the slum-dwellers if they wanted to have their children educated. Those who were willing were transported by a hired bus at 4.00 p.m. to this school. For two hours, five days a week, Shaheen and her friends would teach the children how to read and write. And from humble beginnings of just twenty children in the first year at the Holy Name School, they've now grown to over 1,000 children in about twelve to fifteen schools. Dreams do come true as long as you have the energy and a plan of action.

There's an idea that's been running around in my head for quite a while now. And I've mentioned it on several occasions at various public platforms. It's my theory of second citizenship. What the hell is that? Well, your first duty as a citizen, of course, is in the time of war to help defend your country and in the time of peace to pay your taxes regularly. But other than that, your country asks very little of you.

Your second citizenship is what you owe to the community in which you live. Not just to donate money, but also to donate your time, energy and skills. It's not enough for us to get our bread and butter out of the community we live in. We need to go back to the words of the late US President, John F Kennedy, 'Ask not what your country can do for you. Ask what you can do for your country.' Every educated Indian should be duty bound to get involved with community service. Whether it's volunteering a few hours a week to help an NGO like National Association for the Blind or Spastics Society of India. Or organising a street committee to help keep your road clean. It is pretty clear that unless we citizens help each other, nothing is going to get done. Relying on government bodies to improve matters is like barking at the moon. In the words of a foreign journalist who spent six months in our country, 'India is a First World nation...with a Third World government!'

When Mrs Gandhi was assassinated, I was very upset. I went away to grieve at my weekend retreat in Alibag. I suppose that out of grief comes insight. I sat down and wrote the following lines:

'I am an Indian, not because I am a Hindu or a Muslim or a Sikh or a Christian or a Parsi or a Jew. I am an Indian because if I am not...who am I?'

I showed these lines to several people in the office and they felt that they were very apt for the hard times we were all going through, what with the Sikh riots in Delhi. So that year for the Lintas annual memento, we printed these lines on a small mirror and sent it out to clients, suppliers and other people who interacted with us.

In its own way, it was a message of communal harmony, because no matter what community you hail from or what religion you follow, as soon as you step out of the country, you are an Indian. And that is the only identification you have.

At Lintas, this was our little way of saying, 'We're not just in the business of advertising. We're in the business of motivating human behaviour through communication.' I am always gratified to find that small mirror sitting on desks in offices across the country, even after so many years.

Pubic service is actually private satisfaction.

Chapter 11

THE SOUND OF A
DIFFERENT DRUMMER

*W*hen the British left India in 1947, they left us more than just an excellent railway system and roads and some beautiful buildings. They also left us a legacy of language. And after Independence, there was a great need for Indians to use English. But at that time, anything that did not conform to the King's English was not accepted. It was considered bastardised English. So unless it strictly adhered to the Oxford Concise Dictionary, it was out.

Gradually, Indian novelists felt the need to use English in their own way. Not as an Englishman uses it, but in our own unique way. And this is not Hinglish, which is a fractured English or pidgin English. I'm referring to Indian English, in the same way as we understand American English or Australian English or even West Indian English. It is a language that takes certain colourations from our Indian vernacular and without murdering the English language, creates a new tongue of its own.

Indian English is a voice speaking in English but which is peculiarly Indian.

Indian English is a voice speaking in English but which is peculiarly Indian. R K Narayan's writing is a very good example of Indian English. And in poetry, there's the venerable Nissim Ezekiel who seems undernourished except when it comes to intellect. He has an Indian voice which writes in English, like our playwrights Partap Sharma with *Begum Sumroo* and Mahesh Dattani with *Tara* and *Final Solutions*. Each recreates the English language to suit his purpose. Not so much their choice of words but their sentence construction is uniquely Indian. For instance, ending sentences with 'no', as a question. 'You went to the cinema, no?', which is the equivalent of the Hindi, *'Aap cinema gaye the, na?'* It is a parochial English and it's what most Indians who imagine they speak the Queen's English actually speak.

My first brush with Indian English was a play I did in 1961 called *Bandra Saturday Night*. A group of Catholic students had a zonal competition every year in their parish. Where different groups put on plays.They got judges to come and decide which one was best. It was very popular in those days, and I think it still is in Catholic localities.

One of the groups came to me and asked me to direct them. At that time, I had just finished Arthur Miller's *A View from the Bridge*. I was quite keen to switch over to Indian English because I was inspired by Shanta Rama Rao's adaptation of *A Passage to India,* which was staged in London in 1960. I had said to myself, 'Here is an Indian who has taken an English novel and turned it into a play. Can't we take Indian lives and turn them into a play?' Easy to say, tough to do. The first thing was the problem of a plot.

At that time, I had seen a Hollywood movie called *Marty,* and I found a lot of similarities between the Saturday night syndrome in that movie and the kind of thing we used to do in the Bandra milieu when I was in college. I had mixed with Catholic boys all my life, so much so that I became one of them. We'd sit around and say, *'Arre yaar,* what do we do on Saturday night? I say, Vincy men, let's go to a movie, men.' And Vincy would reply, *'Cheh.* All *bukwas* movies, men.' There was an easy flow from English into Hindi words which gave our speech a colourful Indianness.

So I decided to use the *Marty* plot. It's about a lonely man who is getting to be thirty, and his mother keeps telling him, 'Marty, when are you getting married?' I found the whole Jewish idiom and environment, the whole family concept, very Indian.

I told my group of Bandra actors, 'Let's do some improvisation. Take the plot from *Marty*. Four or five guys sitting around in a restaurant saying, 'What do we do on Saturday night?' and improvise your own dialogue.' There was one irrepressible guy, the jokester of the pack. A chap called Cuthbert Serpes, Cutty. He was very funny and I just fell in love with his lingo. He spoke in a very picturesque idiom.

Together with the lean and quiet Dom D'sa, who's now a top executive at ACC, plus a girl called Jean Kingdom and a few others, we began improvisations. After experimenting, we finally got together a kind of semi-improvised script. I then wrote out the rough dialogue. 'Look, this dialogue is only a guide track. Whenever you want to wing it, go out on your own and improvise. As long as you come back to the track.' Cutty was, in his own words, an ace, simply an ace at this sort of thing.

When we finally performed our play in Bandra at the parish zonals, there was a kind of hush, as Cuthbert began, 'I tell you buggers. What are we going to do? Saturday night has come again. And there's nothing to do. Just farting around, sitting here.' The audience had never heard such language on stage before. The kind of speech that they spoke on the streets every day. Then we heard the first giggles. And as I looked around the audience, I noticed that it was the younger people, teenagers, who were amused. The familiarity of hearing their own Bandra lingo turned them on. I looked around further and found that the elders in the audience were stony faced.

As the play progressed — it was only a half-hour play — there was a distinct division in the audience. The elders looked grim, while the young people enjoyed the characters and the slang they knew so well. It was the language they heard in their homes, in schools and in church. But it was not the kind of English that their parents wanted them to speak.

The play finished and there were two reactions. There was absolutely no applause from the older people. While there was vociferous clapping from the youngsters who just loved it. They were whistling and shouting and cheering. And when the prizes were announced, one of our performers got an award for best actor.

But after the play, the parish priest came to see me.

'Mr Padamsee, this is a very bad show.'

'Really, Father, why do you say it is a bad show?'

'You have made fun of us Bandraites.'

'But that was not my intention. We were keen to depict the lives of Bandraites speaking their own dialect.'

'That is not us. It is a parody of us.'

'I am sorry. The dialogue was never meant to be a parody. It was in fact made up by your own youngsters. They spoke the way they normally speak. We wanted it to be real.'

'Maybe so, but I see this play as a slur on our community and you should apologise.'

So we got into quite a wrangle over that and a deputation of elders came to me backstage. All the over-thirties saying, 'How insulting. This sort of play shouldn't be allowed because it is slanguage, rather than language.' I said, 'I'm sorry. I really believe this is a breakthrough. Bandra should be proud, not ashamed.'

It was a very unusual experiment and I should have continued with it. But, typically, I got diverted to something more interesting for me at the time. However, I always had a nagging feeling that perhaps I should do something more in this area. And so in 1965, four years later, together with the Theatre Group of Bombay, we set up the Sultan Padamsee Playwriting Award for Indians writing in English.

The first play to win the award was Gurcharan Das' *Larins Saab*. It was produced and directed by Deryck Jeffereis, starring Zul Vellani as Lawrence of the Punjab. The second prize was won by Gieve Patel, poet, painter and playwright. He wrote a play called *Princes*. An excellent play where he attempted to write in the English that was the equivalent of Parsi-Gujarati. Extremely difficult, since Parsi-Gujarati itself is a corrupted form of Gujarati and to add to it, he gave it a poeticised flavour. Pearl Padamsee directed Hosi Vasunia in his first role on stage. He and his Parsi family would exclaim, 'Eat chicken. Chicken very good.' There were very few verbs in the dialogue. It was mainly adjectives and nouns. A kind of shorthand English but very effective. Powerful stuff, and yet it was not pidgin English.

By that time, Partap Sharma (Pat) and Asif Currimbhoy were already writing Indian plays in English. One day Pat asked me to direct a play he had written, called *A Touch of Brightness*. The play had been accepted for the Commonwealth Arts Festival in 1965. I readily agreed and we started rehearsing.

The play was set in Kamathipura, Bombay's red-light district. We had some fine actors in it. There were Zul Vellani, Vijaya Mehta (née Vijaya Jaywant and later Vijaya Khote), Pearl Padamsee, Farrokh Mehta and many others. It was written in a medium that was a bit like R K Narayan's English, where each character speaks a kind of ruralised English depending on their background. So Zul was the beggar, Banarasi Babu. Bhabhi Rani, the madam of the brothel and a very colourful character, was played by Pearl.

I think Pearl more or less transmuted Pat's dialogue into her own version of what she thought a Bhabhi Rani would speak. Which is very colourful and full of sound effects, spitting, clearing the throat, snorts and grunts. Indian languages get their impact from the sound effects we utter while speaking. And also from the *mudras* of our body language.

We rehearsed and rehearsed and then we did a preview before going to London. Because I wanted the actors to get used to an audience reaction. I didn't want to open in London cold. Unfortunately, some mischievous reporters sneaked into the preview. Next day in the Marathi press, were headlines: 'This is a play about prostitutes. It will disgrace the fair name of Maharashtra abroad.'

Because of the outcry in the press, the Home Minister of Bombay took strong objection to it. We tried to explain that it did not defame Maharashtra at all. If anything, it told the story of these hapless prostitutes with a certain amount of sympathy. But before we knew it, our passports were impounded and our trip was aborted, literally on the eve of our departure.

Imagine the kind of blow it dealt us. However, there was really very little we could do. We had no powerful friends in the government, and so we had to sit there and lick our wounds. Pat was heartbroken. In fact, he was struck by Bell's palsy which froze the muscles on one side of his face. Undaunted, he sent his play to the censors and they banned it. He asked me what should be the next step. I replied, 'You fight the ban.'

I helped Pat to get hold of Soli Sorabjee, who was at that time a young lawyer about to make his name. Today he is

Solicitor General of India. Soli agreed to take on the case for free. He fought for seven long years till he finally managed to overturn the Maharashtra Stage Performances Scrutiny Board. He found a loophole in the law and had the Board disbanded. Eventually, the play was allowed to be performed.

By that time, I had got myself involved with many other things, so I told the indefatigable Pat, 'Why don't you direct it yourself?' And he did. He staged the production which received reasonable reviews. But seven years had passed and a lot of the *hungama* had died away, so it did not make the kind of impact it should have.

After *A Touch of Brightness,* I decided to hold a playwrights' workshop. I got together people like Pat Sharma, Nissim Ezekiel, Gieve Patel, Sylvie da Cunha, Erna Vachchagandhi and others. We met at Bella Terrace, where I was living at the time. It used to be a bare terrace belonging to a friend of mine, who allowed me to build a flat on it. I designed it as a terrace theatre. The drawing room was the stage, and the terrace was the auditorium.

Out of this workshop emerged a play called *Asylum,* which was written by Erna, based on improvisations that were done in the workshop. The play was then performed at Tejpal Auditorium, with a brilliant young actress, Yasmin Mody, playing the lead role. It was about a Gujarati girl married to a Catholic boy. Though it was a tragic drama, it had funny overtones. Tall, heavily-built Roger Pereira played the husband, with his deep sonorous voice. Pearl was outstanding as the Anglo-Indian lady, Mabel (nicknamed Cleo–fataka). My brother Bubbles played her boyfriend. Dina Pathak, the doyen of the Gujarati stage, stood out as the mother. I was keen that the mother should be very much like my own mother. As I've mentioned on numerous occasions, I've always been obsessed with my mother. So I wanted an ethnic Gujarati actress to play the role.

Dina was petrified at first of speaking in English. She said, 'I can't remember lines in English. How will I act?' But I reassured her, 'It doesn't matter. You can improvise if you get stuck and break into Gujarati.' And she played the role of the mother brilliantly. The audience was in absolute raptures. A very believable character, absolutely down to earth, who spoke with a strong Gujarati accent. However, here and there she did fracture the language because she was speaking in a tongue she was not used to. So there were a lot of malapropisms, which the audience loved.

Again, like *Bandra Saturday Night,* the audience sat with their mouths open, saying, 'Hey, this is terribly familiar.' As it caught on, they began to appreciate it. They told their friends, and this is how *Asylum* became a box-office smash hit. Full houses. In those days, the mid-1960s, the English theatre rarely got a full house. I realised that this was a unique way to get plays written. Get hold of writers, enthuse them through a workshop and see if a play could be improvised and then scripted.

In the Indian English theatre, I think playwrights try and write like Arthur Miller or John Osborne or Tennessee Williams. We looked westward instead of inwards. We should have actually looked at writers like R K Narayan and Mulk Raj Anand and even Khushwant Singh and said, 'These novelists have been writing in English for a long time and they have been writing about things in India. How come we are not looking at them?'

Partap Sharma too, for many years, did not really appeal to me. I felt that though he wrote about Indian characters, his dialogue was heavily influenced by western playwrights. And then suddenly in the mid 1990s, Pat read me a play called *Begum Sumroo* which really struck a responsive chord. 'My God! Pat has at last discovered his own voice. It is not the voice of Arthur Miller or John Osborne. It is Partap Sharma.'

Today, it is a far cry from the early days of Indian English theatre. We have plays written by authors like Girish Karnad and Mahesh Dattani who I think are the two outstanding Indians writing in the English theatre. And perhaps you can add Partap Sharma to that list since *Begum Sumroo*. These are Indians who use the medium of English to talk about their dreams, their desires, their conscious and subconscious, and write about themselves.

Indians who use the medium of English to talk about their dreams, their desires, their conscious and subconscious, and write about themselves.

A tall, handsome man with a beautiful voice, Girish is very proud of the fact that he wrote *Tughlaq* originally in Kannada. When I first asked him to do an English version, he refused. Which I felt was a bit of false modesty, since he had been President of the Oxford English Union when he was there. But I finally prevailed and it turned out to be a very fine piece of work which is used in the syllabus in many universities in India.

Mahesh Dattani is a person with tremendous enthusiasm and a nice gift for dialogue, which I think is the essence of a good playwright. If you can write great themes but can't write crisp dialogue, forget it. Write a novel. That would be better, because in novels you sometimes don't even need dialogue. But in a play, everything is communicated through the mouths of the characters.

I met Mahesh when I was doing a play in Bangalore. He was invited to a party to meet my cast. We got talking and he gave me his translation of Mohan Rai's Gujarati play, *Kumar Ni Agashi*. The next time I heard from Mahesh was when he brought his play *Dance Like A Man* to Bombay. I was very struck, both by the play and by its writing. I went backstage and invited him and the cast for dinner.

We talked till the early hours of the morning. I asked him what he was working on and he said he was developing a play called *Twinkle Tara*, about Siamese twins. The theme dwelt on the role of the girl child in India. I told him that it sounded like just the thing I was looking for. And I offered to produce and direct it. He agreed and said that we'd work on it. So he sent me a first draft and I made a few comments, after which he sent me a second one and I said, 'Okay.' He then told me, 'Look, *Deccan Herald* is organising a playwright's competition in Bangalore. Do you mind if I do a trial production?' So he did and I managed to see a rehearsal while visiting Bangalore.

I found his version interesting, but when he sent me the final draft, I made a few minor changes. But basically, it was all there. My production of *Tara* was very different from his, and it touched a very responsive nerve in the Bombay audience. I have not seen that kind of response for an Indian English play since *Tughlaq*, though it was nothing like *Tughlaq*. There were no grand sets or elaborate costumes. *Tara* is about the girl next door who happens to be crippled. As the play unfolds, you find out why she is crippled. Wonderful characters and a great story. The audience simply adored the play.

I then asked Mahesh about his next play and he said that he did not have any theme in mind. So I told him about an idea that had been running around in my head for the last twenty years. I said I'd get my actors to improvise and asked if he would be interested. He was. I said, 'It's on a communal theme.' And he replied, 'Good. That sounds great.'

So Pearl and Raell organised the improvisation. I just sketched out what my idea was. Mahesh loved it, enjoyed the improvisation and went away to start writing the play. He sent me the first draft for Act I and we corresponded over the phone. He then sent me a draft for the whole play and came up to Bombay and we had a reading in my drawing room. The actors commented on some of the characters, their motivations, and what the loopholes might be. Mahesh then did a final draft and we started rehearsals for what we called *Final Solutions*.

It was about a communal riot that had just happened. Historically, *Final Solutions* was about the 1969 Ahmedabad riots. But since the play was eventually produced in 1994, everyone assumed it was about the Bombay riots that had just taken place. So it had a tremendous impact. It was about prejudice. It was about appeasement. Even though it talks about Hindus and Muslims, *Final Solutions* is a play that touches any Indian who comes from almost any background. It is a very human play.

English as a language with an Indian voice is a very important movement in this country. Whether we're talking about playwrights or poets or novelists or film makers. Because there is a generation that always grows up in a kind of no-man's land, after a colonial power leaves. They seem to belong to the past, live in the present and have a great nostalgia for what was. But they can't come to grips with what is and what is going to be.

On the other hand, Hinglish is a fractured English which uses the English language of the Indian streets in a fractured way to elicit laughs. It is a masala English where a lot of Indian words creep in. Today it is very common to find Hinglish used in advertising, on stage, and especially on the music channels like MTV and Channel [V].

Many people are under the impression that the advent of Indian English in advertising began with the slugline, *Humko Binny's Mangta,* in the late 1980s. But as early as the 1960s, Lintas created advertising for Mafco, where we took Hindi sentences and used a kind of Indianised English to pun on the word 'peas', But we weren't the pioneers. Hindi cinema had already been using this language for years.

Hinglish is a fractured English which uses the English language of the Indian streets in a fractured way to elicit laughs.

This was even before Bharat Dabholkar made the Amul Butter campaign famous at Da Cunha Associates. And now every Tom, Dick and Hari has switched over to using Hindi words in the Roman alphabet. My current favourite is a Situations Vacant ad for a Hindi copywriter: *Roti, kapda aur McCann.*

Has advertising in English in India got an Indian voice? The simple answer is no. Advertising was invented in the United States and as far as we are concerned, we still look to Madison Avenue for guidance and inspiration. However, advertising created in Hindi, Marathi, Gujarati and our other Indian languages, very often has a unique and piquant flavour of its own. Lintas' late great Hindi Copy Chief, Balwant Tandon, was the father of this movement. Roots are relevant. The rest is window dressing.

Don't reinvent the wheel. Adapt it.

Chapter 12

HOW TO CREATE A BRAND
THAT CREATES WAVES

*O*ne of India's breakthrough campaigns started when the young, debonair, Gautam Singhania of the JK Chemicals Group came to Lintas one day. 'I have the know-how to make a very good quality condom. It's Korean technology and it's ahead of the rest. Unfortunately, I don't know much about the condom market. Can you study the market and help me position this product?'

There was no name, no brief, and very little to go by. All Gautam had was a dream and he wanted to know how to go about executing it. Now, Gautam is a very dynamic man. He's a guy who likes ideas and gets very involved in them. He doesn't necessarily say, 'Look, I want all the data and all the boring facts and figures.' He says, 'Give me bright ideas. Ideas that will make my eyes dance with delight.' Gautam wanted to hit the ground running. He loved to slam the table and say, 'I want a campaign next week.' Of course we realised that this was impossible, but we were stimulated by his enthusiasm.

When we landed the account, the agency reaction was lukewarm. The idea of creating advertising for a condom caused a bit of a giggle. I think the general feeling among the agency bigwigs, especially the wiser brains on the financial side, was, 'Hold on. Let's check it out. If this is not something that is going to fly, let's not even attempt to get it off the ground. Or we'll end up spending a lot of expensive time and energy, only to find out that the market is too small to be worthwhile.' But to me, and maybe this is because I'm from the theatre, any project that sounds exciting, no matter how small it may be, makes me say, 'Let's go for it.'

Immediately, I appointed a brand team headed by Jayant Bakshi, the gentle giant, who was at the time the chief of Lintas: Bombay 2. The brief I gave him was, 'You have an opportunity to create a óne-in-a-million brand from scratch. Let's not rush into the advertising before we've investigated the market perception on condoms. Let's find out the reason there's eighty-eight per cent awareness of Nirodh, the leading brand, but only two per cent usage.'

Within five weeks, Jayant and his team were ready. He highlighted the fact that the Focus Groups (100 per cent male) were unhappy with the quality of Nirodh and most other brands. They felt the family planning appeal or even protection against AIDS was not strong enough to override their distaste for the product.

So Jayant, Kersy Katrak, our Executive Creative Director, and other bright sparks at the agency put our heads together and exchanged views and ideas on condoms and family planning. The first thing we did was define the target group. If you don't define your target group, the demographics, psychographics and so on, you are dead.

The audience here was people who had a latent need for some kind of sexual protection. That is, protection against having a large family or against STD. But they found that most of the current brands available were distasteful. A condom by its very nature is an irksome thing and has to be used at an inconvenient moment. People could not quite get over that barrier and the fact that it destroyed your mood and pleasure. Secondly, they did not have a brand that appealed to their lifestyle. We assessed that the target group would be in the 18-30 age bracket. People who were thinking of marriage, were newly married or married with one or two children.

Then we tabled everything, including the research reports that I had been involved in with MARG, who had done extensive work in the northern states. We included all the insights we had culled from there. Plus my supposition that you could never get a man to use Nirodh because it was anti-pleasure.

It was a product designed to go against the very activity for which it was devised. You can't wear a condom unless you have an erection and as soon as you think of Nirodh, you lose your erection. So you're going backward. I even checked this out with a lot of my friends. It's like saying, 'I'm very hungry.' And someone replies, 'Eat porridge.' I hate porridge and there goes my appetite, boom!

Condoms were being sold on the premise that they were good for you. And I think marketers realised a long time ago that if you told children, or even adults, that anything was good for them, it immediately meant that it was distasteful. It was good for you but not pleasurable, and if sex was pleasurable, what the hell were you doing with an unpleasurable product?

So we tried to think of ways to make this product enjoyable. My basic idea was, 'Can we have a pleasurable condom? So when the user hears the brand name, he says, 'Wow. It's a turn on. Not a turn off.' That was the essential positioning difference between our brand and any other condom that had ever been advertised.

I love the word, oxymoron. I think one of the most powerful creative devices is the oxymoron. It thrives on contradiction. Like Hindustan Lever is a 'local multinational.' So I said, 'Why can't we have a sexy condom?' Which is almost the opposite of what a condom is. Yet, it seemed so logical. A condom should be sexy, it should be almost like an aphrodisiac. Well, maybe that's stretching it a bit! But it should definitely be an upper rather than a downer.

A lot of people on the Strategy Review Board felt that this was dangerous ground to tread on, this whole area of sex and making it pleasurable. Dangerous from the point of view of government intervention and censorship. They also felt that it wasn't the reason why people wore condoms. They used condoms for safety, protection, family planning. So they felt that it should be a very conservative, family-type product. It shouldn't be seen as raunchy hungry young men looking for sex.

There was a very spirited defence put up against going the sex route. And instead opting for the safe route. As protection against AIDS. But we found that it was the wrong button to press. If you scare the devil out of people for having unprotected sex, they get turned off. They don't read your advertisement. They don't want to think about AIDS.

If you want to sell a condom, don't tell your target audience, 'Unless you wear a condom, you'll get AIDS and die.' Young people love to flirt with death. They imagine they are immortal. That's why they ride mobikes at ninety kilometres an hour. They can have unprotected sex and will never get AIDS. God has blessed them! This is the psychology of your macho consumer.

So the debate at the SRB was whether to go the emotional way or the rational way. The sex route or the safe route? Most of the board tended towards the rational route because it seemed to be the stronger reason why. But eventually the tide turned when I said, 'To enter the head, aim at the heart.' In any case, the creative team

To enter the head, aim at the heart.

found the sex route more exciting.

It sounded very good in theory, but the real crunch came when we moved from concept to execution. The first thing to do was to find a name with a built-in descriptor. From the name would flow everything. The packaging, the look of the ads, the feel of the campaign, everything. And we played around with names like Tiger and Panther and Macho. All in the area of male virility. But these names ignored the female completely, and we felt that giving her pleasure was the real secret of male performance.

So we brainstormed. And then we came up with the name Kama Sutra. What could be better in India than the word Kama Sutra? Everybody knew it. It's universal for sensual pleasure. It meant sex without saying the forbidden word, S-E-X. It was culturally acceptable. It had the right status connotations.

It's important to understand that breakthrough advertising not only has to have a unique concept, it must also have a unique insight: The consumer will only wear a condom if he feels it's going to maintain his erection, not depress it. The next step was to go about turning that into a reality.

Breakthrough advertising not only has to have a unique concept, but it must also have a unique insight.

If you want to build a brand, and not just a nine-day wonder, it is very important to realise that whatever campaign idea you come up with, it must have legs. It must have the capability of running for a considerable period of time, so that it can build the brand.

We fiddled with a lot of words and visuals. Early on we realised that even though the word Kama Sutra was advantageous, people would hesitate to go up to a shopkeeper and ask for it by name. So we coined the phrase, 'Just ask for KS.' Which itself became a very sexy term. On campus, girls would whisper to each other, 'Do you think he's a KS guy? Sexy, I mean.'

Now, with a brand name like Kama Sutra, the immediate visual image that comes to mind is Khajuraho. So the original campaign had a whole lot of graphics of ancient Indian temple sculpture. But we discovered that the young thought this to be too traditional, too old-fashioned.

Therefore we decided that the campaign must have a contemporary look and appeal. We paid great attention to detail. Right down to the colour, the special shade of magenta pink we chose. The Kama Sutra campaign was a breakthrough in advertising in many ways. It was the first time that a condom campaign came out and said that condoms are for sex, for love-making... not for blowing balloons! Remember, our line was, 'For the pleasure of making love.' Not for protection.

Another thing that was commented upon was the sperm squiggles. That was just the

Vivid mnemonics make valuable brand properties.

visualiser's crazy concept. I fought tooth and nail to have them knocked out, but the creative team overruled me. I finally gave in but I warned them that it was going to cause a lot of unnecessary flak. I expected that people would think it was in bad taste. 'How dare you have sperms running around a condom advertisement!' I suspected that they'd either cause an outrage or they'd be completely missed. As a matter of fact, the sperms were well remembered, but did not cause an outcry. So I was wrong on both counts. Even today, you draw those two squiggles on a piece of paper, and people will tell you that's from the Kama Sutra ad. Vivid mnemonics make valuable brand properties.

For any brand-new brand, two things are vital. One, a memorable, distinctive name, that is preferably a descriptor of the brand benefit. Two, a symbol that expresses the brand personality. We were keen that this personality be typified by the model we selected. We felt that she had to exude tremendous sex appeal. She was so central to the campaign that we had to be certain that we got the right model.

As it so happened, around the time we were creating the campaign, Gautam Singhania, being the kind of young spark that he was, met Kabir Bedi's daughter Pooja at a party and asked her if she'd like to model for Kama Sutra. She agreed and so Gautam asked us at the agency what we thought of her. Knowing Kabir, I said, 'I don't think Kabir is going to look at this in a friendly light.' But as it transpired, Kabir said to Pooja, 'You do what you think is best.'

Pooja Bedi was an aspiring starlet who symbolised sexiness at that time. A tall girl, with a ripe figure and flashing eyes, and a delicious pout, she had been seen more in movie gossip magazines than on the silver screen. She wore miniskirts, which were considered daring, and plunging necklines. She was known to have a wild tongue, and she'd say anything she wanted off the top of her head – 'What's wrong in having an affair?'

When Gautam brought Pooja to us, he said, 'Look, she wants an amazing amount of money.' At that time, Pooja was asking for seven lakh rupees, which was unheard of. In those days, the top model was being paid a lakh and a half rupees. Here was someone who was asking for nearly five times as much. But Gautam said that he was willing to pay it, if she signed up for two years. Everyone was aghast. 'You can't do that! You'll ruin the market for everybody.'

I said, 'Look, I don't usually say that the client is right, but my gut feel tells me, "Let's go with Pooja." She strikes me as the kind of flamboyant character who will have a publicity aura that will go beyond the ads. Having her in the campaign is synergistic with the atmosphere we want to build around Kama Sutra. She is young, modern and vivacious. The perfect personality we want for our brand. She is not just a department store mannequin, but a cool, sexy cat.

'She also tends to shoot from the hip and say outrageous things. It always makes for good copy because our press is sex hungry. She's terrific at sound bites which we can write for her: "I don't condemn sex. I condom it. That's why I'm the Kama Sutra girl."'

The photo session took place in Goa. I myself wasn't there. But from what I heard, Pooja was very conservative. She was not keen to reveal too much. She kept her shirt slightly unbuttoned but that was about it. It was very clear that there would be no bare breasted shots. And she had a 'No Nipple' clause in her contract. I think she got the idea from something she had read somewhere in an American magazine. She said, 'I'm willing to reveal everything except the nipples. Because nipples means you are nude. Up to the nipples, you are not nude.'

What was interesting was that during the shoot, the photographer also took shots of two other models for *Debonair* magazine. And these models were nude. However, when the Kama Sutra ads were released alongside the centrespread, some people assumed that the nude centrespread too was Pooja. Which is totally incorrect. It was not Pooja.

When we finally presented the campaign, which was designed by Adi Pocha and Priya Correia-Affonso, Gautam was ecstatic. Here was a client who wholeheartedly agreed, 'Yes! This is it.' But I think there were a few others in his company who were a little apprehensive. After all, the Singhanias are a conservative firm. But Gautam was a bit of a maverick. His father however, felt that since Gautam was in charge of this project, the ultimate decision should be his.

When we released the campaign, we didn't realise the extent of the sensation it would cause. It created enormous shock waves. But none of us had any idea that the Kama Sutra ads were going to be blown out of proportion. And we certainly did not expect such an unreasonable reaction. After all, Kama Sutra is an accepted word. It just happened to be linked to a condom, that's all. If it was linked to a perfume, I don't think there would have been such a furore.

The flak we received was, 'How can you talk about sex like this in public?' and 'How can you show sexy pictures?' Actually, the pictures were not very sexy. There was no female nudity. In fact, the whole campaign, if you look at it objectively, has extremely good taste. Pooja Bedi is completely clothed in every ad. She's wearing a shirt and not even showing any cleavage. It was Marc Robinson, the male model, who was bare chested.

And yet we got complaints saying we were exploiting the female form. It was actually the media who picked it up and made a huge hue and cry over it. But then the media always looks out for sexy ad stories. A few years ago, it was the Tuffs shoes campaign. Before that, it was MR Coffee. Before that, Kama Sutra.

We were really taken aback, but we stood firm. Then I got a letter from the Advertising Standards Council of India (ASCI) asking me to show cause why the ad should not be withdrawn. Our defence was simple. I wrote back saying,

'What element of the ad is disturbing you? Is it the word, Kama Sutra? It's a perfectly decent word, it's one of our famous texts. There is no cleavage. There is no sex at all in the copy. Go through every word and if you find anything offensive, we will remove it. There is nothing wrong in saying "For the pleasure of making love" because that is the product description.'

Sex, like beauty, is in the eye of the beholder. We just told them to look more closely at the ads. They couldn't believe what they saw. Which just goes to prove that sex, like beauty, is in the eye of the beholder. Sensuality is not on the printed page, it is in the area that lies between the eyes and the brain. It appeals as much to your sense of aesthetics as to the libido. None of the complaints held up.

Actually, the thing that offended people was Pooja Bedi. She was symbolic of the liberated, 'don't give a damn' woman. And her demeanour was very sensual. Her eyes closed, lips parted. Her expression turned people on, as it gave them the impression that she was having an orgasm. Pooja Bedi soon became the Sharon Stone of India. The floodgates opened and she was offered every sexy role possible on the Hindi screen. Until that time she had done only one film which wasn't even released.

One of our media innovations was to book all the ad space in a single issue of *Debonair*. We bought the whole damn thing which caused quite a commotion and really rocked the boat. We also pasted a condom on the centrespread so that a reader got a condom free. It caused an uproar because it became associated with the Debonair nudes. But there was nothing nude about the Kama Sutra ads. Nothing.

We spent about twenty-five to thirty lakh rupees on the

first burst, which caused this huge impact. People thought we had spent five crores, but it was the multiplier effect of the media that caused Kama Sutra to become a part of the language, and an international news item. It was widely written about, not only in Indian papers, but even abroad. *The London Telegraph* called it 'The new awakening of sex in India.' And because of all the media hullabaloo, questions were even raised in Parliament, about advertising and censorship.

Today if you mention Kama Sutra, people will first recall the condom and only secondly think of Vatsayana's book. Ask anyone to name a brand of condom and they'll immediately hit on Kama Sutra. The second choice will be Nirodh. Even though Nirodh has spent crores and crores of rupees over a forty-year span.

However good the advertising and the product, if it's not available when you want it, forget it.

For thirty-five lakh rupees, the client got an excellent deal. The thing was, he had a limited budget and his big problem was distribution. We had expected modest sales and our predictions were way off the mark. If I recall correctly, he ran out of stocks within the first two months. Everyone in India, especially the English-speaking public, knew about it. So his sales figures should have gone through the roof. But he couldn't distribute his product. And that's one thing advertising teaches you. However good the advertising campaign, however good the product, if it's not available when you want it, forget it. Nobody will say, 'I'll wait till next week to get Kama Sutra.' No, they'll say, 'I want it now. If you don't have it now, what else have you got?'

Once the client had sorted out his distribution problems, we were ready for the next phase of the plan. We decided we needed to advertise on television, and so we called up three or four producers. Which is a Lintas rule worldwide. You don't just select a producer from the top of your hat. You invite competitive quotes from three or four of them. We decided on Shyam Ramanna for various reasons. One, his was the lowest quote. Two, the other producers were busy and could only shoot after three months. And three, I myself had very high regard for Shyam, as he had recently done the MRF and the Kawasaki cheetah films for us.

As expected, Shyam did a superb job. He used a soft blue colour, which was very important to convey the right ambience and mood. Unfortunately, the film ran head-on into censorship problems. Our script had a man in a boat and a girl in the shower, and unlike the press campaign, the TV commercial was definitely sexy and certainly erotic. The models had a distinct wet look about them. So, as you may expect, it was not allowed to be shown by Big Sister, DD.

Then we created a fifteen-second film to be aired on DD, while we showed the original on cable TV. The Doordarshan version is extremely simple and non-sexy. Pooja Bedi is playing chess with her friend, Marc Robinson. She's looking at him and he's looking at her and she's looking back at him. A lot of glances are exchanged and then he says, 'Check' and she picks up all the pieces and sweeps everything off the table and says, 'Mate'. And this is Kama Sutra, for the pleasure of making love. But even this film ran into trouble.

What irked me about the entire Kama Sutra exercise was that people shied from calling a spade a spade. A condom is for sex, but for years everyone had been saying that it's for family planning. Yes, it is true that it does keep the sperm from reaching the ovum. But if you want to popularise it, then you can't position it as prevention against disease or for contraception. You can't sell a medicine if it tastes foul. The old days of castor oil are out. Sell castor oil with a strawberry flavour, or with a spearmint flavour. Now you're talking!

If it's desirable, it's buyable.

One of the phrases I coined in Lintas to make trainees aware of this concept was, 'If it's desirable, it's buyable.' That is the heart of the Kama Sutra campaign. We made the condom desirable. Therefore it became buyable. It was something that people went out to buy and would wear. It became a kind of a fashion statement. Like wearing a pair of Nike shoes or Levi's jeans.

I wear Nike shoes because I understand I look great. My girlfriend loves to see me in them. It has nothing to do with running. I've probably never even jogged in my life. But wearing them makes me feel that I'm being accepted by the 'in' crowd.

So in the same way, wearing Kama Sutra makes you feel that you're with it. If you're not wearing Kama Sutra, you're not 'happening'. In fact, I feel the next campaign for Kama Sutra should have a line to the effect of, 'The well-dressed man wears Kama Sutra in bed all the time.'

Kama Sutra was a breakthrough in advertising because people exclaimed, 'My God! You are saying the forbidden in an ad.' But there was nothing in it that was salacious or prurient. It was a very clean campaign and if you look at it again and again, I challenge you to find anything obscene about this first KS campaign.

The fact is at that time quite a few teenagers were indulging in sex in college. Women in India were beginning to think that they too had the right to derive pleasure from sex. It was no longer just a man's prerogative. So in a way, perhaps Kama Sutra came along at just the right time, when sex in India was finally coming out of the closet. And perhaps in its own way, KS has been a catalyst for whatever sexual liberation has happened here in the last decade or so.

There is an apocryphal story that did the rounds in the early 1990s, about the sultan of sex, Kushwant Singh. It seems at a party he gave, a young accolyte burst in shouting 'Hi, KS.' Khushwant jumped to his feet: 'Don't call me that. People may get the wrong idea!'

When there's a fusion between
the 'what' and the 'how'
you get advertising brilliance.

Karen Lunel for Liril, 1976

Kavita Chowdhry as Lalitaji for Surf, 1987

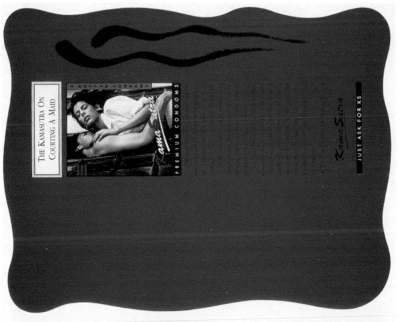

Pooja Bedi and Marc Robinson for Kama Sutra, 1990

how fixed are fixed deposits ?

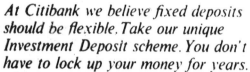

At Citibank we believe fixed deposits should be flexible. Take our unique Investment Deposit scheme. You don't have to lock up your money for years. We accept even 15-day deposits. Bring along any idle money you have. We will put it to work. We pay a very handsome interest. □ The amount can be a mountain or a molehill. We will work out an Investment Deposit plan to meet your needs. Or if you prefer, open a Savings Account. Either way, it's nice to have a growing interest in the bank. Citibank.

FIRST NATIONAL CITY BANK

we print your name on every cheque

IN CALCUTTA: 9 BRABOURNE RD. & AT 1 MIDDLETON ST. □ BRANCHES ALSO IN MADRAS BOMBAY NEW DELHI

AP for Citibank, 1965
(Copywriter of the Year Award)

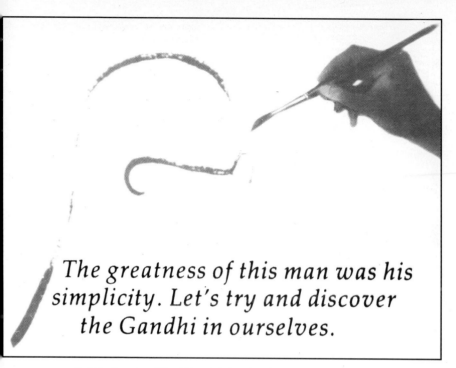

The greatness of this man was his simplicity. Let's try and discover the Gandhi in ourselves.

Public Service film (Gandhi drawing by Imtiaz Dharker)

On 31st January history will be re-created. Will you be there?

Indo-British Films invite you to the re-creation of the funeral of Mahatama Gandhi—on the 33rd anniversary of his martyrdom.
Join the cast of actors playing Pandit Nehru, Sardar Patel, Lord Mountbatten, Maulana Azad and other historical person – ages who paid the final tribute to Bapuji.

Gather along Rajpath this Saturday at 9.30 a.m., 31st January

A historic event is being filmed for posterity — you can be part of it.

AP's ad for *Gandhi*, 1981

Whitening Strikes with RIN

Lintas ad for The Village restaurant, 1989
(Created with Anita Sarkar and B V Patil)

The Muscleman for MRF Tyres, 1966

Cherry Charlie for Cherry Blossom Shoe Polish, 1989

You'd think the world would have learnt a lesson.

Between Hiroshima and Nagasaki, 230,000 people perished. Both cities vanished. But it didn't stop man from amassing enough nuclear arms to obliterate mankind thousands of times over. And this evil has multiplied only because you don't know what kind of death rains down on you from a nuclear bomb. Please make it a point to see this exhibition, because its the one thing the proponents of nuclear arms don't want you to see. **Nehru Centre Upto February 19   11.00 a.m. to 7.00 p.m.**

HIROSHIMA & NAGASAKI

NEVER AGAIN

McCann Erickson ad for 'Hiroshima-Nagasaki Never Again' Exhibition, 1998
(Created with Alvin Saldanha and Pradeep Padwal)

Chapter 13

HOW TO CREATE A STAR,
NOT A COMET

*T*he first time I met Sharon Prabhakar was at a party in Juhu (a Bombay suburb). She was singing, and I was quite struck by the quality of her voice. What intrigued me and attracted me was her freshness. She didn't have a very well-trained voice, but she had a lot of feeling and a lot of emotion.

The next time I came in contact with Sharon was when I was doing *Jesus Christ Superstar.* I was very keen to cast Sharon as Mary Magdalene, which is the leading female role in *Superstar.* Unfortunately, she was flying for Air-India at that time, and she couldn't really make all the shows, because she never knew when she'd be pulled out on flight. So we hunted and found another girl to play that part, but I still felt that Sharon had a tremendous emotional quality.

Some years later she came to me and said, 'I've got this contract to sing at the Oberoi Hotel and it's a marvellous opportunity. Do you think you could train me?' So I got in touch with my good friend Noel Godin, who really knows much more about music and singing than I do. I am not basically a music man. Although I do love music and I have done musicals, funnily enough, I do not come from a musical background.

So Noel and I worked on Sharon and tried to give her some poise and pizzazz on stage. We asked her to sing the famous Judy Garland song, *Somewhere Over the Rainbow,* and found that her voice had a very appealing quality. She had a nice break in her voice — she could pour on the emotion.

It was some time later that Sharon came to me and said, 'I'm very keen to do something on the stage.' And around the same time I was seriously considering doing *Evita*. Now *Evita* is such a huge back-breaking production that I thought why don't we just do a sort of mini version. So we put on something called *Razzle-Dazzle*. The first half was a medley of songs including *Somewhere Over the Rainbow*. The second half was the condensed *Evita*.

At this point, I realised that Sharon needed some professional vocal training. Though Sharon's mother was a very accomplished pianist and had taught singing and music in several schools all over India, Sharon herself hadn't taken singing lessons. So I contacted one of the last opera trainers around — Hyacinth Brown. I asked Hyacinth if she would take on a pupil. That's how we arranged for Sharon to take tuitions from the legendary teacher.

Hyacinth taught her breathing and taught her projection. But perhaps over-taught her. Sharon began to elocute and to sing in a kind of operatic voice, which was not really what I had in mind. But her power increased enormously because she had learnt how to breathe correctly.

And this is something I tell all actors. 'For God's sake, get your breathing right.' It's the first thing they teach you in drama school. If your breathing is right, you can bring your voice out, you can do marvellous things. It's like going to a gymnasium and doing weight training. After a while your body begins to respond to you because your muscles are tuned up. Before you go on stage, it's important to tune up your voice. Whether you're going there to act or to sing.

So Sharon got this fantastic training and Zing! Bang! Boom! Before anyone knew what was happening, we plunged into the big version of *Evita*. It was my own interpretation of

Evita. I had always seen many parallels between Eva Peron and Indira Gandhi. So naturally these similarities became the highlight of my production. *Evita* was the biggest success the English theatre in India had ever known. It ran and ran and

Improve on your own performance. You are your own best pacesetter.

ran. It ran for almost five years. Sharon and I worked very closely together. And one thing led to another...and this, of course, led to marriage. Almost every night after rehearsals, we'd be in our drawing

room, working out the mechanics of how she could give more power to the role. We did 150 shows or more of *Evita,* and after every show I would say, 'Okay, darling. It was great, but it could be greater.' I can be a hell of a bore in that sense. Perhaps it's got something to do with my childhood in an Irish school, where they taught me that 'Every day I grow better and better.' So it's always trying to improve upon yesterday. Don't improve on somebody else's performance. Improve on your own performance. You are your own best pacesetter.

Besides running for five years, *Evita* was also responsible for creating a whole new galaxy of stars. There was Sharon, of course, who went on to become a pop icon. There was Shiamak Davar, who had just a little dance role. Today, he's one of Bombay's leading choreographers. There was Rachel Reuben who went on to become a top model. Suneeta Rao, who is now a pop star. Alisha Chinai, who too became a pop star. There was Javed Jaffrey, who's a major television personality now. Karla Singh, who's not only a top choreographer but also an excellent actress. Roger Drego, who did the sound, is today India's finest sound engineers. Viraf Pocha, who handled the lights, is now one of the most sought after lighting directors. And, of course, Mr Rehmatali, whose Shobiz company built the magnificent sets, is India's most trusted décor constructor.

There was Brian Tellis, who filled in for Keith Stevenson as Peron. Brian has gone on to become one of Bombay's finest compères and radio jockeys, and now runs his own event management company. Then when Dalip Tahil (playing Che) dropped out because he got a break in movies, Shiamak Davar took over his role. Suneeta Rao replaced Alisha Chinai. And that's how theatre grows talent. Even when people substitute for other people, if they have got the talent, they get confidence and then go on to make careers for themselves. It's all a matter of getting an opportunity and getting a chance to be showcased. Because a play like *Evita* just ran and ran, you had a chance to hone your talent.

After *Evita,* Sharon and I agreed that if she wanted to become a singer and wanted to earn money, she needed to go into playback singing. Now, playback singing is in Hindi but the problem was that Sharon's Hindi was weak. So she got herself a *guruji*, and she began to take lessons with him. He would come over and do *riyaz* daily.

In the meantime, I also advised her, 'Let's do a play in Hindi so that you get totally confident in the language.' We worked with a movie that had starred Goldie Hawn, *Butterflies are free,* and got it converted into a Hindi play. I felt that Sharon was ideal for the role. One might think, 'From Evita to Goldie Hawn? That's pretty crazy.' But it wasn't crazy, because Sharon in real life is a very bubbly personality. Very Goldie Hawnish.

So we did this play in Hindi and it was quite a success. That's how Sharon got used to speaking Hindi dialogue without stammering and stuttering. Then she met Bappi Lahiri, the top Hindi film music director, who said to her, 'I believe you are a singer. But can you sing in Hindi?' She nodded. Her first song for Bappi was *Meri jaisi haseena*. It was a great hit and it went on to win the all-India award for the best song of the year. For a while Sharon dabbled in playback singing, but rather sporadically.

One of the big things I discovered about Sharon was that she not only speaks Punjabi but she also enjoys herself most in Punjabi. So we developed another show for her which became quite a rage. It was called *The Sharon Spectacular.* Sharon has tremendous vivacity on stage, and so we developed an opportunity for her to rap with the audience. In Punjabi. She interacts with the audience in three languages, Punjabi, Hindi and English. She has the ability to hold them in the palm of her hand. I think she developed this when I was working with her on her Oberoi routine. It's what Frank Sinatra calls 'Working the room.' Which means that you are able to work the audience and make them part of the show.

Now this is unusual, getting the audience involved as part of the show. By God, it's damn difficult, and you've got to have nerves of steel. Very often, you'll get a heckler who says, 'Hey! You hit a false note there.' And Sharon would reply, 'Welcome to the club. Because you hit a false note right there.' Boom! That ability to improvise a witty answer has the whole audience roaring with laughter. And what could have been an insult is now turned into a comic squelch.

After *The Sharon Spectacular,* the next big thing we found for Sharon was *Cabaret.* The Liza Minelli film. But I said, 'I'll work out a different version.' So I went back to the source work which was a story by Christopher Isherwood. From there I extracted a kind of scenario and that's how we did the musical *Kabaret,* spelt with a 'K.' Why 'K?' Because in the Germany of the 1930s, they used to have what was known as café theatre or kabaret theatre. And it was mainly political and satirical. It wasn't cabaret as we know it, with cabaret dancers et al. That's why I insisted we spell it with a 'K.' I didn't want people to think it was some tawdry cabaret dance show.

Still, *Kabaret* did have sex appeal, but at the same time, it had a social and political satirical edge. Furthermore I adapted the original to our idiom. So, as I mentioned earlier, Hitler's Brownshirts became saffron shirts. Which brought us a lot of interesting comments. Some of them quite nasty, I might add. However, many thinking people said, 'Yes, there are elements of fascism creeping into this country.' Remember, this was as early as 1988 when the Congress Party looked like being the Government for ever and ever.

In *Kabaret,* Sharon not only had to sing but she had to act as there was quite a bit of dialogue. It was not like *Evita,* which was all singing. *Evita* is what is called a Rock Opera. There is no dialogue. It's fascinating to see the transition of a singer into an actress. Too many of our pop crooners don't know how to put meaning into the lyrics they are singing. Acting is meaning with emotion . You have to learn how to phrase, how to underline, how to bring out the sense of what you are saying or singing. Feeling without meaning is empty.

In *Kabaret,* there was this one scene which I was crazy about, and I must have spent zillions on it. Half the budget went on that one damn scene. It was a song called *Mein Herr.* There's Sharon in a bowler hat with a chair. The scene opens and she's alone in a solo spotlight. As she starts singing, by magic, you suddenly see six Sharons behind her. And you say, 'How the hell can that be?' And behind those six Sharons, you can see another twelve Sharons. I worked it with mirrors and a gauze scrim.

Sharon Prabhakar's rise to stardom can be attributed to her ability to work tremendously hard. She is one of the hardest workers I know. She really puts everything into anything she does. And for me, there are two types of people. There are 100 percenters. And there are the rest. I believed this even way back in the 1960s when I was the Films Chief of Lintas.

There are two types of people. There are 100 percenters. And there are the rest.

I was looking for an assistant at the time, and quite by chance, I found soft-spoken, unassuming Shyam Benegal in the copy department working under Gerson da Cunha, who was the Copy Chief. Shyam was then an unknown struggling copywriter. I said to Gerson, 'Look, if you don't mind, I see tremendous film possibilities in Shyam. And I think he'll be better off in my department than in yours.' And Gerson, in his usual generous manner said, 'Okay Alyque, give him a try.'

So Shyam came over to the films department, and he was really perfect. He was first and foremost a painter. Secondly a poet. And thirdly, he was obsessed with becoming a film maker. So I said, 'Shyam, you can cut your teeth on ad films.' In those days we were making one-minute ad films. And Lintas was the largest producer of cinema commercials in the country because of our client, Hindustan Lever. We used to do something like fifty films a year. One a week. It was a killing schedule. We were under tremendous pressure all the time.

We were in the movie studios almost every night. Why night? Because the models were all working girls. Secretaries and so on. A lot of them came from the Christian and Anglo-Indian communities. Parsis too. Since they all had daytime jobs, they would only be available at night to shoot. We would smoke and drink gallons of coffee to stay awake. Food was forgotten. We would go to bed at six in the morning and get up at twelve noon. We would start working on the script and be back in the studio by nine in the evening. This went on round the clock. I think that's where I developed an ulcer. Shyam too. In fact, everyone in the ad film business developed ulcers.

Everyone who works with me seems to crossover from theatre to advertising and vice versa. So people from Lintas would suddenly find themselves in theatre, and theatre folk would suddenly find themselves in advertising. I told Shyam, 'Look, you've got a knack for this. Have you worked in the theatre?' He said, 'Yes, I have done a bit.' So I said, 'You are an artist. Could you help out with the make-up?' I was doing a play at that time called *The Madwoman of Chaillot,* which needed a very stylised kind of make-up.

Pearl was playing a role and doing the costumes. In fact, looking after the whole production. Pearl had a cousin, Neera Chatterjee, who was helping her with the costumes. And day after day, while everyone was on stage, Neera and Shyam would be sitting in the dressing room. They got talking and eventually fell in love and the rest, as they say, is history. Oh, these fairy-tale backstage romances!

For my next play as well, Shyam designed the make-up. Then he moved across to ASP, the Birla ad agency, as Films Chief, before he set up his own unit and made his first feature film *Ankur.* Which I still think, in many ways, is his best film. (Incidentally, a lot of people's first work is their best.) It had everything. It had passion. It had a great story. It was obviously something which was lying within Shyam Benegal. Like *Ankur,* which means the seedling, it was a seed in him and then it flowered.

I believe the best training for anyone in movies is the theatre. Look at Naseeruddin Shah. Look at Amitabh Bachchan. Shabana Azmi, A K Hangal, Balraj Sahni, Prithviraj Kapoor. All theatre people. It is theatre that hones talent. It is the cradle of acting. Everyone will tell you that. From Robert De Niro to Jack Nicholson to Al Pacino to Marlon Brando.

Anyone who wants to get into movies must first get on to the stage. That is where they will learn the discipline of acting and character development.

Anyone who wants to get into movies must first get on to the stage. That is where they will learn the discipline of acting and character development. And for anyone wanting to get into advertising, theatre is the best discipline.

Gerson came to me one day and said, 'Look Alyque. I've got this young man here called Kabir Bedi. He is a model who wants to be a film maker. Will you take him in your films department?' I said, 'Sure, Gerson.' At that time Shyam had left, and I had no one. So Kabir became my Films Deputy and eventually the Films Chief of Lintas. He not only made ad films but he also acted in ad films as a model. So he got a double income out of advertising.

And then I said to Kabir, 'Have you done any theatre work?'

'Yes. In St Stephen's College. I have done a bit of Shakespeare.'

'Great! I am casting a new play. It's called *Tughlaq* and it's by Girish Karnad.'

'Yeah, yeah, I've heard of it. It's been done in Hindi.'

'Good. I'm doing the English version.'

It really is a terrific play. Without a doubt, the best play written in English by an Indian. So we got into rehearsals. To play the lead, I was gambling with a new talent. We were spending big bucks with massive sets and elaborate costumes. The late Pilloo Pochkanawalla, the famous sculptor and my dear friend, did the sets. Pearl Padamsee did the costumes in conjunction with the costume designer of the movie *Mughal-e-Azam*.

Kabir was acting with an array of very senior talent. We had various veteran actors of the Bombay stage, all playing one-scene roles. There was Gerson, Usha Katrak — another brilliant actress of the time (who played the female Caesar in my mini production of Shakespeare's play in the 1970s), Bomi Kapadia — who is still as active today as he was fifty years ago, and is one of the best comedy actors this country has ever seen in the English theatre; plus Kersy Katrak, the late Protap Roy, and Zafar Hai, who is now a well-known film maker. Every scene featured a star performer.

And against this galaxy of stars, a very young Kabir was going to play the lead role. We worked very hard together for about six months, on his voice, on his posture, on his gesticulation, on his articulation, on everything. I also sent him to weight-training classes, because, I said, 'Kabir, you've got a good body, but it's a little unmuscled.' He had never done any weight training before. He said, 'Okay, Alyque, I'm on. But you know, it's very boring going for weight training on my own. Do you mind coming along?' Bloody hell! Every morning I had to get up at seven o'clock, go across to Talwalkar's Gym and do weight training with Kabir. Of course, after a week, I dropped out because it was exhausting. But Kabir continued and he developed a superb body.

As usual, I had an obsession. To me, *Tughlaq* is about a man who was not ready to be emperor, but was catapulted on to the *gaddi* owing to the death of his father. I was very obsessed with Jean Genet's famous quote, 'Once you wear the emperor's robes, you become the emperor.' Remember, Indira Gandhi became Prime Minister when her father died, because there was no one else fit to take over. She was pushed into the role and then gradually she became the role. Narasimha Rao, another former Indian Prime Minister, is another example. A sort of faded backroom diplomat. Suddenly he becomes leader of the nation and finds the guts to usher in Liberalisation. The heat of the spotlight turns a wallflower into a vibrant orchid. Turns an ordinary man into a mighty emperor.

The heat of the spotlight turns a wallflower into a vibrant orchid.

I was haunted by this 'man into myth' idea. One day at the gym, I saw Kabir in his briefs doing his weights. It hit me. 'My God! What a beautifully muscled back. What a well-sculpted body he's got now.' It suddenly came to me in a flash. I saw a bare forked animal, a vulnerable naked man. And I saw him being dressed in the robes of the emperor, and when he turns to face the audience, he is the emperor.

And that's what my version of *Tughlaq* was all about. I asked Girish, 'Do you mind if I put in a prologue?' He said, 'Look Alyque, I wrote the play many years ago. Don't ask me what it means. Don't ask me about your production, just do it. I won't come to a single rehearsal. I swear to you I won't interfere. You forced me to translate my own Kannada play into English. I have done it. I don't want to hear anything more about it. I will come to opening night and that's it.'

So our prologue, which was less than two minutes long, had Kabir in the nude with his back to the audience. Well, not quite nude. He was wearing a kind of a fisherman's *langot*. Just a thin string running across his buttocks but otherwise totally nude from the rear view. And on either side of him were two servitors in Moghul outfits, holding all his robes. To an eerie sound track, they dress him from head to foot. Eventually they put the emperor's *pagdi* on his head. He turns to face the audience and lo and behold, a bare forked animal has now been transformed into the powerful Emperor of Hindustan.

At this point, the audience let out a huge gasp because a) Kabir is a very handsome man and b) the transformation was so incredible. Of course, it created a scandal. And scandal always creates an audience. So it became a compulsion to never miss the opening of *Tughlaq*. An amusing sidelight was the tussle I had with Kabir every show just before the curtain opened. I would pinch the string of the *langot* into a thin line which was nearly invisible... and he would try and stretch the cloth as wide as he could to cover his naked buttocks. By the intensity of the audience's gasp, you could tell who had won the battle of the *langot* that night!

While *Tughlaq* was running, Kabir became a movie star. B R Chopra, who worked with me on many Lux film commercials with movie stars, said to me, 'Hai Bhagwan!' This man must be in my next movie.' He grabbed Kabir and so we had to close *Tughlaq* which was still running to packed houses.

Of course, Kabir then went on to Italy, where he played the heroic *Sandokan,* and became a mega Italian TV star. Teenagers used to beg him to autograph their thighs. Giant forty feet cut-outs of Kabir as *Sandokan* dotted the Italian landscape. From there Kabir tried his luck in Hollywood. However, I am happy to say that Mr Sandokan manages to squeeze in an *Othello* and a Ramakant (in *Vultures*) for me, while shuttling between Hollywood and Bollywood. Like Naseeruddin, Kabir knows that the theatre, not cinema, is the touchstone of acting.

The common thread, the connecting link between Kabir, Shyam and Sharon (and Shiamak, Karla, and dozens of others whom I've worked with in their early years), is dedication. Hundred per cent dedication to improving their skills. They work at it ceaselessly. Twenty-four hours a day, they are thinking and working at their craft. I have seen Shyam slaving over a script, day after day, night after night. And it's the same with Sharon, Kabir, and anyone else who dreams of becoming a star. The vital ingredient is pure dedication. Then, as in Zen, you and your work become one.

Andy Warhol said that everyone
will be famous for fifteen seconds.
But it all depends on which
fifteen seconds fate grants you.

CONCLUSION, BUT NOT THE END

*M*y story has been one of riches to rags to rugs to riches. I moved from the riches of Kulsum Terrace to rags when I had to leave and fend for myself. In Lintas, I was introduced to the Unilever principle that the size of the rug in your cabin grows as you move up the corporate ladder. And when I finally left Lintas, I was medium rich again.

I retired from Lintas after a pretty good innings and I had a fleeting impression that I was retiring from advertising. But that was not to be. Because the world of ideas does not leave you alone. Retirement is only a physical thing whereas the world of ideas is mental.

After forty years in advertising (three in JWT and thirty-seven in Lintas), I asked myself, what does a man who has had a variety of experiences in communication do with the rest of his life? Mind you, I might fall down dead tomorrow, in which case there would be no problem. But what if I went on for another twenty years or more? Then what do I do?

I did a SWOT analysis on myself. And I realised that my greatest strength lies in ideation and organisation. I am able to cross-fertilise very quickly and then focus on an action plan. Turning ideas into action is what I enjoy most. Looking back over this fifty-year span, I realise I have an unusual aptitude for observing and analysing human nature and formulating an insight. This applies to every area of work that I get involved in, whether theatre or advertising or public service or even family matters.

So I set up my own company, APA — Alyque Padamsee Associates who are Image and Marketing Consultants. I have a group of people who work with me, but I myself act as the *agent provocateur* of insights and ideas. APA has provided consultancy services to various clients such as McCann Erickson Advertising, the *Indian Express* Group of Newspapers, Modi Entertainment Network, Repro India Ltd, Crest Communications, ActionAid and others, which has kept me in touch with the Big Idea world of advertising and communications.

My basic enjoyment in life is to constantly ideate. I'm like a butterfly that flits from meeting to meeting, conversation to conversation, book to magazine, television to newspapers to other media. My brain picks up phrases, ideas, images, and then I cross-fertilise them and discover insights for my clients.

For instance, why is ice cream sold in hot countries on the taste appeal instead of the cool appeal? Another one: Multichannel surfing would be impossible without your 'remote'; so you'd probably stick to the same channel and not switch to another during a commercial break if remotes were banned. Since all men love flirting, why don't married men try flirting with their wives? (What becomes dull in a marriage is not your partner… it is your imagination.) Whoever branded the theatre district in New York as 'Broadway' deserves an award for bringing in millions and millions of tourists from all over the world. The same branding applies to Hollywood. (And now, God help us, Bollywood!) If you want to change the culture, change the system. Just as Kerry Packer changed the culture of cricket by changing the system from five-day Tests to one-day tournaments.

If you want to change the culture, change the system.

I believe India is a superpower when it comes to brains. Forget hardware and software, we manufacture brainware. We could be the Brain Centre of the world in the next century. Japan became the hi-tech superpower in the 1970s and 1980s. It was a combination of performance and projection. And that, in my book, equals image. I have a crazy Big Idea. Why not hold a symposium, say in Washington DC. The theme would be Momentum for the Next Millenium — An India Perspective. We would get together at this symposium all the brilliant Indian brains that have individually shone like stars in the world firmament in the last decade. Outstanding brains like Amartya Sen (Nobel Prize winner for Economics), Zubin Mehta (the world's leading western music conductor), Sabeer Bhatia (Hotmail whizkid), Arundhati Roy (world famous novelist), Dr Vinod Dham (inventor of the Pentium chip), Dr Amar Bose (inventor of Bose Sound Systems), Rana Talwar (CEO worldwide of Chartered Bank), Deepak Chopra (spiritual guru), Swraj Paul (top British industrialist), Rajat Gupta (world head of McKinsey), Victor Menezes (international head of Citicorp), Rajesh Gangwal (new CEO of US Airways), Ismail Merchant (top Hollywood producer), etc. So instead of individual stars, we would have a constellation which would give India the kind of positive glow we sorely lack. Each of these stars could project their ideas of what the world could look forward to in the next 50 years. Then instead of the ancient glory of the Taj Mahal and the begging bowl of Mother Teresa, Image India would be the brilliance of the human mind.

In the world of ideas, there is no retirement. There is only an extended afterlife. As long as your grey cells are active, even if your body is slowing down, you can still be effective. You can get other people to act as your arms and legs and you can continue to be the brain behind it all. I've found that ever since I've become a consultant, my brain is more active than it ever was in all the years I worked in Lintas.

Fortunately, I am still physically able to action many of my ideas. When it comes to theatre, I am more than just a consultant. I actively direct plays. I actually go on stage and tell my actors what I want from them, and often show them how to do it. I go to the workshop where the sets are being made, and I might occasionally pick up a hammer myself. I go to the recording studio where the music director is ready to compose the background score and hum him the tune I have in my mind.

When it comes to public service activities too, I get involved in the execution. Because I find that there are very few executors in this area. I like to poke, prod, stimulate, provoke... the municipality, the education system, the government, and many other organisations which I feel are in need of certain social reform. I'm very keen on getting fully involved in a family planning operation where we not only create communication ideas, but we actually provide a family planning service through APA.

I enjoy getting involved in myriad activities. At any given time, I've got at least twenty projects on hand. Nearly everyday the phone rings and a voice will say, 'Alyque, are you interested in...?' And before they can even say what, I say, 'Yes.' I'm one of those greedy people who's always interested in taking on something new. The only thing I'm not interested in is talking about the 'good old days'. The 'good old days' are today . And tomorrow is even more 'good' than yesterday.

I feel that as long as your brain, and more importantly your memory, is functioning, you can go on for as long as you like. You are the sum of your parts and if you remember your life vividly, in terms of what you've done, what you've learnt, what stimulations you've had, you will find that you are sparking as much as you did in your thirties. But now your computer brain bank is overflowing with rich experiences.

My advice to people over the age of sixty is to keep the memory sharp. Force yourself to remember things. The brain is a muscle. Exercise it regularly and it will remain strong.

Retirement for me has meant more time for ideas and more time for stimulating other people to turn these ideas into actions. So although this is the conclusion to my book, it is certainly not the end. Like death, retirement too is only a new beginning.

If you've enjoyed this book and have kept it on your library shelf...instead of on your toilet roll, hold your breath. The sequel is coming: *Everyone is in Advertising.*

THE EXPERIENCE
OF THE EXPERIENCE

*H*ow did I who had sworn never to even write an article, actually write an entire book? The real villain of the piece and the person who instigated me was the tall, bespectacled and forceful David Davidar, Chief Executive and Publisher of Penguin India, whom I met at a party many years ago.

'Alyque, have you ever thought of writing a book on advertising?'

'I've thought about it a million times and I'm never going to do it.'

'Why ever not?'

'Because I hate writing. I've been a copywriter all my life and I've developed a bug against actually sitting down to write anything.'

'Anyway, think about it. You should give it a whirl.'

And so I thought about it and somehow David's words worked on my emotional energy. A week later I called him up. 'Listen, I won't do a book on advertising alone. I'll do a book on the cross-pollination between advertising and theatre. Because I'm basically a theatre man who stumbled into advertising in order to make a living. But advertising has helped my theatre and theatre has helped my advertising.'

Then a headline came into my mind. I felt that the book should be called 'A Double Life', because that's what I've been leading for the past so many years. I have been full-time in advertising as well as in theatre. Alongside, I've always been interested in public service activities, so that has been the third stream. Till I retired it was a minor stream, but it has now turned into a major river.

The next thing was to figure out how to go about writing the book. At first I thought I'd escape to my palm tree-lined beach house at Alibag (across the harbour from Bombay). Since I'm hopeless at writing — I find writing with a pen or even typing very laborious — I thought I'd speak into a pocket tape-recorder, and then get it transcribed.

I wrote four chapters that way, with the help of my ever-eager assistant, Peter Fernandes, and then I dried up. I just couldn't find the stimulation to continue. I became bored. I found it a wearying task.

When you find something a task, you write a dull, lifeless kind of prose.

And when you find something a task, you begin to write a dull, lifeless kind of prose. Funnily enough, I've never suffered from 'idea's block', but this time, 'writer's block' was a stonewall I couldn't break through.

I then asked several friends, among them Anita Sarkar, Anvar Ali Khan and Vikram Doctor, to help me out. We dabbled around a bit but never got anywhere. Then one day I was talking to my good-natured friend, the roly-poly 'Bugs' Bhargava Krishna, about my predicament and he asked me, 'Have you ever spoken to Arun Prabhu?' I said I hadn't. 'Have a chat with him and see. Bounce it off him.' So Arun came over to my place and we discussed a few ideas. I liked the way he responded and before I knew it, I gave him my famous pocket tape-recorder.

After that it was really his energy that drove the book. He would call up my secretary, fix an appointment and then sit down and ask me provocative questions to which I would give replies. It was a kind of 'As told to...' situation. Arun had tremendous patience. After I had spewed forth all the suff in my mind, Arun would prune it, but basically, it's still as if I'm speaking to the reader rather than writing.

This book also owes a lot to many other people:

My wife Sharon, for her support throughout.

My youngest daughter Shazahn, who stimulates me constantly.

My eldest daughter Raell, who's wonderfully intelligent and mature.

My foster son Ranjit, who has been my comic muse for the last thirty years or more.

My son Quasar, who's full of lateral thinking.

Pearl, a wise friend, philosopher and guide.

My late sister, Jerry Sayani, who's been a rock in my life.

My late brother Bubbles, with whom I enjoyed so many stimulating conversations which I miss.

Cynthia Mascarenhas, for her undying faith that this book would eventually see the light of day.

Gita Coelho, Arun's mother, for her constant help and support.

-Alyque Padamsee, January 1999.

A NOTE ON
ARUN PRABHU

Sixteen years of Jesuit education at St Stanislaus' High School and St Xavier's College (both in Bombay) taught Arun Prabhu how to write. Armed with a BA in 1993, he entered the big bad world of Indian advertising. After three years spent with leading advertising agencies — Sista Saatchi & Saatchi and Trikaya Grey — Arun decided to take the plunge and become a freelance consultant. Besides the many advertising campaigns he's been involved in, Arun's writing talents have featured in various publications such as *Indian Express, Mid-Day, Afternoon Despatch & Courier, JAM* and *Island.*

LIST OF PLAYS DIRECTED BY AP

1951	:	THE KILLERS by Ernest Hemmingway
1952	:	ANTIGONE by Sophocles
1952	:	DR FAUSTUS by Christopher Marlowe
1953	:	SHE STOOPS TO CONQUER by Oliver Goldsmith
1953	:	THE WAY OF THE WORLD by William Congreve
1953	:	AN IDEAL HUSBAND by Oscar Wilde
1954	:	THE TAMING OF THE SHREW by William Shakespeare
1955	:	CANDIDA by Bernard Shaw
1957	:	SHISHON KE KHILONE (*Hindi* adaptation of The Glass Menagerie)
1958	:	OF MICE AND MEN by John Steinbeck
1958	:	SHAYAD AAP BHI HANSEN (Original play in *Hindi* by Rifat Shamim)
1959	:	LONG DAY'S JOURNEY INTO NIGHT by Eugene O'Neill
1959	:	ALL MY SONS by Arthur Miller
1960	:	A VIEW FROM THE BRIDGE by Arthur Miller
1961	:	SARA SANSAR APNA PARIVAR (*Hindi* adaptation of All My Sons)
1961	:	BANDRA SATURDAY NIGHT
1962	:	THE MADWOMAN OF CHAILLOT by Jean Giraudoux
1962	:	JULIUS CAESAR by William Shakespeare (Radio Production)

1962	:	THE ZOO STORY by Edward Albee
1962	:	THE DEATH OF BESSIE SMITH by Edward Albee
1962	:	HELLO OUT THERE by William Saroyan
1963	:	OTHELLO by William Shakespeare (Radio Production)
1963	:	THE CRUCIBLE by Arthur Miller
1964	:	HAMLET by William Shakespeare
1965	:	A TOUCH OF BRIGHTNESS by Partap Sharma
1966	:	THE WORD by Partap Sharma
1966	:	ASYLUM by Erna Vatchaghandy
1967	:	BED ROOM by Zarina Sayani and Freny Bhownagiri
1968	:	O DAD, POOR DAD, MAMA'S HUNG YOU IN THE CLOSET AND I'M FEELING SO SAD by Arthur Kopit
1968	:	BURY THE DEAD by Irwin Shaw
1968	:	TRIAL BALLOON (Theatre pieces devised by Alyque Padamsee)
1969	:	THE PERSECUTION AND ASSASSINATION OF JEAN-PAUL MARAT AS PERFORMED BY THE INMATES OF THE ASYLUM OF CHARENTON UNDER THE DIRECTION OF THE MARQUIS DE SADE by Peter Weiss
1970	:	TUGHLAQ by Girish Karnad
1971	:	MEDEA by Robinson Jeffers
1972	:	MIRA by Gurcharan Das
1973	:	THE BIRTHDAY PARTY by Harold Pinter

1974	:	JESUS CHRIST SUPERSTAR by Tim Rice and Andrew Lloyd-Webber
1975	:	VULTURES by Vijay Tendulkar
1975	:	INHERIT THE WIND by Jerome Lawrence and Robert E. Lee
1975	:	WHO'S AFRAID OF VIRGINIA WOOLF? by Edward Albee
1976	:	EXIT THE KING by Eugene Ionesco
1976	:	A STREETCAR NAMED DESIRE by Tennessee Williams
1977	:	MAN OF LA MANCHA by Dale Wasserman and Joe Darion
1979	:	RAZZLE-DAZZLE/EVITA by Alyque Padamsee
1979	:	JULIUS CAESAR by William Shakespeare
1980	:	A STREETCAR NAMED DESIRE by Tennesse Williams
1981	:	PAGAL KHANA adapted by Ismat Chugtai into Hindi
1981	:	DEATH OF A SALESMAN by Arthur Miller
1983	:	EVITA by Tim Rice and Andrew Lloyd-Webber
1984	:	ALL THE KING'S MEN by Robert Penn Warren
1986	:	AAP KI FARMAISH (*Hindi* adaptation of Request Concert)
1986	:	TITALI (*Hindi* adaptation of Butterflies Are Free)
1986	:	TARANTULA TANZI by Claire Lukham
1986	:	MAHA DADA (*Hindi* adaptation of All the King's Men)

1987	:	SUICIDE IN B FLAT by Sam Shepard
1988	:	KABARET (Adapted by Alyque Padamsee)
1990	:	OTHELLO by William Shakespeare
1990	:	MISS JULIA by August Strindberg
1991	:	TARA by Mahesh Dattani
1992	:	BUTTERFLIES ARE FREE by Leonard Girshe
1993	:	DEATH AND THE MAIDEN by Ariel Dorfman
1994	:	FINAL SOLUTIONS by Mahesh Dattani
1995	:	ROSHNI by Alyque Padamsee and Louis Banks
1997	:	BEGUM SUMROO by Partap Sharma
1998	:	ODD COUPLE by Neil Simon

MAJOR BRANDS AP HELPED TO BUILD

1. Liril Soap
2. Rin Detergent Tablet
3. Dalda Vanaspati
4. Cherry Blossom Shoe Polish
5. MRF Tyres
6. Kama Sutra Condoms
7. Spartek Tiles
8. Kitply Plywood
9. Park Avenue Clothing
10. Reynolds Pens
11. Timex Watches
12. Closeup Toothpaste
13. Lifebuoy Soap
14. Captain Cook Salt
15. Surf Detergent Powder
16. Jet Airways
17. Monte Carlo Clothing
18. Johnson's Baby Powder
19. Ponds Cold Cream
20. Lipton's Tiger Tea

CHECKLIST FOR
PRODUCING A PLAY

1. Cast the play
2. Present Budget to Managing Committee
3. Photocopy the Scripts
4. Write for Copyright
5. Submit Script to Censors
6. Committee for Programme Advertisements
7. Look for Sponsors for Shows or Sold Out Shows
8. Book Hall for Rehearsals and Shows
9. Rehearsal Schedule
10. Plan the Set (and Moves)
11. Apply for All Licences
12. Start on Costume-making
13. Print Tickets
14. Prepare Posters/Car Stickers/Banners/Hoardings
15. Person to Sell Tickets
16. Start on Set Construction
17. Collect Small Props and Furniture
18. Inform Make-up man and Dhobi
19. Design Lighting and Order Extra Lights
20. Backstage Crew Including Prompter and Professional Stage Manager
21. Choose Music
22. Start Advertisements in the Press
23. Arrange TV Interviews
24. Take Photographs for Press and for Displays

25. Press Conference (Handouts, Photos and Invitees)
26. Print Programme Brochure with Ads
27. House Management – Ushers and Brochure-sellers
28. Organise Party for Cast & Crew
29. Photo Album of Rehearsals and Play
30. Scrapbook with Reviews, Announcements, Pre-publicity Clippings, Postcard and Programme Brochure
31. Tape-record the Entire Play in a Small Studio (with Music, SFX, etc.)
32. Videotaping

CHECKLIST FOR BUDGETING A PLAY

Expenses
Copyright Fees
Sets
Furniture Hire
Licences
Hire of Hall for Dress Rehearsals Plus First Set of Shows
Publicity
Hire of Premises for Rehearsals (Electricity)
Printing
Properties
Costumes
Additional Lights
Additional Sound System (for Musicals)
Additional Audio-Visual or Effects projection
Cartage
Tips
Refreshments (for Rehearsals)
Transport/Taxis
Postage, Phones, Photocopying, Courier
Party after Opening Night
Fees to : Author, Producer, Set Designer, Choreographer,
          Music Director, Lighting Director, Cast and Crew
Cost of Recording of Play at DR on Video or Audiotape
Cost of Photos for Press and for Cast

Income

Advertisements in Programme Brochure

Sponsors for Shows

Sale of Tickets

Sale of Brochure (Posters, T-shirts, etc.)

Total Income   =   Rs.

Total Expense =   Rs.

PROFIT   =   Rs.

CHECKLIST FOR AD PRESENTATIONS

Venue :   Book Date
                 Time
                 Place
                 Inform Participants

Recce Trip :   Take Measuring Tape and Sketch Pad
                 Acoustics
                 Lighting
                 Controls
                 Blackout Possibility
                 Electrical Points
                 Alternative Power Supply
                 Projection Space (Back and Front)
                 Tables for Projectors and Props
                 Audience Sight Lines
                 Seating Arrangements
                 Décor
                 Display Space

Visual Aids :   Blackboard
                 Chalk
                 Duster
                 Chartboard
                 Charts
                 Felt Pens
                 Screen
                 Overhead Projector Acetates
                 Carousel Projector Trays

```
                     Video Monitor/Videoscope
                     VHS Player
                     U-Matic Player
                     PC & PC Projector
                     Remote Controls
                     Operator
Cue Sheets :         Pointer
                     Test Tapes, Slides, Acetates
                     Rehearse with Visual Aids
Props :              Product Display
                     Ad Display
                     Logo Display
                     3-D Props for Presentation
                     Guard Books
                     Layouts
Sound System : Mikes (Floor, Table, Lapel, Cordless)
                     Amplifiers
                     Mixer
                     Tape Deck
                     Speakers
                     Note Each Presenter's Sound Levels
Lighting
Presenter
Script
Audience
```

Props :	Visual Aids
For Emergencies:	Torch
	Cellotape
	Black Tape
	Masking Tape
	Tweezers (for Slides)
	Scissors
	Blank Slides
	Masking Fluid, Brush
	Stapler
	Rubber Solution
	Blade
	Slide Mounts
	Calculator
	Thumb Tacks
	Suppliers – Phone Numbers
For the Speakers:	Script, Notes
	Cues Marked
	Adjust Lighting
	Adjust Mike Level

Mineral Water Bottle

Leave Behind Documents

Names of Key People to Be Addressed

Audience

Aids :   Seating Plans

                  Pens

                  Pencils

                  Ashtrays

                  Refreshments (Timing, Menu)

Last Check by Stage Manager :

                  All Equipment Switched On

                  Operators/Presenter Ready with Cue Sheets

                  Lights Brought to Start Position

                  All Tapes/Visual Aids at Start Position

                  Amplifiers at Pre-Set Position

PROBLEM SOLVER

Now that you have read *a double life,* please feel free to ask me any questions on advertising, theatre or public service. Fill in and mail the form below.

My question is: _____

_____

_____

_____

_____

_____

_____

Name: _____

Occupation: _____

Designation: _____

Address: _____

_____

Phone No: _____ Fax No: _____

Mail To: Alyque Padamsee,
          AP Associates, Christmas Building,
          Westfield Estate, Warden Road,
          Bombay 400 026, India.